D1070289

The Working Class in American History

A list of books in the series appears at the end of the book.

Solidarity and Fragmentation

SOLIDARITY
AND FRAGMENTATION

Working People
and Class Consciousness
in Detroit
1875–1900

RICHARD JULES OESTREICHER

UNIVERSITY OF ILLINOIS PRESS

Urbana and Chicago

Publication of this work was supported in part by a grant
from the Andrew W. Mellon Foundation.

Illini Book edition, 1989
© 1986 by the Board of Trustees of the University of Illinois
Manufactured in the United States of America
1 2 3 4 5 P C 5 4 3 2 1

This book is printed on acid-free paper.

Library of Congress Cataloging in Publication Data

Oestreicher, Richard Jules, 1947–
    Solidarity and Fragmentation.
    (The Working class in American history)
    Includes bibliographical references and index.
    1. Labor and laboring classes—Michigan—Detroit—History.   2. Social
classes—Michigan—Detroit—History.   3. Alien labor—Michigan—Detroit—
History.
4. Detroit (Mich.)—Industries—History. I. Title. II. Series.
HD8085.D6038   1986   305.5'62'0977434   85-1030
ISBN 0-252-01225-9 (cloth   :   alk. paper)
ISBN 0-252-06120-9 (paper   :   alk. paper)

To Pam—her imprint is on every page.

Contents

LIST OF TABLES

LIST OF FIGURES

Acknowledgments

Many people have helped, advised, prodded, and supported me during the years I struggled to understand Detroit workers; without their assistance I would never have finished this book. Norman Pollack and Peter Levine guided me through the dissertation. Many others read all or part of this manuscript and made useful suggestions for revisions, including James Soltow, Don Lammers, Ken Waltzer, Ron Edsforth, David Montgomery, James Barrett, Fred Jaher, Olivier Zunz, and Maurine Greenwald. My colleagues and students at the University of Pittsburgh have consistently encouraged me. The University of Pittsburgh's Faculty of Arts and Sciences awarded me a summer research grant, and the American Council of Learned Societies supported me with a fellowship. Olivier Zunz of the University of Virginia not only generously gave me an advance copy of his manuscript on Detroit and access to his raw data on the 1880 census, but also took several hours out of his own busy schedule to help process the data into a form that would be useful to me. Tom Featherstone helped to find most of the illustrations in this book. He and Annie Featherstone also fed and housed me during two research trips to Detroit and their daughter Megan cheered me up. Many other people helped in small and large ways; I cannot mention them all, but their generosity has not been forgotten. Parts of two chapters have been published previously, and I would like to thank the publishers for permission to use them here. An earlier version of most of chapter 3 appeared in *Labor History* (22, no. 1 [Winter 1981]) as "Socialism and the Knights of Labor in Detroit, 1877–1886." Part of chapter 7 appeared in a slightly different form as "Industrialization, Class, and Competing Cultural Systems: Detroit Workers, 1875–1900," in *German Workers in Industrial Chicago, 1850–1910: A Comparative Perspective*, edited by Hartmut Keil and John B. Jentz (DeKalb: Northern Illinois University Press, 1983).

Finally, there is my family. Pam, my wife, typed, edited, retyped, counseled, soothed, flattered, and nagged, all as necessary. My son Daniel arrived in time to provide final encouragement. My parents stimulated my early interest in history and taught me a sense of justice which has inspired me throughout.

INTRODUCTION

"We'll have to fight," Gnomon, a local worker-poet, advised his fellow Detroit workers in 1883, "And by force take our right . . ."

> So we had better prepare
> (For revolution's in the air)
> To get our rights at the polls if we can;
> But if they beat us there
> Let oppressors beware,
> We'll have our rights, if we take them man to man.

By 1886 many Detroit workers seemed prepared to do what Gnomon had urged.[1] A few were secretly drilling with .44-caliber Winchesters "at the outskirts of the city under cover of darkness."[2] Over 6,000 workers struck for shorter hours in May, and in September 10,000, one out of every four workers in the city, marched behind socialist printer Judson Grenell, the grand marshall of the Labor Day parade. In November they elected Grenell and four other nominees of the Independent Labor party to the state legislature.[3]

Gnomon, Grenell, and other labor activists were inspired by the vision of a cooperative commonwealth where each worker would have an equal voice and together they would decide what to produce and how to produce it. No one who wanted to work would have to beg for it, and no one who did work would have to accept conditions which insulted one's dignity or endangered one's health. All who worked would be able to live a decent life and each would be rewarded for individual effort. Workers could make this dream come true if they recognized their common interests and organized as a class to fight together.[4]

What made such dreams seem possible in the 1880s was the emergence of a working-class *subculture of opposition:* an interlocking network of formal institutions and informal practices based on an ethic of social equality, cooperation, mutual trust, and mutual assistance. Strikes, marches, political victories were the most visible indicators of its existence, but its roots lay deep in working-class experiences—in the century-old republican traditions not only of America but of England, Ireland, France, and Germany as well; in the cooperative work practices developed by many skilled trades; in the memories of neighborly kindnesses; in the sense of community that existed where people who worked together also lived on the same blocks, went to the same churches, drank in the same saloons, and watched their children grow up playing together on the same streets. Such experiences gave intense meaning to a word like *solidarity*.

But such experiences were far from universal. In a large and rapidly growing city, half of one's workmates might be newcomers. Small workshops drew on neighborhood work forces. But in 1890 a large factory like the Michigan Car Works drew its 1,500 workers from many parts of the city. When the factory whistle blew at the end of the day workers scattered in several directions. Perhaps the car painters who worked together knew each other, but how many car painters knew more than a handful of the 500 foundry workers who made the wheels and axles in another building? What did the native-born printer who set type at the *Free Press* for $2.50 a day and lived with shopkeepers and clerks in a mixed West Side neighborhood have in common with the dollar-a-day Polish street laborer? What meaning did class solidarity have in a city where the working class was fragmented into groups with such different experiences? And what traditions were most important when an Irish Catholic and a Scotch-Irish Orangeman entered the same factory? In 1886, both solidarity and fragmentation were fundamental parts of working-class life in Detroit. The possibility of any dreams of cooperative futures depended on the ability of Detroit's workers to resolve the tensions between these two very different parts of their experience.

This book is about Gnomon and Grenell, about the workers who marched with them, and also about the many more who did not. What vision moved those who joined them? What rights did they fight for? And why did others who labored under similar conditions refuse to join them? How did the lives of all of the city's workers change as a result of their decisions? What legacy did they leave the next generation? What can answers to those questions tell us about the changing nature of class relations during the years when America became the world's leading industrial nation and about the sources of class consciousness and the barriers to it?

The answers to these questions will be organized around four themes. First, in chapter 1, we will look at the process of industrialization and the differences in the positions of different types of workers within the industrial system. What did workers have in common because they were workers? In the 1880s, socialists like Grenell believed that industrialization would eradicate all social and economic distinctions among workers, leaving a clear separation between the working class and employing class. But industrialization proved to be more complicated than this theory of proletarianization and polarization had predicted.

Second, in chapter 2, we will look more closely at Detroit's working people. Who were they? What else besides their work determined how they thought about themselves and how they acted? Judson Grenell was a printer, but he was also native born, the son of a radical republican Baptist preacher who had joined the Underground Railroad. And what of Mrs. Grenell, who had also been a printer until she married Grenell and left the trade to raise his children?[5] Thomas O'Donnell, who deserted Grenell's Independent Labor party in the closing days of the 1886 campaign, was an Irish Catholic.[6] Henry Kummerfeldt, a socialist cigarmaker born in Hamburg, Germany, spent many of his evenings singing in a German socialist men's choir or reading his countryman Robert Reitzel's radical anticlerical literary journal, *Der Arme Teufel*. Reitzel's paper, however, outraged some of Kummerfeldt's fellow German workers.[7] How did such differences in ethnicity, religion, tradition, sex, race, family, and personality affect the willingness or capacity of workers to act together as a class?

Third, in chapters 3 through 6, we will look at the class institutions and organizations workers did create, especially at the Knights of Labor, and their relationship to the subculture of opposition. How was the rise and fall of the Knights intertwined with the possibilities for oppositional cultural institutions?

Finally, in chapter 7, we will look at the legacy of the Knights and the subculture of opposition. What was their long-term impact on workers' organization and consciousness and on the patterns of class relations in the city? And what can the test case of late nineteenth-century Detroit tell us about the nature of class and class consciousness in American history?

Recreating the world of Detroit's workers in order to answer these questions is a process of detective work. A subculture of opposition is almost by definition partially clandestine. Deciding what Detroit workers thought about their work, their bosses, their lives, their place in the world depends on inference and supposition: many pieces of the puzzle are missing. We must proceed with caution, aware of these methodological complexities and avoiding simplistic conclusions. But despite these problems a clear picture emerges. An important sequence of events took place: advocates of class solidarity struggled to overcome a complex set of fragmenting influences in order to create a working-class movement. That movement seemed to be successful for a brief period in the mid-1880s, but by the early 1890s, as the institutions of the oppositional subculture collapsed, the movement lost much of its force. While notions of worker solidarity and the rights of labor had become part of popular culture, a more narrowly circumscribed labor movement faced new competition for workers' loyalties from liberal capitalists like progressive mayor Hazen Pingree. Well before the rise of the automobile industry completely transformed Detroit's economic and social terrain, the credibility of a cooperative commonwealth, of a working-class social reconstruction, had sharply receded.

Scholars have generally depended on two intellectual traditions— Marxism and modernization theory—to understand working-class behavior and consciousness. Neither classical Marxism, with its emphasis on proletarianization as a result of the development of productive forces, nor modernization theory, with its emphasis on the conflicts between tradition and modernity, are adequate theoretical bases for analyzing what happened in Detroit. Instead, I have argued that social change in Detroit produced intertwining tendencies toward class solidarity and fragmentation, both tendencies simultaneous outgrowths of the consequences of industrialization and urbanization, both increasing together. How working people felt about these conflicting possibilities varied over time. Consciousness was never a simple reflection of class interests nor a direct product of the arrangement of social structure. In a contradictory social environment, there was always an inner tension in which the extent of class consciousness was a function of concrete opportunities for its expression. When such vehicles, e.g., the Knights of Labor, thrived, class consciousness increased; when they did not, it declined.

No two cities were exactly alike. In Pittsburgh, the Knights of Labor peaked earlier than in Detroit but survived longer. In Chicago and Milwaukee, the labor movement remained stronger and more influential politically. Yet in the last quarter of the nineteenth century, nearly every city in industrial America went through a cycle of events which mirrored what happened in Detroit. Visions of a cooperative economy within a democratic republic sustained a variety of workers' activities between 1860 and the 1890s. But by the turn of the century, this "distinctive . . . moral universality" of labor reform had been shattered.[8] In the new political economy of the early 1900s, while strikes were more frequent and often more violent, while the social distance between workers and other classes was greater than before, workers were more fragmented. The making of the American working class had not produced, in Edward Thompson's words, a set "of common experiences" which allowed American workers to "feel and articulate the identity of their interests."[9]

NOTES

1. Gnomon, "The Rights of Man," in *The Spectator* (Detroit), November 10, 1883. Gnomon was a frequent contributor to Detroit labor papers in the early 1880s.

2. *Labor Leaf* (Detroit), December 30, 1885; *Evening News* (Detroit), September 5, 1887.

3. See chaps. 4 and 5 for discussions of these activities.

4. *Three Stars* (Detroit), January 1880; *Labor Review* (Detroit), August 1881; *The Unionist* (Detroit), March 1882; Judson Grenell, "Autobiography," unpublished manuscript (Clearwater, Florida, 1930), Michigan State University Archives and Historical Collections, pp. 30–31.

5. Grenell, "Autobiography," pp. 1–3, 27.

6. *Labor Leaf*, September 15, October 20, 1886. See chap. 5.

7. "Men Who Make Your Cigars," unidentified newspaper clipping dated July 28, 1889, Detroit Labor Leaders File, Labadie Collection, University of Michigan, Ann Arbor, Michigan, hereafter cited LC; *Der Arme Teufel*, December 6, 1884; Adolf Edward Zucker, *Robert Reitzel* (Philadelphia, 1917), pp. 31–36, 39.

8. David Montgomery, "Labor and the Republic in Industrial America: 1860–1920," *Mouvement Social* 3 (1980): 201–15.

9. E. P. Thompson, *The Making of the English Working Class* (New York, 1963), p. 9.

SOLIDARITY
AND FRAGMENTATION

1

LIVING AND WORKING IN DETROIT

> My godfather was in Detroit and wrote me that he had
> paper on the walls, shoes, meat every day, fresh bread, milk,
> water in the house, beer on the corner, soup, and plenty of
> money. From that time I was crazy to come . . . I am 28 years
> old and have worked as long as I can remember; yes, since I
> was five years old; always in the fields, for nothing; first to
> help my father; then for wages, but my pay was never more
> than $5 a month and I had to sleep in the stable with the
> cattle . . . I had to make my own shoes and my food was usu-
> ally beans, onions, soup, sauerkraut, pork once in a long
> time, and lard for butter, with a pinch of salt.
>
> A Detroit Polish immigrant, c. 1905

Most Detroit workers came from somewhere else. Like the Polish laborer who joined his godfather in Detroit just after the turn of the century, they came looking for steady work and good wages.[1] Six of every
ten workers in late nineteenth-century Detroit had been born outside
the United States, eight of every ten outside of the state of Michigan.[2]

Detroit was one of the chain of industrial cities stretching along
the Great Lakes and through the Ohio Valley from Buffalo and Pittsburgh in the east to Chicago and Milwaukee in the west. These cities
expanded rapidly between 1870 and 1900 as they formed an industrial
heartland that processed iron, timber, and agricultural commodities.
Pittsburgh, Cleveland, Detroit, and Chicago all grew quickly—faster
than the rest of the country, faster than the rest of the Midwest, faster
than other American cities of comparable size. In each case, industry
expanded even faster than population, and the cities were transformed
from medium-sized regional marketing and transportation centers to industrial metropolises.[3]

Detroit did not grow as fast as Chicago and Cleveland, its chief
lake port rivals, but workers arriving at the Michigan Central Railroad
Depot at the foot of Jefferson Avenue would already have spotted many

Table 1. Growth of Detroit Population and Industrial Work Force, 1880–1900

Year	Population	Industrial Workers
1880	116,340	14,500 (est.)[1]
1890	205,876	34,535[2]
1900	285,704	45,707[2]

Sources: *Twelfth Census*, 1900, vol. 1, p. lxix; vol. 8, p. 994.

1. Totals for 1880 included salaried officials, clerks, etc. In 1890 and 1900, when these were differentiated, they made up 9.6 and 10.6 percent respectively of manufacturing employees; hence, the 1880 estimate is 10 percent below the census total of 16,110.

2. Manufacturing wage earners.

of the factories where they would soon be working. The main lines of the Michigan Central, the Detroit and Milwaukee, and the other railroads wound through the warehouse district along the Detroit River, where new factories had been springing up since the late 1860s. Detroit's population more than doubled between 1880 and 1900, while the number of industrial workers tripled.[4]

Varying Industrial Experiences

Perhaps relatives were waiting at the train station to greet the new arrivals. Our twenty-eight-year-old Pole probably looked for his godfather, who had sent him the money to make the trip. Together they boarded the streetcar back to one of the East Side Polish neighborhoods, where corner groceries, cigar stands, saloons, and other small shops, some of them run by earlier Polish immigrants, lined the business streets and where small frame houses were crowded together in residential neighborhoods. On Sunday they walked to St. Casimir or the Blessed Heart of Mary, the nearby Polish Catholic churches, to hear Father Gutowski or Father Kolasinski say mass and give a sermon in Polish.[5] If there had been a young German seamstress on the same train, she could have followed them onto the same East Side streetcar, but she would have gotten off a few blocks earlier in the German neighborhood along Gratiot Avenue, where half of the city's German families lived. An Irish family might have headed in the opposite direction, to Corktown on the West Side, where 40 percent of the Irish families lived.[6]

4

Other workers would not necessarily have sought these ethnic neighborhoods. If he knew no one in Detroit, a union printer would probably have looked for the gathering spot of local journeymen, secure in the conviction that his union brothers would honor the tradition of helping a fellow craftsman "on the tramp." Seven blocks up Larned Street from the Michigan Central Depot he would have found Tim Gorman's Saloon, the "Printers' Headquarters" for over twenty-five years. As he walked in the bar, he would know that someone here would put him up until he found work or help him on to the next town if "the trade" was dull in Detroit.[7]

The tramping printer was not an anomaly of his trade. Even in good times a steady flow of unemployed and unattached workers arrived in the city in search of work. Some of this flow was seasonal. Great Lakes sailors, for example, were laid off as shipping traffic declined in the winter. Yet even in June of 1891, at the height of the shipping and building seasons, a Detroit *News* reporter complained that 160 unemployed workers were crowded into a free lodging house on East Larned Street.[8]

To the printer drinking with newly found comrades at Tim Gorman's, the sailor stranded in an overcrowded flophouse, or the eager young Polish immigrant, the city must have seemed like three very different places. Yet each faced a common problem: he needed a job. As they scanned the newspaper ads or questioned relatives and new acquaintances, they heard the names of many companies. No single industry dominated the city's economy. No firm was so large that it was an obvious first choice. Industrial growth in Detroit had been increasingly diversified. In 1870, Detroit's economy had still been based more on its position as a commercial and transportation center than on its industries. Only one-fifth of its work force had been employed in industry, and over 2,800 of these 10,000 industrial workers were in the building trades. Even by nineteenth-century standards there was not yet a single large factory; the two biggest, two railroad car construction companies, had only 703 workers between them.[9]

As Detroit became an industrial city in the next three decades, several of the hundreds of new manufacturing firms grew dramatically. Pingree and Smith started a shoe factory with eight shoemakers in 1866. By 1890, they employed 700 workers in the largest shoe factory west of New York City. When Parke Davis opened in 1867, the future pharmaceutical giant was no more than a big drugstore. By 1896, the company employed 1,200. The Michigan Stove Company, which opened

5

Table 2. Firm Size and Distribution of Factory Employees in
Detroit, 1896

Firm Size	0–99	100–499	500+
Number of factories	793	61	8
Number of employees	12,584	10,626	6,495
Percent of total factory employees	42.4	35.8	21.9

Source: Michigan Factory Inspectors, *Fourth Annual Report of Inspection of Factories in Michigan* (Lansing, 1898).

Note: Figures based only on those factories actually inspected and on those workers actually at work at time of inspection. Since 1896 was a depression year, many large firms were operating well below capacity, and two of the largest were completely idle at the time of inspection. Using figures reported for number of workers employed when running at full capacity would yield fourteen factories of 500+ with 26.2 percent of the theoretical full-capacity work force. In addition, each plant of the Michigan–Peninsular Car Company was counted as a separate factory, and several were placed in the 100–499 category. There is, however, a major bias in the other direction: based on census figures, the total number of factories would be over 2,000 (1,746 manufacturing firms in 1890, 2,847 in 1900), thus more than 1,000 small firms were not included in the factory inspections.

in 1871, employed 1,500 by the late 1880s. The railroad car companies, still the largest factories, were approaching the structure of what business historian Alfred P. Chandler calls the "modern business enterprise" containing "many distinct operating units . . . managed by a hierarchy of salaried executives." In 1892, the Michigan Car Company merged with the Peninsular Car Company and the Detroit Car Wheel Company to form the Michigan–Peninsular Car Company. Under the leadership of the McMillan family, the millionaire leaders of the state's Republican party, the company reorganized production to coordinate the flow of materials through the many steps of the manufacturing process and expanded its work force from 3,000 to 9,000 by the turn of the century. By 1917, renamed the American Car and Foundry Company, it ranked thirty-third among American industrial corporations.[10]

But along with these larger factories industrialization also brought a proliferation of smaller firms, most of them no bigger than the small family-owned workshops that had predominated in 1870. Eight large factories employed more than 500 workers each in 1896, yet their combined work forces made up less than one-quarter of the city's total industrial work force; sixty-one medium-sized factories employing between 100 and 500 workers represented a much larger share of the industrial work force, more than a third, while more than 40 percent of the industrial workers worked in small shops with fewer than 100 employees.[11]

Newly arrived workers thus found themselves in a varied industrial economy. Even if they were looking for work in only a single industry, they would find sharp contrasts. The Michigan Stove Company employed 1,500 iron workers in 1889; the tiny Cooperative Foundry, fifteen. Pingree and Smith's mechanized factory competed with 119 custom boot and shoe shops which, together, employed only 216. Two of the tobacco companies, Daniel Scotten and Brown Brothers, were among the city's fourteen largest firms, but they shared the market with more than 100 "buckeye" cigar shops—small shops in which the owner, a skilled hand roller, worked along with a stripper and perhaps

Table 3. Class Composition of Detroit Work Force, 1890

Class	Number	Percent
Business people and entrepreneurs	6,930	9.5
Professionals	2,055	2.8
White-collar wage earners	10,783	14.8
Working class	53,191	72.9
Total	72,959	

Source: *Eleventh Census*, 1890, vol. 1, pt. 2, p. 664.

Businesspeople and entrepreneurs: gardeners, florists, nurserymen, and vine growers; restaurant and saloon keepers; bankers, brokers, and officials of banks; livery stable keepers and hostlers; merchants, dealers, and peddlers; manufacturers; publishers; hotel and boarding house keepers.

Professionals: clergymen, engineers (civil, mechanical, electrical, and mining) and surveyors, physicians and surgeons, professors and teachers.

White-collar wage earners: officials (government), agents (claim, commission, real estate, insurance, etc.) and collectors, bookkeepers, clerks, commercial travellers, salesmen, musicians and music teachers, accountants, clerks and copyists, stenographers and typewriters, saleswomen.

Working class: barbers; bartenders; engineers and firemen; laborers; watchmen; policemen; detectives; boatmen; coachmen; pilots; sailors; draymen; hackmen; teamsters; messengers; packers and porters; steam railroad employees; street railway employees; apprentices; bakers; blacksmiths and wheelwrights; boot and shoemakers and repairers; brassworkers; brewers and maltsers; cabinet makers and upholsterers; carpenters and joiners; harness, saddle, and trunk makers; iron and steel workers; machinists; marble and stone cutters and masons; painters, glaziers, and varnishers; plasterers; plumbers; printers, engravers, and bookbinders; steam and boat builders; stove, furnace, and grate makers; tailors; tinners and tinware makers; tobacco and cigar factory operatives; wood workers; housekeepers and stewardesses; laundresses; nurses and midwives; servants; telegraph and telephone operators.

one or two others.[12] Such differences would have concrete meaning as people found their new jobs. Detroit was a blue-collar city. By 1890, the working class made up nearly three-quarters of the city's work force, but in such a diversified economy, there were sharp variations in the wages, working conditions, and future prospects of different types of workers. Living and working in Detroit might be very different for the Polish peasant, the stranded sailor, or the tramping printer.[13]

For the Polish peasant, finding work seemed easy. The knowledge-able godfather brought him down to the car shops. A bribe to the fore-man—a bit of snuff—and it was settled. At first his $1.10 a day prob-ably seemed like a lot. Even with what he paid for room and board there was a little left over for what must have seemed like luxuries: an occasional cheap cigar, a beer at the saloon after work, a holiday car ride to the park on Belle Isle. But the work was very hard—six ten-hour days, with only a quick thirty-minute lunch to break up the steady work rhythm; cold in the winter, hot in the summer—probably much harder than he had expected. At least that is what three car shop laborers interviewed by the State Bureau of Labor Statistics said in 1892. Two construction laborers, a Pole and a German, agreed. "It's much better in Germany," the German concluded, "Don't have to work so hard"; and his Polish friend concurred, "It's better in Poland."[14] And quickly he learned that he could not count on the little luxuries to make the hard work seem worthwhile. There were frequent layoffs, even in good years, when wages ceased but rent and food bills continued. In 1892, the car shop laborers worked an average of only 36.5 weeks. In the depression years after 1893, the shops shut down for months several times. During such periods, if the laborer had mar-ried and started a family, he might face poverty every bit as serious as what he had left behind in Poland.

Unskilled workers in Detroit quickly learned that if they were to maintain any margin over minimum subsistence or any security against frequent layoffs, the family needed more than one income. Women and children went to work. Close to half of the city's working-class families may have found themselves in this position. At $1.10 per day, for ex-ample, even if there were no layoffs, the car shop worker could not ex-pect to make over thirty dollars per month, yet judging from budgetary information collected by the State Bureau of Labor Statistics, a worker with several children would need that much just to cover rent and food. It was disproportionately from these families that the growing female and child labor forces were recruited.[15]

Census takers found 1,153 children between ten and fifteen at work in 1880, but canvassers from the State Bureau of Labor Statistics disputed the accuracy of these figures. They found nearly twice as many child workers in 1884 (2,065, 4.6 percent of the work force) and cautioned that even this figure was unreliable. "The parents conceal, in many cases, the fact of employment," explained the director of the State Labor Bureau. Investigators discovered that the number of working-class children between ten and fourteen not attending school was more than double the number reported working and suspected that most of the children not attending school were in fact working. Of those reported employed, nearly 70 percent of the boys and 57 percent of the girls worked as factory hands for wages less than half those of an adult: an average of $3.30 per week for boys and $2.62 for girls. Contemporary apologists for child labor often claimed that such children worked to support their poor widowed mothers, but the Labor Bureau's statistics effectively refuted this myth. Children worked because they were poor. Only 10.2 percent of the male children in the survey reported deceased fathers, but 68.9 percent had fathers who were unskilled laborers.[16]

By 1890, nearly one worker in four was female. Women workers were overwhelmingly young and single. Five out of six began working before they were seventeen; most quit before they were twenty-five. They usually lived at home and contributed the wages they earned as factory workers and domestics to a common family economy. As they married and had children, they left the factories or the middle-class homes. While prescribed sex roles certainly had much to do with this decision, it made economic sense as well. Their average wages had often barely matched those of their little brothers. Few domestics made more than three dollars per week; women factory workers averaged eighty-two cents a day in 1886, but many female factory workers made

Table 4. Detroit Women Wage Workers, 1892: Age at which They Began Work

	10 or less	11–13	14–16	17–19	20–25	Over 25
Number	34	850	3,776	722	152	37
Percent	0.6	15.3	67.8	13.0	2.7	0.7

Source: Michigan State Bureau of Labor Statistics, *Annual Report*, 1892, p. 144.

Table 5. Age of Women Workers in Detroit, 1892

	Under 16	16−20	21−25	26−30	31−35	Over 35
Number	481	3,285	1,508	508	113	126
Percent	8.0	54.6	25.0	8.4	1.9	2.1

Source: Michigan State Bureau of Labor Statistics, *Annual Report*, 1892, p. 139.

far less. The female employees in a candy factory made between fifty-nine and sixty-nine cents a day; the women in a large box factory averaged less than three dollars per week. Working at home, married women could find other ways to supplement the family income. Careful management could stretch a meager income, and married women earned extra cash by taking in boarders, doing laundry or sewing, and gathering scraps of paper and wood off the streets for heating their homes in winter.[17]

The situation of skilled workers, who made up perhaps a third of the working class in the 1880s, was quite different from that of these unskilled families. The gap between skilled craftsmen and unskilled laborers represented a division among workers that was nearly as significant as the separation between workers and other classes. Skilled workers were artisans; their trades bore some of the characteristics of a profession: limited numbers, years of training and experience, specialized knowledge common only to craft members, ability to perform tasks that could not be done as easily or as well by someone else. Unskilled laborers were ditchdiggers or factory hands or servants. Anyone could learn to do their jobs in a few hours or at most a few days—perhaps not quite as well as someone with experience, but well enough. Laborers averaged wages of $1.33 a day in 1884. Many crafts averaged nearly twice as much: bricklayers earned an average of $3.06; machinists, $2.24; carpenters, $1.97. If our tramping printer found a spot in a union shop, he could expect to make at least $2.50 per day.[18]

But the differences between skilled and unskilled labor were not only economic. Union printers worked in a shop governed by rules the workers had helped to make. They chose the foreman and they could remove him if his demands on them became objectionable. As automatic typesetting machines were introduced in the 1890s, union typographers were still able to maintain sufficient shop floor control to dictate the pace of transition and insure an adjustment as hand typographers learned how to operate the new machines.[19]

Table 6. Daily Wages of Detroit Workers, 1884

Wage Rate	Number of Workers	Percent Total Workers
$1.00 or less	566	6.57
$1.05–1.50	3,863	44.86
$1.55–2.00	2,391	27.77
$2.05–2.50	1,108	12.87
$2.55–3.00	439	5.10
$3.10–3.50	144	1.67
$3.75–4.00	64	.74
Over $4.00	36	.42

Source: Michigan State Bureau of Labor Statistics, *Annual Report*, 1884, pp. 84–87.

Yet even within the ranks of skilled labor there could be large variations in working patterns. All union printers, for example, theoretically worked under the same rules, but in fact conditions in the many small job shops were quite different from those in the composing rooms of the city's daily newspapers. At the newspapers, union printers had won the eight-hour day by the 1890s while many job shops were still working ten hours. Printers in these small shops were continually complaining of employers' attempts to chisel on union rates, bypass union work rules, subcontract parts of jobs to nonunion shops, and violate state safety and sanitation codes.[20]

Or consider the variations that State Bureau of Labor Statistics investigators found in the city's iron foundries in 1890. Workers in the Cooperative Foundry worked fifty-two weeks a year in a small shop they controlled themselves. Only three of the ten workers questioned had lost time during the year, two for illness and one who took a week's vacation. Wage rates were relatively uniform for similar work. A laborer and two apprentice molders earned $9.00, $9.00, and $8.25 per week respectively. Skilled molders earned between $15.00 and $18.00. A small German firm, F. Huetteman and Company, hired fellow Germans and German-Americans and maintained a similar pattern of steady work and relatively uniform wage rates. These small firms had reputations for amiable work relations. But in the large stove companies, skilled workers waged a virtual guerrilla war with management throughout the 1880s as they objected to management efforts to redefine work rules and to divide workers by introducing the "bucks system" of subcontracting. Under this arrangement, artisans were paid a piece rate for the finished products, and they hired helpers out of their own

11

wages to do the "drudge work requiring no skill." The bucks were usually children or Polish or Italian men who "work for a pittance, three or four of them often getting less than one skilled molder."[21]

As the state survey revealed, craftsmen had been unable to maintain the uniform standards they sought. At the Michigan Stove Company, one German-born molder who had arrived in the United States with $2.00 in his pocket nine years before was now laid off, and he listed his net worth as 0. A German stovemounter in the same shop who had arrived with only $1.00 twenty-two years later listed his net worth at $2,000, including a $2,000 home that was half paid off, a $150 savings account, and a $4,500 life insurance policy. The company paid a thirty-six-year-old German molder $8 a week—when he worked. He had been laid off for twenty-six weeks that year. A Danish-born molder of the same age earned $18 per week and only missed four weeks. His property was worth $3,000. An American-born patternmaker had property worth $9,000. A German metal polisher with five children earned $7.50 per week and claimed $200 in possessions. The same company employed all of these workers, yet the differences in their salaries, experiences, habits, and wealth raise questions about how they conceived of themselves and each other.[22]

Differences between trades were even more marked than those within a single craft. Some artisans found their jobs mechanized out of existence; others found declining opportunities as they tried to compete against machines. Different industries had very different rates of skill dilution, while rapid expansion of some industries meant that demand for some skills expanded faster than supply. In 1892, despite the threat of typesetting machines and other changes in printing technology, the Detroit Typographical Union was able to report a 12 percent increase in average wages over the last five years. Skilled handroll cigarmakers did not fare so well. Their average wages declined from $1.76 per day in 1883 to less than $1.50 in 1889, despite a rapid expansion of the industry, as competition from machines and unskilled women and children increased.[23]

Technological change destroyed opportunities, but it also created new ones. In 1890, there were no electrical workers in Detroit. By 1900, there were 525. Industrialization must have looked very different to an electrician or a cigarmaker.[24] These differences between industries and within industries are crucial to understanding how workers reacted to their lives in Detroit. They had come from different places, faced different receptions, found different situations. If they had faced the same conditions in each shop, on each work gang, such differences might have come to seem less and less important. But in Detroit in the 1880s and 1890s, conditions were not the same everywhere. One factory was very different from another. In a highly diverse and rapidly changing economy, a whole range of work methods, levels of mechanization, types of firms, and patterns of employer-employee relationships existed side by side in different industries and sometimes in the same industry. Nineteenth-century Marxists assumed that industrialization would overwhelm the fragmented loyalties and varied attitudes of workers, eliminating all gradations of status and conflicting interests among workers. The actual process of industrialization in Detroit was far more complex than a simple theory of proletarianization. Industrialization created new differences in status and consciousness as it wiped out some of the old.[25]

What Did Workers Have in Common?

Workers came from different places, and found work in different firms with significant differences in wages, working conditions, and job security. As they settled in, such differences did not disappear. Experiences varied and these variations had an important impact on how Detroit's workers thought about their lives.

Prospects varied as well. A significant minority could eventually hope to escape the working class. Among a sample of Detroit workers traced from 1880 to 1890, 18 percent of the skilled workers and 14 percent of the unskilled and semiskilled had moved into white-collar, business, or professional positions by 1890. Projecting these mobility rates over a work life would suggest that perhaps as many as a quarter of the unskilled and semiskilled workers and a third of the skilled workers would eventually rise out of the working class (such a projection makes some optimistic assumptions, however).[26]

In the shorter run, many people changed jobs, and some of those changes were for the better. Improvement was possible. The laborer who entered a skilled trade earned more and probably found the work more satisfying. Yet regardless of differences and regardless of long-range prospects, being a worker involved some common realities. Every morning the factory or the trolley barn or the unfinished sewer line was still waiting. Skilled and unskilled alike had to hurry to beat the factory whistle, and once inside all workers faced the inherent nature of the wage relationship: dependence on wages, subordination to

13

the wills of supervisors and owners, insecurity, and the feeling of relative deprivation that came from recognition that your energies—even if you were well paid and fairly treated—went to the enrichment of someone else. Workers could bargain, negotiate to change particular aspects of their jobs, or refuse a job if the demands were unreasonable, but no worker could live for long without a job.

Wage dependence and insecurity went hand in hand. Even the most skilled and highly paid artisans had few cash reserves to tide them over layoffs, illnesses, or injuries. Layoffs were a consistent part of workers' lives. In 1890, a prosperous year, 18 percent of Detroit's workers were unemployed for one month or more. In 1896, a depression year, 81 percent of the workers questioned by state investigators reported lost time—an average of fifty-eight days. Some industries routinely laid off workers on a seasonal cycle. In the metal trades, many foundries and casting departments shut down on hot summer days; 58 percent of all metal trades workers reported layoffs in 1890. Carpenters faced layoffs during winter, an average of nine weeks in 1885.[27]

These patterns of intermittent unemployment not only reduced annual incomes but also created serious uncertainties for workers. Even where the family budget was sustained by several wage earners, prolonged layoffs could mean disaster. Only 5.2 percent of the workers surveyed by the State Bureau of Labor Statistics in 1885 had savings accounts, while an 1892 survey made up mainly of skilled workers found only one worker in four with any liquid assets.[28] With little or no savings, unemployment or illness could mean near starvation after only a few weeks. Prudent individuals might make plans to deal with regular and expected seasonal layoffs: arranging credit with the regular grocer, putting off rent or house payments, picking up odd jobs. But there was no way to predict events like the shutdowns of the car shops, which laid off and rehired in response to fluctuating orders. Nor could anyone know when an accident or injury would strike. At thirty-seven, Jacob Hauser was still a young man. He had been a highly skilled brewery worker until a fall put him out of action in 1876. He was an immigrant, but he was no greenhorn: he had lived in Detroit twenty-five years. But for two years after the accident he had not been able to work regularly. Neighbors had helped, but when he applied to a local charity in 1878, he was penniless, with five small children and a month behind on the rent. Robert O'Hara was in similar shape that year. He had been unable to find steady work for a year and a half since the factory where he had worked burned down. Ann McFarland lived in a tiny garret and occasionally found a little light work. She had lived like this for ten years since her husband, a sailor, was killed in a ship fire.[29]

These are not isolated examples. In 1890, nearly 1,700 families were forcibly evicted from their homes for nonpayment of rent. State Labor Commissioner John McGrath was appalled at the evidence of "destitution and wretchedness" his investigators uncovered in Detroit: "In our cities they send their wives and children into our streets and alleys and backyards, gathering paper, fuel, and garbage. At the tearing down of an old building, or the tearing up of an old pavement, they appear in swarms, as if by magic, and carry away the rubbish, which they use for firewood and for building additions to their tenements."[30]

Public welfare programs or private charities like the Detroit Association of Charities, formed to "repress street begging and to better the conditions of the honest and deserving poor," gave only occasional help: a load of coal for a family without heat, a few dollars to forestall an eviction for past due rent, or help in finding a job. Thousands of families turned to them for emergency assistance. Five thousand received help from the Poor Commissioners in 1877; the Detroit Association of Charities considered 2,236 cases in 1883. But workers who asked for help from the association had to face humiliating questions from investigators who described applicants in their case records as "unreliable . . . habitual drunkards . . . beggars." An unemployed carpenter had refused to go through this ordeal in the winter of 1884, even though his daughter was sick with diphtheria, the house was freezing because his coal had run out, and he had thirty-five dollars in unpaid grocery bills and overdue rent. Neighbors, concerned about the impact of the cold on the little girl, applied to the city Poor Commissioner, who sent a half ton of coal.[31]

Workers turned to charities or public welfare out of necessity. There were no government unemployment programs, no workmen's compensation law, and few companies had systematic sick leave, unemployment, or accident insurance policies. Not a single one of the 133 employers questioned about employee benefit programs by the State Bureau of Labor Statistics in 1892 reported contributing to employee benefit funds. About half (56 percent) claimed to provide some relief for sick employees, apparently at their discretion, depending on their judgment of the merits of the case. Employers who did emphasized that they did so out of a spirit of charity, not out of any legal obligation. A

Detroit building contractor expressed what seems to have been the dominant spirit among Detroit employers: any relief "is entirely out of sympathy in proportion as they have been faithful employees."[32]

Union and fraternal insurance programs provided one alternative to charity or public relief. Nearly three-quarters of the trade unionists in Detroit in 1892 (73 percent) were covered by some union illness or disability benefits like the printers' five-dollars-per-week sick pay, about 40 percent of the regular minimum union wage scale. But at no time in late nineteenth-century Detroit did more than one worker in four belong to a labor organization, and for most of the period the proportion was far lower. About one worker in three (29 percent in 1890, 34 percent in 1896) belonged to a fraternal society. Most of these societies paid death benefits to cover funeral expenses; some also had sick or unemployment insurance. Unionized workers and those who belonged to fraternal societies clearly preferred these alternatives to private charities or public welfare. Among a sample of 688 Detroit Association of Charities cases (over 95 percent working class) only 11 percent reported membership in "beneficial societies." Of the seventy-four who did, only nine belonged to labor organizations, only twenty-one to religious or secular ethnic fraternal societies.[33]

The insecurities of wage labor were an important common thread cutting across many of the other differences in workers' backgrounds and experiences. The prevailing native middle-class culture stressed the value of independence and self-reliance, but even workers who fully believed in these virtues could never know when they, too, would need the help of neighbors, friends, or fellow workers.

Labor organizers consistently tried to build on this natural interdependence by pointing out that the threat of insecurity was not simply the product of divine providence. In a regular column in the Detroit *Labor Leaf* entitled "Labor's Risks," the editors recounted gruesome details of frequent accidents: "John Troy, a car washer for the Detroit City Railway Company, had his left leg broken last night by getting caught between a car and post at the Baker Street Barn . . . Thomas W. Byrne of Robinson and Byrne, pressmen, had his arm caught in the cogs of a printing press Saturday night . . . Charles Bowlsby, M.W. of Eureka Assembly, had the end of two fingers on his right hand badly crushed by a tire upsetter at Girardin's carriage factory . . . Oscar Jefferson, a boy in Pingree and Smith's shoe factory, was killed yesterday by an elevator crushing his head." Workers suffered, they argued, because employers drove them, forcing people to work under unsafe conditions which inevitably led to accidents, working them beyond their natural endurance until their health broke down.[34]

A carpenter who had quit his job in a seed box factory agreed. Workers there, he explained, were "compelled to keep up with machines." Three nights a week the factory ran three extra hours. Men who refused mandatory overtime were fired. The extra pay was little consolation. "At night when they quit work, and come out into the fresh air, the men can be seen hawking and spitting, and they blow great quantities of black walnut dust from their nostrils. If they look up from their work or stop to blow their nose, the machine gets ahead of them, and they lose caste with the foreman, and are liable to be discharged." In summer, when other carpenters made $2 or $2.50 per day, the factory's employees still earned only the $1.25 winter wage, but they kept on in order to avoid the forced winter layoff of other carpenters. Men who could not keep up with the machines were discharged, as was anyone who complained. "It is the policy of the firm not to have any discontented workmen in their employ," they were told. Older workers could not stand the pace but were still "turned out like old horses, to search for a living . . ." The carpenter had himself been forced to quit. "I do as much as any average man," but "I could not stand the extra night work. Every evening I was choked up with walnut dust."[35]

According to labor leaders, city and state factory inspection and sanitary laws, which should have prevented such conditions, were rarely enforced. In 1881, Detroit had passed a sanitary inspection ordinance, but in 1885, the *Labor Leaf* claimed that "to the knowledge of the oldest printer he [the health officer] has not visited a single printing office, except one on especial complaint, and that is as bad now as it was two or three months ago, when the health officer ordered it ventilated." In June 1887, the paper reported the death of John P. Lowry, the seventh printer to die of consumption in Detroit that year, and suggested that the excessive tuberculosis rate among printers (two and one-quarter times the average for the rest of the state's adult male population) was the result of overwork in cramped, poorly ventilated workshops.[36]

An examination of state factory inspectors' reports indicates that labor activists' complaints about lax enforcement of protective legislation were not without foundation. A state factory inspection law passed by the Michigan legislature in 1893 created a system of state inspectors mandated to visit every factory in the state at least once a year and with the authority to order compliance with regulations governing elevators, guard rails, machine guards, fire escapes, blowers, structural dangers,

17

washroom facilities, and prohibiting employment of children under fourteen. Detroit inspectors issued 1,670 citations in their first four years of operation and were unable to obtain compliance with their orders in 26.4 percent of these cases.[37]

Inspectors complained that ineffective enforcement was the result of inadequate funding for the agency, but the attitudes of the inspectors were clearly a factor as well. The law, for example, stipulated a minimum of forty-five minutes for workers' dinners unless the inspectors agreed that special circumstances made this impossible and gave their permission for a shorter dinner break. In 1897, Detroit inspectors found 318 firms operating with less than forty-five-minute dinner breaks and issued 318 special permissions.[38]

Correspondence between P. A. Loersch, the secretary of the Detroit Trades Council, and the State Labor Department is equally revealing. When the Trades Council called violations of the child labor section of the law to the attention of the director of factory inspection, the director argued, contrary to the law, that children should be allowed to work when the head of the family was laid off. "It seems a necessity that a child should be allowed to contribute to family support . . . It seems to me this is only common humanity." In a confidential communication to the factory inspectors, the director advised the use of "discretion" and "good judgment . . . for while the law seeks to provide for the safety and health of all employees of manufacturing establishments, it is not the intention to demand anything unreasonable or impossible of owners or operators of such establishments."[39]

Employers' attempts to maintain work discipline added another source of insecurity in addition to layoffs, illness, or accidents. A streetcar driver on the Fort Wayne and Elmwood Avenue line complained to a Detroit *Labor Leaf* reporter about the uncertainty that disciplinary practices produced. "We don't know at night whether we will go to work in the morning . . . They discharge a man and never tell him why; they never let him know he is discharged until he comes down in the morning ready to go to work, and finds his name is not on the slate." He drove fifteen hours a day without breaks for meals. "At the end of every trip we have twelve minutes to turn the car around, take the horse . . . and hitch him to the car when we are ready to start; this leaves us about eight minutes of the twelve to eat our meals if it is meal time. When I first came on the road, I used to take two sessions at my meals, but now I can eat a pailful in five minutes. A fellow needs some whiskey on top, though, to force it through." On Saturday, he added, "when-

18

ever the shows are late," some drivers were forced to work past quitting time without extra pay. "A man's a slave that drives a car, sir." [40]

When the *Labor Leaf* ran a series of such accounts in 1884 and 1885, some local businessmen were outraged by the articles. Frank Pingree was so angry after an article appeared in the *Labor Leaf* describing Pingree and Smith's work rules that he threatened to discharge the entire shop unless he was told who had talked to the *Leaf*. The foreman at Ferry's, Mr. Ward, threatened any employee seen with a copy of the *Labor Leaf* would be fired. When an article appeared accusing him of forcing his employees to contribute to a Christmas gift for him, a practice reported by workers in a number of other companies, he forced seventy-two of the women under him to sign a declaration under threat of discharge denying the truthfulness of the piece. Many of those who signed the denial admitted they had not even read it. Anyone seen buying the *Labor Leaf* was subject to immediate dismissal. Another Ferry employee, Susie Kahl, came to the *Leaf* office to report on the treatment of the little children, "oldest not over twelve . . . ," who tore open packages of seeds. A small child, Kittie Fuchs, reportedly an asthmatic, fainted shortly after the forewoman had refused her a break to get a drink of water. Miss Kahl bitterly described the scene: "When she came to, she said, 'Please, Aggie [the forewoman], let me rest for five minutes?' And in a mean, cross way, Aggie said to her, 'If you don't go to work right away, I will tell Mr. Davidson to get another girl in your place!' The poor little child was so sick and frightened that she did not know what to do. I tell you, sir, sometimes, it seems as though God ought to destroy the persons who have charge of the rooms in that warehouse." [41]

The language of the account might strike some modern readers as overly dramatic, but the realities described were serious. A week later, the *Leaf* reported, both Susie Kahl and Kittie Fuchs had been discharged. A spotter stationed outside the *Labor Leaf* office by the general foreman saw Miss Kahl enter and reported it. Three weeks later the *Labor Leaf* itself was forced out of its offices when the owner of the building and an adjoining print shop that printed the paper decided that a description of the lack of ventilation in an anonymous Detroit print shop had been based on his establishment. [42]

The threat of dismissal was the ultimate sanction upon which the entire system of labor discipline rested, but employers attempted to enforce punctuality, steadiness, and consistency by other methods as well. At Newcomb, Endicott, and Company, workers suffered one-dollar fines for tardiness, even if only one minute late. Metcalf's fined its workers for talking on the job five cents per offense. At Pingree and Smith, shoemakers were docked for an entire case of shoes if even one was not up to quality standards, although the company packed and sold the supposedly inferior shoes along with the rest. One shoe only "showed a little wrinkle on the toe; drawn like, you know," the laster explained. He was docked for the whole case. The Ferry Seed Company insured promptness by locking the door at 7:00 A.M., preventing women who were late from entering. They were allowed in at noon with the loss of a half-day's pay. A similar practice at Gay, Toynton, and Fox candy factory was reported to have been the cause of death of three women who were unable to get out the locked door when the building caught fire.[43]

Not all employers resorted to such practices, but the question of work discipline was at its heart a reflection of the contest of wills common to all wage labor. Employers hired workers because they hoped to make a profit, but what they bought with the money they paid out in wages was only a *potential* for labor. The employer was buying the worker for a specified period of time. To actually realize a profit the employer had to insure that the worker produced goods of greater value than the wage during that time. The more work the employer got out of the worker, the higher the profit. The employer's interest was to make the worker work as steadily, as carefully, as intensely as possible. Any time the worker leaned on his shovel, or walked away from her machine, or stopped to get a drink of water, from the employer's point of view, potential labor and thereby potential profit were wasted.[44]

While a kindly employer might voluntarily try to avoid the full implications of this dilemma, in a competitive economy no employer could survive for long if he maintained wages or working conditions much better than those of his competitors. Even the most militant trade unionists recognized this. Many trade union activities, as well as more widespread informal practices of self-regulation among workers, were geared to establishing standards: setting floors for wages and ceilings on the level of effort expected. To trade unionists, a "fair-minded" employer was one who treated his employees politely, maintained the generally accepted standards in his industry, and did not try to chisel extra profits by pushing people or cutting rates—in effect, one who accepted the wisdom of trade union efforts to set standards of working conditions.[45]

Thus, variations in management practices did not remove the need for workers to take action to limit the consequences of an adversary relationship. The most efficient, or the most ruthless, employers set the pace for everyone else. Regardless how satisfactory or unsatisfactory a particular job may have seemed to an individual worker, every worker who decided when to slow down or when to speed up, every worker who kept an eye out for the foreman, every worker who needed just a bit more explanation of how to do the next task was taking such actions every day. Even the nicest boss was still a boss, and even the most privileged and fortunate workers were affected by the general conditions of other workers in their trade.

Finally, all workers faced the frustration of a relationship in which the results of their skills, their creativity, and their efforts went to someone else. If the employer made unwise management decisions and the firm faltered, they would be let go. As a tinsmith explained to the interviewer from the State Bureau of Labor Statistics, employers treated workers "like any other piece of machinery, to be made to do the maximum amount of work with the minimum expenditure of fuel." A lumbermill worker agreed that they were used just like any other piece of machinery "to be speculated on and worked to their utmost capacity in good condition, but to be cast aside as worthless when out of repair."[46]

But the profits, when they worked well, went to their employers. "I experience every day," complained a hostler, "that my employer, who works neither so hard nor so long as I do, lives in luxury while I am reduced to a bare living, and that must be wrong, as I know that our Creator certainly entitled me to the same enjoyment of life's blessings as him." Workers did not need a familiarity with Marxist theory to come to something close to a labor theory of value. It came from experience. A machinist observed, "My employer pays me $1.75 and charges his customers from $5.00 to $15.00 for the same."[47]

Class systems do not necessarily breed the antagonism these workers felt. Greater inequalities than existed in Detroit have been accepted as quite legitimate.[48] But the authoritarian regimes workers experienced in Detroit workplaces sharply contradicted the egalitarian rhetoric that even their employers used to justify the system. No Detroit employer tried to rest his claims to wealth or authority on Divine Right or hereditary privilege. Republican values and an ideology of equal opportunity reigned supreme. Many Detroit employers, like millionaire mayor and shoe manufacturer Hazen Pingree, were self-made men and proud of it. We claim "no special privileges," he explained in a speech to the Detroit Chamber of Commerce in 1895. "All should be upon an equal footing."[49]

The very logic of Pingree's argument was the basis of labor organizers' indictment of accumulated wealth. As a columnist in the *Advance and Labor Leaf* put it: "We are often told that the millionaires of today were working for wages thirty or forty years ago, and the millionaires of thirty or forty years hence, will be the men who are now working for a dollar or two per day. These delusive statements are intended to reconcile the toiler to the condition to which monopoly is disposed to consign him. No wage worker ever has or ever can become a millionaire by honest labor. The first step towards the accumulation of a million is to cease to earn a living and go into the business of skinning others." [50]

Labor activists joined employers, newspaper editors, and politicians in celebration of a new industrial way of life, in admiration of the wonders of new mechanical marvels, and in appreciation of the potential of new technologies for liberating human beings from age-old material scarcity and physical drudgery. The activists, most of them editors and columnists for the *Labor Leaf* who were hired to write the labor page which the Sunday *News* established in the 1880s to appeal to its working-class readers, devoted part of nearly every page to descriptions of manufacturing processes or reports of new machines. But as a resolution at the Socialist Labor party's July 4th celebration in 1879 explained, the present arrangement of society gave industrial progress a threatening character to workers as "mechanical science . . . tends to degrade rather than elevate the laboring classes; destroying the comparatively independent position which their skill or handicraft afforded." [51]

More and more trades faced this threat. As companies expanded, they reorganized production, and much of that reorganization was aimed at cutting costs by replacing skilled and expensive hand labor with simpler, cheaper, and more mechanized production methods. Each trade experienced this threat in different ways: for the shoemaker, it was the McKay pegging machine; for the cigarmaker, the mold; for the printer, the typesetting machines; and even for the lordly molder, the aristocrat of the metal trades, the bucks system. The differences were important; some trades weathered transformation of their industries far better than others. But even when they were able to make the transitions, as the hand compositors did to the typesetting machines, workers faced a personal and group crisis which could be resolved only after years of anxiety and conflict. When the first typesetting machines were introduced in Detroit composing rooms, 30 percent of the hand compositors were laid off. Printers were able to maintain wage rates and working conditions only because the printing industry continued to expand more rapidly than the increases in productivity from the new machines, and because the strong local printers' union was able to insist that employers hire only union compositors as machine operators and pay them at union rates as they learned the new machines.[52]

But while the development of "mechanical science" seemed to be a mixed blessing to workers, their day-to-day experiences demonstrated that all who made industrial progress possible were not on an "equal footing." They worked with their hands, wore overalls, work shirts, or cheap dresses, and carried their lunch buckets to work. But the clerks, bookkeepers, accountants, and managers worked in clean offices, in suits and ties. Many went around the corner to a restaurant to lunch. When the workers returned home many of them greeted wives, sisters, and daughters who had spent the day cleaning the homes of bookkeepers, accountants, and managers. Half of the non-working-class families in Detroit in the 1880s had domestic servants, while fewer than 1 percent of working-class families did.[53]

Some of the social boundaries between classes were fuzzy. Few neighborhoods were solidly working class. Carpenters lived next door to bookkeepers or even occasionally to the proprietors of small workshops. The barkeeper at the local saloon may have been a retired printer who still kept up on union affairs, the corner grocer a retired artisan who had saved his money carefully to open the store. Yet despite such ambiguities in the social boundaries of classes, and despite the differences in workers' experiences, all workers faced common problems growing directly out of their position in the wage relationship—dependence on wages and the insecurity that went with it, the conflict and frustration inherent in authoritarian work settings, and pervasive evidence that they were receiving less than their fair share of the wealth they created. Their experiences, their homes, their lives contrasted markedly with those of the managers, superintendents, and employers whom they helped to enrich.

These problems and these contrasts drove many of them to action. Workers did not come to a sense of opposition quickly or easily, but once they did, the potential implications were far-reaching. A shoemaker in a shoe factory almost apologized in 1885: "I am no crank; I am no tramp; I am no agitator; I am no lazy fellow who wants to be fed from others' earnings. I am willing to work as most men are . . ." But he saw poverty and increasing discontent, "men in despair . . . and now it is time something is done . . . if a change is not soon devised, trouble must arise." [54]

Many, if not most, workers were similarly dissatisfied. In a poll conducted by the State Bureau of Labor Statistics in 1885, nearly 80 percent of those who answered the question thought their pay was unfair, and the explanations many of them offered suggest it was not merely the amount they thought unfair, but also the nature of the wage relationship. But if it was "time something was done," what was it that should be done, who should do it, and how should they go about it? [55]

Labor organizers had one set of answers: working people had to ignore differences in background and experience in order to act together to change the rules which governed the industrial system. Organizers often disagreed among themselves about what changes were needed and what actions would bring about those changes, but they agreed that any solutions to workers' problems depended on collective action of workers in their own behalf. But for workers to act as a class, they had to have a sense of common position, common plight; i.e., class consciousness. As we have seen, Detroit workers did have some common problems, and clear differences existed between their life styles and those of the business and white-collar classes. A typical Detroit worker of the 1880s worked a sixty-hour week at manual labor for about ten dollars. The work was tiring and left little time or energy for much else except on days off. Regular wages or the combined incomes of several wage earners were usually sufficient for basic physical needs for an average family of five—food, clothing, shelter—in a minimum style, but typical wages left little surplus for amusement or savings. Without savings, there was little to fall back on if someone became seriously ill or the primary wage earner was laid off. Layoffs and unemployment were common enough that most working-class families faced poverty periodically. In bad times the differences between skilled and unskilled could evaporate quickly. The worker's family lived in a small frame house, probably near their church. The homes contained basic utilitarian furniture; about half the homes had sewing machines, hardly any had musical instruments. About two-fifths of the working-class families were buying their homes, and slightly more than three-fifths rented. [56]

These things most workers had in common with each other. But in many other crucial aspects, workers were different from each other: work experiences, skill, background, nationality, attitudes, ambitions, religion. While they faced common problems, their perceptions of the meaning and importance of these problems were filtered through different cultural and social visions. Different perceptions could mean very different responses.

NOTES

1. Peter A. Ostafin, "The Polish Peasant in Transition: A Study of Group Integration as a Function of Symbiosis and Common Definitions" (Ph.D. dissertation, University of Michigan, 1948), p. 71.

2. *Tenth Census*, 1880, vol. 1, pp. 471, 876; *Eleventh Census*, 1890, vol. 1, pt. 2, p. 864; Michigan State Bureau of Labor Statistics, *First Annual Report* (Lansing, 1884), pp. 112–13, 128–30. (Michigan State Bureau of Labor Statistics Reports will hereafter be cited SBLS and the year.)

3. Allen R. Pred, *The Spatial Dynamics of U.S. Urban-Industrial Growth, 1800–1914* (Cambridge, 1966), chap. 2; JoEllen Vinyard, *The Irish on the Urban Frontier, Nineteenth Century Detroit, 1850–1880* (New York, 1976), pp. 124–25.

4. *Eleventh Census*, 1890, vol. 1, pt. 1, p. 370; *Twelfth Census*, 1900, vol. 1, p. lxix; Melvin G. Holli, "The Impact of Automobile Manufacturing upon Detroit," *Detroit in Perspective*, 2 (Spring 1976): 177; Melvin G. Holli, *Reform in Detroit, Hazen S. Pingree and Urban Politics* (New York, 1969), pp. 4–6; Silas Farmer, *History of Detroit and Wayne County and Early Michigan* (Detroit, 1890), pp. 802–36.

5. Ostafin, pp. 74–78; Sister Mary Remigia Napolska, *The Polish Immigrant in Detroit to 1914* (Chicago, 1946); Olivier Zunz, "The Organization of the American City in the Late Nineteenth Century, Ethnic and Spatial Arrangement in Detroit," *Journal of Urban History* 3 (August 1977): 453–57.

6. Zunz, 453–57. For further descriptions of Detroit's neighborhood structure, see also Olivier Zunz, *The Changing Face of Inequality: Detroit from 1880 to 1920* (Chicago, 1982); David M. Katzman, *Before the Ghetto, Black Detroit in the Nineteenth Century* (Urbana, 1975), esp. chap. 2; *Eleventh Census*, 1890, vol. 4, pt. 2, pp. 219–27.

7. Detroit *Evening News*, April 3, 1891.

8. *Evening News*, January 26, 1891; case histories of many unemployed workers can be found in the casebooks of the Detroit Association of Charities in the United Community Services Collection, Archives of Labor and Urban Affairs, Wayne State University, Detroit.

9. *Ninth Census*, 1870, vol. 1, p. 785; vol. 3, pp. 682–83; Holli, *Reform in Detroit*, p. 4.

10. Holli, *Reform in Detroit*, pp. 5–7; George N. Fuller, *Michigan, A Centennial History of the State and Its People* (Chicago, 1939), pp. 536–40; Farmer, *History of Detroit and Wayne County*, pp. 804–6; Alfred D. Chandler,

Jr., *The Visible Hand, The Managerial Revolution in American Business* (Cambridge, 1977), pp. 1–3, 359, 511; "Among the Molders," unidentified Detroit newspaper clipping dated June 16, 1889, "Detroit Labor Leaders" file, Labadie Collection, University of Michigan, Ann Arbor, hereafter cited LC.

11. *Twelfth Census*, 1900, vol. 8, p. 994; *Fourth Annual Report of Inspection of Factories in Michigan* (Lansing, 1898), pp. 12–47. See note to table 2 for a discussion of factory size statistics.

12. "Among the Molders"; *Eleventh Census*, 1890, Compendium, pt. 2, pp. 102–5; "Men Who Make Your Cigars," LC; Farmer, *History of Detroit and Wayne County*, p. 831.

13. *Eleventh Census*, 1890, vol. 1, pt. 2, pp. 664–65. For additional data on the composition of the work force, see Richard Oestreicher, "Solidarity and Fragmentation: Working People and Class Consciousness in Detroit, 1877–1895" (Ph.D. dissertation, Michigan State University, 1979), pp. 17–20, 25, 48–50, 503–7, 513–19.

14. Ostafin, p. 71; *Evening News*, April 27, 1891; *SBLS*, 1893, pp. 750–53. These statements are not included here to assert that wage rates and the standard of living in Detroit were lower than in Germany or Poland. What they do suggest is that despite objectively higher living standards, a tough work regime made life in Detroit still seem qualitatively difficult.

15. *SBLS*, 1893, pp. 780, 789, 1042–1108, 1117; *SBLS*, 1884, p. 847. Monthly rents of Detroit factory workers surveyed in 1892 averaged $8.91. Typical monthly food budgets were over $4 per adult; i.e., a family of six (assuming four children equalled two adults) would need over $16 per month for food. Over half (51 percent) of workers surveyed in 1884 made $1.50 per day or less.

16. *Tenth Census*, 1880, vol. 1, p. 876; *SBLS*, 1884, pp. 62–65, 71–75, 80–81.

17. *Eleventh Census*, 1890, vol. 1, pt. 2, pp. 664–65; *SBLS*, 1892, pp. 2–4, 132, 139, 144, 154, 160; *SBLS*, 1886, p. 274.

18. *SBLS*, 1884, pp. 86–87; "Labor Day Review," 1892, p. 11. Based on the relative distribution of wage rates within the working class, it would appear that artisans made up slightly more than one-third of the working class, unskilled laborers about another third, and semiskilled workers slightly less than a third. The last group would include a variety of workers whose jobs involved some skills and experience but who were not full-fledged artisans. In many trades, however, especially those undergoing technological change, the distinctions between artisans and other workers were breaking down.

19. Herman Koss, "A History of the Detroit Typographical Union No. 18," (M.A. thesis, Wayne State University, 1950). Detailed discussions of union work rules can be found in the Minute Books of Detroit Typographical Union No. 18 in the Archives of Labor and Urban Affairs.

20. *Fourth Annual Report of Inspection of Factories in Michigan* (Lan-

sing, 1897); Koss, pp. 27–42; *The Detroit Printer*, April 24, 1896; *Advance and Labor Leaf*, June 11, 1887; *Labor Leaf*, December 3, 1884, February 15, 1885.

21. *SBLS*, 1891, pp. 134–35; "Among the Molders", LC; *Evening News*, June 5, 6, 9, 1887.

22. *SBLS*, 1891, pp. 2–25.

23. "Labor Day Review," 1892, p. 11. *SBLS*, 1884, p. 86; "Men Who Make Your Cigars," LC.

24. *Eleventh Census*, 1890, vol. 1, pt. 2, p. 664; *Twelfth Census*, 1900, vol. 2, pt. 2, p. 558.

25. Clyde Griffen, "Workers Divided: The Effect of Craft and Ethnic Differences in Poughkeepsie, New York, 1850–1880," in Stephen Thernstrom and Richard Sennett, *Nineteenth Century Cities* (New Haven, 1969), is an excellent example of the impact of similar differences in a smaller industrial city.

26. Vinyard, *The Irish on the Urban Frontier*, pp. 320–23, 404–8. Vinyard's intention was to compare the mobility rates and property ownership of Irish, German, and native families. Her mobility sample is thus made up of first and second generation males of these three ethnic groups. Projecting the 1880–1890 mobility rates out of the working class for thirty years yields an expected total rate of 45 percent for skilled workers and 36 percent for unskilled and semiskilled workers. These estimates strike me as too high for several reasons. First the sample excludes those immigrant groups (notably Poles) who were both most recent arrivals and at the bottom of the ethnic hierarchy; a more representative sample of the entire working class would probably yield lower initial rates. Second, the thirty-year projection assumes that people would continue working on average to age seventy, an unlikely assumption. Twenty-year projections for mobility out of the working class would be 33 percent and 26 percent respectively. Third, long-term studies of career mobility in other cities found initial ten-year mobility rates were not matched in successive decades. Career mobility out of the working class in Boston and Poughkeepsie in this era was 26 percent and 31 percent respectively for skilled workers and 28 percent and 15 percent respectively for low manual workers. Stephen Thernstrom, *The Other Bostonians* (Cambridge, 1973), p. 237.

27. *Eleventh Census*, 1890, vol. 1, pt. 2, pp. 664–65; *SBLS*, 1897, p. 171; *SBLS*, 1891, p. 153; *SBLS*, 1885, p. 252.

28. *SBLS*, 1886, pp. 230–31; *SBLS*, 1893, p. 781.

29. Detroit Association of Charities, cases 14, 11, 18, United Community Services Collection, Archives of Labor and Urban Affairs, Wayne State University. The archives prohibits the use of actual names of charity applicants. The names used here are fictitious.

30. *Evening News*, January 4, 1891; *SBLS*, 1884, pp. 180–81.

31. Farmer, *History of Detroit*, pp. 645, 666; Detroit Association of Charities, Case Record Books.

32. *SBLS*, 1893, pp. 1284–88. The employers' sample included both Detroit firms and some outstate firms.

33. Detroit Association of Charities, Case Record Books, 1878–1891. These results should be approached with caution. Applicants may have considered it in their interest to conceal other possible sources of aid, and they may not have considered membership in labor and ethnic organizations relevant to the question as worded. (Earlier forms asked: "Does, or did your husband belong to any beneficial societies? Do such societies give you any aid, and how much a week? In later years there was simply a blank for "club or benefit society.")

34. *Labor Leaf*, March 26, 1887, November 17, 1886, August 6, September 10, 1887. Detroit legislators elected by the Independent Labor party repeatedly introduced bills for safety legislation and were responsible for the passage of several acts.

35. *Labor Leaf*, December 3, 1884. For additional descriptions of working conditions see Oestreicher, pp. 111–22.

36. *Labor Leaf*, June 11, 1887; *Thirty-Seventh Annual Report of the Secretary of the State Board of Health of the State of Michigan for the Fiscal Year Ending June 30, 1909* (Lansing, 1910), p. 96. The exceptionally high rate of tuberculosis among printers has been studied by several authorities including James A. Miller, M.D., "Pulmonary Tuberculosis among Printers," International Congress on Tuberculosis (Washington, D.C., 1908), vol. 3, pp. 209–16; George A. Stevens, "The Health of Printers, A Study in Industrial Hygiene," *Twenty-Fourth Annual Report of the Bureau of Labor Statistics, 1906* (Albany, N.Y., 1907), pp. lxxxix–clii; Rosamond W. Goldberg, *Occupational Diseases in Relation to Compensation and Health Insurance* (New York, 1931), pp. 63, 68–70, 77. All emphasize the importance of factors in the work environment. Miller and Stevens stress inadequate ventilation, sanitary conditions, and lowered resistance from overwork. Goldberg argues that printers suffered from low-level lead poisoning from handling lead type. The level of exposure was generally too low to produce acute symptoms of lead poisoning but chronic lead poisoning lowers resistance to infection—thus explaining susceptibilty to tuberculosis.

37. *First Annual Report of Inspectors of Factories in Michigan, 1894* (Lansing, 1894), p. 1; *Fourth Annual Report of Inspectors of Factories in Michigan, 1897* (Lansing, 1897), p. 4.

38. *Fourth Annual Report of Inspectors of Factories in Michigan, 1897* (Lansing, 1897), p. 50.

39. Executive Office *Reports*, correspondence files, B 182, F 9, nd, Michigan State Historical Commission, Lansing, Michigan.

40. *Labor Leaf*, January 14, 1885.

41. *Labor Leaf*, January 7, 1885, December 31, 1884, January 7, 14, 21, 1885. Three separate cases of foremen extorting Christmas gifts from employees are described.

42. *Labor Leaf*, January 28, February 25, 1885.

43. *Labor Leaf*, March 4, 1885, January 28, 1885, December 24, 31, 1884, December 10, 1884, December 7, 1884.

44. This argument is developed further in Harry Braverman, *Labor and Monopoly Capital, the Degradation of Work in the Twentieth Century* (New York, 1974), and Richard Edwards, *Contested Terrain, the Transformation of the Workplace in the Twentieth Century* (New York, 1979).

45. *The Union Label* (Detroit), vol. 1, no. 13, September, 14, 1895.

46. *SBLS*, 1885, p. 158. This section of the 1885 *Report* was based on interviews made throughout the state of Michigan, and the residences of particular respondents were not identified.

47. *SBLS*, 1885, pp. 1499–51.

48. See Barrington Moore, Jr., *Injustice, the Social Bases of Obedience and Revolt* (White Plains, N.Y., 1978), pt. 1, for a discussion of when inequalities are accepted as legitimate and when they are not.

49. Hazen Pingree, speech to the Detroit Chamber of Commerce, Hazen Pingree Papers, Burton Historical Collection, Detroit Public Library. David Montgomery, *Beyond Equality* (New York, 1972), discusses the nature and significance of republican values. Herbert Gutman, *Work, Culture and Society in Industrializing America* (New York, 1977), discusses employers' struggle for legitimacy in chaps. 1, 5, 7.

50. *Advance and Labor Leaf*, August 24, 1889.

51. *The Socialist* (Chicago), July 12, 1879.

52. *Evening News*, August 14, 1892; David Montgomery, "Workers' Control of Machine Production in the Nineteenth Century," in *Workers' Control in America* (Cambridge, 1979); John Laslett, *Labor and the Left: A Study of Socialist and Radical Influences in the American Labor Movement, 1881–1924* (New York, 1970); Irwin Yellowitz, *Industrialization and the American Labor Movement, 1850–1900* (Port Washington, N.Y., 1977); Alan Dawley, *Class and Community: The Industrial Revolution in Lynn* (Cambridge, Mass., 1976).

53. *SBLS*, 1884, pp. 140–41; *Eleventh Census*, 1890, vol. 1, pt. 2, pp. 664, cxci. For a fuller discussion of class differences in living standards, see Oestreicher, pp. 30–33.

54. *SBLS*, 1886, pp. 165, 158.

55. *SBLS*, 1886, pp. 149–50.

56. *SBLS*, 1884, p. 142; *SBLS*, 1886, pp. 53, 231. About half the homeowners questioned said their homes were mortgaged.

2

CLASS SOLIDARITY AND COMPETING CULTURAL SYSTEMS

> Rise up in struggle—act like men not like old wives . . .
> organize yourselves . . . under the flag of the proletariat we
> hold high . . . God helps those who help themselves.
>
> Charles Crouse, temporary secretary of the
> Detroit Social Revolutionary Group, 1885

Charles Crouse's letter to the local radical German weekly, *Der Arme Teufel*, reveals something of the convictions of a worker who would have described himself as "class conscious."[1] Crouse was outraged, outraged like Robert Reitzel, the paper's editor, by a world which should "belong to all . . . but in practice is something completely different. Der Arme Teufel [the Poor Devil] . . . doesn't own a foot of ground in the whole wide world, while every day people pass by my office who own so much land that one of the Twelve Tribes could have lived comfortably on it."[2] But Crouse was also frustrated. It seemed perfectly clear to him that in such a world all workers everywhere had to stick together, but his Social Revolutionary Group could not muster more than 100 workers in 1885, and the local unions included only a bit more than one Detroit worker in ten. To Crouse the reality of class conflict was so self-evident that cowardice could be the only reason more workers did not step forward.[3]

At one time or another, Crouse's disappointment with his fellow workers was echoed by nearly every other labor leader in Detroit. The "stumbling block in the way of progress," wrote a *Labor Leaf* correspondent in January 1885, "is the *apathy* of . . . those who ought to be most interested." "The masses are dull of apprehension, and cannot comprehend abstract ideas," veteran organizer John Francis Bray warned his fellow agitators in 1883. Some were more charitable than Crouse, recognizing fear of employer repression, or the lack of experience of recent immigrants, but most admitted they were puzzled about why more workers did not protest against their condition.[4]

30

Class consciousness and the vision of class solidarity that flows from it are abstractions. They are abstractions grounded in real and concrete experiences—the day-to-day conflicts and antagonisms of people who face each other from opposite sides of the wage relationship—but the abstractions are generalizations which go well beyond these immediate experiences. As a generalized analysis of the world, the class-conscious vision assumes that the relationship between all bosses and all workers is fundamentally the same. In some ways this is never true. Personalities vary; each boss and each worker is a unique individual; each person behaves a little bit differently from the next. No two jobs are exactly alike. A class analysis ultimately is an argument that these variations are unimportant. Workers in many times and places have accepted this argument that the similarities in their experiences were more important than the differences. If most workers in Detroit seemed unwilling to accept it, if the differences were important, moral exhortations were unlikely to make them see the world differently. To comprehend why those differences were important we need to know how they understood their lives in Detroit.

Detroit's Workers: Who Were They?

While we have many case studies of workers in individual communities, few scholars have attempted to develop a general theory which might tell us under what conditions workers are likely to view the world according to a class analysis.[5] But recent studies of such nineteenth-century American industrial towns as Lynn, Fall River, Troy, and Cohoes are suggestive. Class consciousness was strongest in Lynn and Troy, where workers had both highly developed work cultures that conflicted with employers' attempts to change work organization and a highly developed sense of community outside the workplace. Where the work force was culturally diverse and traditions of autonomous artisans were not well established (Cohoes), or the sense of community was weak (Fall River), class consciousness was less important.[6]

None of these communities was quite comparable to Detroit; all were relatively homogeneous, single-industry towns. In contrast, Detroit was a diverse industrial city. As we have seen, this meant that workers found themselves in a variety of economic circumstances. But even more important was how workers' different backgrounds led them to interpret those circumstances. Who were they?

In early nineteenth-century Lynn, we could easily answer the question, who were the workers? They were native-stock shoemakers, their families and relatives. The impact of variations in wages, skill, work experience, and sex roles was mitigated by a tight network of family, kin, and neighborhood interdependence. While there was a significant minority of more transient workers, what Alan Dawley has called "floaters," and by mid-century a new influx of Irish immigrants, floaters and immigrants could be integrated into this stable core community. Similarly, in Troy the skilled ironworkers formed a stable central core, their sense of artisan solidarity reinforced by a common Irish heritage and the overlap between class exploitation and ethnic discrimination.[7]

In Detroit's working class there was no comparable homogeneous core, no simple answer to the question, who were Detroit's workers? In 1890, among every 100 workers in Detroit there were fourteen native-stock white Americans (that is, natives of native parents), twenty-six Germans, five Irish, six British, ten English Canadians, two French Canadians, three native blacks, twenty-five children of immigrants, eight immigrants of other nationalities. Each of these ethnic fragments of Detroit's working class had its own center of stable homeowners, kin networks, and community associations, but these core communities were largely separate, based more on ethnic than class identity.[8]

Each nationality occupied a different position within the local economy. Immigrants were older, on average, than natives. But despite the younger age structure of the native white population, native white workers disproportionately held the better jobs and were nearly absent from the lowest-paying industrial occupations. The group advantage of native white workers increased over time. In 1880, just over half of the native white workers occupied skilled positions. By 1900, the proportion was two-thirds.[9] As they aged their individual advantage was also likely to increase. JoEllen Vinyard found that between 1880 and 1890 nearly half of the native workers she traced experienced upward mobility while only slightly over one-quarter of the Irish and German workers did.[10]

Differences between the economic positions of immigrant groups were as significant as those between natives and immigrants. British and English-speaking Canadian immigrants were less likely to enter business, professional, or white-collar occupations than native whites, but like native whites they occupied a disproportionate share of the most desirable working-class jobs. British workers arrived in Detroit with craft skills learned in the world's most advanced industrial nation and often with money in their pockets. English metal trades workers surveyed by the State Bureau of Labor Statistics in 1890, for example,

Table 7. Occupational Composition of Detroit Ethnic Groups, 1880–1900

Occupational category	Year	*Percent of total ethnic group in each category by year*						
		Native White[1]	Canadian[2]	British[1]	Irish[1]	German[1]	Polish[1]	Black[1]
High white collar	1880	10.2	1.2	3.0	0.8	1.3	1.2	0.8
	1900	10.5	5.2	2.9	2.6	1.2	0	0
Low white collar	1880	44.0	15.9	24.7	16.8	12.5	30.6	6.2
	1900	45.4	32.8	29.1	17.9	15.5	5.7	6.9
Skilled worker	1880	23.9	31.8	42.1	23.5	43.9	17.6	25.4
	1900	29.7	35.4	46.0	23.7	42.8	32.5	20.8
Semiskilled or un- skilled worker	1880	21.9	51.0	30.2	59.0	42.4	50.6	67.1
	1900	14.5	26.6	21.9	55.8	40.5	61.8	72.3

Source: Olivier Zunz, *The Changing Face of Inequality* (Chicago, 1982), tables 1.5, 9.1.

1. Native of native parents, British of British parents, etc.
2. For 1880 includes both French and English Canadian; for 1900 only English Canadian.

reported that they had had an average of $177.09 on arrival in the United States, more than five times the averages of Poles ($30.66), Germans ($28.99), or the Irish ($27.02). Over half of the male British workers in Detroit in 1890 were artisans in construction or industry. They were overrepresented in nearly all skilled trades, but particularly concentrated in the most elite categories of metal trades and construction. Accepted by natives as fellow Anglo-Saxons, they easily made the transition into skilled positions in American industry. Only 42 percent of the British workers in Detroit were unskilled or semiskilled in 1880, only 32 percent in 1900, a smaller proportion than among native whites.[11]

Canadian immigrants to Detroit did not include as large a proportion of highly skilled craftsmen as the British, but they benefitted from their ready access to the Detroit labor market. Many were commuters from Windsor across the Detroit River, and most of the rest had moved to Detroit from the small towns and farms of Detroit's prosperous Ontario hinterland. They were immigrants only in a legal sense: their process of relocation had been no more difficult than that of natives coming from small towns in Michigan or northern Ohio. Once in Detroit they were virtually indistinguishable from natives; there were no distinctively Canadian neighborhoods and no distinctively English-Canadian ethnic organizations.[12]

The position of German workers, the largest single ethnic group in Detroit's working class, was quite different from that of the English-speaking immigrants. The German community in Detroit was far more working class (86 percent in 1890) than the British (72 percent in 1890) or Canadians (72 percent in 1890). While there was a large German business class, Germans were proportionately underrepresented in both professional and high white-collar occupations and in such low white-collar occupations as bookkeepers and clerks. One-third of German workers were laborers, half were unskilled or semiskilled. Within industry Germans were underrepresented in the high wage sectors. While close to half of the German workers were artisans, like the English bringing craft skills and industrial experience with them, they arrived poorer and found the transition into high-skill positions more difficult than English-speaking immigrants. More important, the most characteristically German crafts—cigarmaking, shoemaking, tailoring, brewing, coopering, woodworking—were those most immediately threatened by skill dilution. German craftsmen bore the brunt of technological change far more dramatically than natives or English-speaking immigrants.[13]

Poles were the most recent arrivals in 1890. After a trickle in the 1870s, Polish immigration expanded dramatically in the 1880s. By 1890 Polish workers may have outnumbered native workers in Detroit, although the failure of census workers to accurately identify Poles makes it impossible to say for sure.[14] Over 90 percent of the Polish immigrant work force were workers, and like the Germans, most of the remainder were small storeowners. But in contrast to the Germans, Poles were excluded from many skilled trades. Most came from agricultural villages and some had been craftsmen in their villages, but in Detroit they often found entrance to their crafts closed. Most Poles worked as laborers or factory hands as they filled the bottom rungs of the job hierarchies in heavy industry and construction. Two-thirds were unskilled or semiskilled in 1900.[15]

Detroit's Irish workers occupied a position in the economic structure below that of the most successful English-speaking immigrants, like the British, but despite a lack of skills, the Irish fared better than the Poles. The Irish had arrived poor and with few craft skills. The heritage of their lack of skills was still clearly evident. Nearly three-quarters of the Irish workers were unskilled or semiskilled in 1880 (a higher proportion than the Poles.) [16] But by the end of the century their longevity was beginning to pay off; their situation was improving. In their 1890 survey of Detroit's metal trades, for example, State Bureau of Labor Statistics investigators learned that Irish metal workers had been in the United States an average of twenty years compared to twelve for the Germans and eight for the Poles. Many had accumulated considerable property. They reported an average net worth of $1,303.18, a higher average than any other nationality in the industry except the British, more than double the average of German metalworkers and triple the average of Poles. Irish-born workers were still 70 percent unskilled or semiskilled in 1900, but a larger proportion of these unskilled or semiskilled workers found jobs in the more highly paid categories of unskilled labor (notably transportation.) By 1900, the percentage of first-generation Irish workers had fallen to less than 5 percent of Detroit's working class, and their children occupied nearly as favorable a position as native white or British workers. [17]

The experiences of Detroit's black workers form a special case quite different from that of any of the European immigrants. Generally descendants of escaped slaves who had migrated to Detroit from nearby parts of Michigan, Ontario, Ohio, or Indiana, they had been in Detroit longer than any of the immigrants but occupied the lowest position in the ethnic hierarchy. Blacks were more preponderantly working class than even the Poles, but they were systematically excluded from most industrial jobs, including the most poorly paid or disagreeable. In such basic industries as shipbuilding, shoemaking, or brewing, there was not a single black worker in Detroit in 1890, while blacks made up less than 0.5 percent of the work forces in woodworking, printing, iron- and steel-making, and furniture manufacturing. In only one male (painters) and one female industrial job category (dressmakers) did the percentage of blacks approach their proportion of the city's working-class population. [18] Most blacks worked as domestic servants, in related service occupations like barbering or waiting on tables, or as longshoremen. Servants and laundresses made up 74.9 percent of the black female work force in 1890, while 60.7 percent of the black male work force were servants, laborers, or barbers. Barbering was one of the few trades in which it was possible for a black man to gain some measure of independence by owning his own shop. The fate of Detroit's black barbers illustrates the fundamental difference between the position of blacks and immigrant workers who were also initially forced into the bottom of the job hierarchy. In 1870, 53 percent of Detroit's barbers were black, but by 1910, only 7.3 percent were black, as blacks had been displaced by Italians and other immigrants. In 1884, one-quarter of the shops had been black-owned; by 1908, blacks owned less than one in fifty. Thus, while newly arrived immigrant workers found opportunities opened up as positions were vacated by earlier arrivals moving up into better jobs, blacks found that the influx of eastern and southern Europeans pushed them further down. The color line in industry and the patterns of racial discrimination in other occupations amounted to something close to a caste system for blacks.[19]

These economic differences between the various ethnic fragments of Detroit's working class were reinforced by residence patterns, church parish structures, ethnic voluntary associations, and marriage choices. Neighborhood life in Detroit was marked by ethnic conflicts. Native workers, a minority in an immigrant city, had a tendency to think of themselves as embattled and beleaguered by immigrant hordes. They organized into nativist lodges like the American Protective Association and the Patriotic Sons of America and pressured trade union leaders to push restrictive legislation against immigrant workers. "The country is swarming with foreigners taking my labor away from me," one worker complained to the State Bureau of Labor Statistics investigator in 1885. A woodworker accused Germans and Canadians who "were just over" and "speak no English" of working for at least fifty cents per day less "than Americans."[20] Such sentiments became even more widespread in the depression years of the next decade as the APA actively intervened in local politics, and even the *Michigan Catholic* endorsed a Detroit Trades Council campaign for enforcement of federal legislation against the importation of alien contract labor. An American brakeman expressed the idea more succinctly, if not diplomatically, in 1894, when he urged that "we chase the Dagos back to Italy."[21]

But immigrant-native hostility was not the only form of ethnic conflict. Ethnic groups were seriously divided by religion, and Germans, Poles, and the Irish were in sharp competition for jobs and political influence. These rivalries, as well as the positive functions of ethnic institutions, help to explain ethnic residential patterns. The city was composed of dozens of ethnic enclaves.

Ethnic neighborhoods were never completely homogeneous. In no Detroit neighborhood did the proportion of residents of a single nationality approach 100 percent. But the neighborhoods with a preponderance of a particular nationality developed an ethnic identity. More than two-thirds of the Polish families living in Detroit in 1880 lived in the Polish East Side neighborhood; half of the Germans lived in a corridor along Gratiot Avenue on the near East Side, while 40 percent of the Irish families lived in a single neighborhood: Corktown on the West Side.[22]

The nature of the ethnic communities varied somewhat in size and social composition. Some German and Polish neighborhoods included occupational as well as ethnic clusters—blocks made up largely of German craftsmen or Polish laborers—but generally ethnic neighborhoods included people of all social classes. Ethnic communities were capable of functioning as self-contained units for recent immigrants or those who spoke no English. Nearly half of Detroit's immigrants had been in the United States less than three years in 1890 (46.4 percent), and more than a third (34.4 percent) spoke no English. The Germans, for example, not only had their own churches, saloons, businesses, and factories, but also eight newspapers including three dailies, their own labor unions, and their own citywide labor federation, the Central Labor Union.[23]

The ethnic community often started around a church. The first Polish neighborhood in Detroit grew around St. Albertus, the Polish Catholic church established in 1871 at East Canfield and St. Aubin on the city's East Side. In the 1880s the rapidly increasing Polish population settled around it as the city expanded on the north and west and areas on the East Side were vacated by earlier settlers. By 1890, the northern part of all the East Side wards contained large Polish neighborhoods.[24]

Nearly all of the city's Catholic churches served a particular nationality, and pressure for creation of new ethnic parishes was a major source of discord within the Catholic church. Detroit had sixteen Catholic churches in the early 1880s; seven were identified as Irish or primarily Irish, four as German, two as Polish, and two as French. These ethnic churches provided social cohesion for their neighborhoods and helped to maintain ethnic solidarity where residential patterns were mixed. Catholic parochial schools were also organized on an ethnic basis with different orders of priests and sisters and instruction in native languages as well as in English. The Polish churches, St. Albertus and St. Casimir, were served by Franciscans who taught in both Polish and English. Two German parishes maintained girls' schools with sisters from Milwaukee who spoke both German and English. St. Anne's, the French parish, likewise maintained its own school.[25]

Most Protestant congregations were also organized on an ethnic basis in the 1880s. Among forty-three Protestant congregations studied by Ralph Janis, in only one case were less than 85 percent of the church members drawn from one ethnic group. As Janis concluded: "Yankees almost never prayed with Germans or members of any other ethnic group, even if they shared similar or identical religious beliefs . . . And the same held true for Germans, whether Protestant, Catholic, or Jewish, and for Irish and French Detroiters. The only exception to this universal religious ethnocentrism were a few of the city's younger churches." [26]

Voluntary associations complemented ethnic churches and schools. Organized both as parish societies like the Polish St. Joseph's Society or secular orders such as the Sons of Poland or the Ancient Order of Hibernians, voluntary associations had active social programs including dinners, dances, dramatic and musical presentations, and celebrations of national holidays. Most also provided many other services: neighborhood information centers, advice and assistance in finding jobs or in dealing with city agencies, insurance, and care for the sick or unfortunate. Occasionally they functioned as the nucleus of political organization or as a substitute for trade unions. Even when voluntary associations did not have explicitly ethnic purposes, they usually recruited more members from one ethnic group than from others.

Ethnic differences were also maintained through resistance to intermarriage. Polish, German, and Irish men married women of their own nationalities, and this tendency carried over into the second and even third generations. In a study of three generations of the members of an East Side Polish parish, Peter Ostafin found that all forty-six first-generation family heads had married Polish wives. But even more surprising, among their children, of those who married (eleven never married), 109 of 111 had married spouses of Polish origin, and all but one of their eighteen grandchildren who were married at the time of the study had also married Polish Americans. [27] German and Irish men were also likely to marry women of their own nationality. In 1880, for example, 91 percent of married German males were married to German women, and 85 percent of married Irish males were married to Irish women. The tendency did not carry over into the second generation as strongly as it did among second-generation Poles, but two-thirds of the second-generation German men married women of German descent, and half of the second-generation Irish men married women of Irish descent. Where intermarriage did take place, marriage preferences suggest the impact of long-standing ethnic rivalries. Germans and the Irish rarely married each other, for example, an indication of continuing German-Irish hostility. In both cases, if they did not choose members of their own ethnic group they usually married native-stock Americans.[28]

Thus, Detroit's workers lived in separate communities within the city, communities which occupied different economic positions within the industrial economy, and communities which they actively maintained by their choices of residence, religious practice, associational life, and marriage partners. As workers within these communities, they faced the problems of wage labor, and class conflict was part of community life, but they viewed their problems as workers from the perspective of their own cultural system.

Each of these communities was a unique cultural system, with a mutually reinforcing set of values, symbols, informal personal associations, and formal institutions. None of these communities was culturally and socially homogeneous, but the divisions within the cultural system all had common meanings based on a single frame of reference. Native employers and native workers both used the rhetoric of a common equal rights tradition to justify their actions even when they faced each other from opposite sides of a picket line. German freethinkers and German clerics argued morality far more easily—and far more regularly—with each other than with their counterparts or antagonists of other nationalities.

Labor organizers sought to inculcate a moral code and build a culture of working-class solidarity which transcended ethnic differences. The evolving structure of Detroit's industries provided opportunities where this was possible. While workers in small workshops were often predominantly one nationality, the city's large factories all recruited ethnically diverse work forces. At night they might go home to separate neighborhoods, but during the day natives and Poles, Irishmen, and Germans met each other in the car shops, the stove works, on the construction sites, and in the shoe factories. Even where this was not the case, in many crafts workers of different nationalities developed very similar work cultures.

Competing Cultural Systems

If workers of different nationalities were to come together into a single subculture of opposition, they had to build on these common experiences without threatening the values or institutions any particular group of them found important. In order for us to understand the possibilities and the problems of building such a culture of opposition, we will look first at the four most important ethnic cultural systems—native white, German, Polish, and Irish.[29]

Native Whites

As a minority within a minority native white workers in Detroit occupied an ambiguous social position and displayed an ambivalent cultural and ideological identity. Only 20.8 percent of Detroit's population was native white in 1890; fewer than half of the native Americans were working class. There were few predominantly native working-class neighborhoods, few distinctively native working-class social or cultural organizations. Most native workers lived intermingled with a mixed Anglo-Saxon lower middle class composed of native, Canadian, and British white-collar wage earners and small businessmen. These neighborhoods, running up the center of the city above the business district and into the near West Side, were overwhelmingly Protestant and Republican.[30]

We can get some sense of how native workers were integrated into the social networks of middle-class neighborhoods by looking at the leadership of the fraternal organizations which provided much of the organized social and cultural life. Typically, a minority of skilled workers joined several businessmen and white-collar wage earners. For example, in 1881 the leadership of the Detroit lodges of the Ancient Order of United Workmen, a quasi-masonic fraternal society, included two skilled workers, five clerks, a lawyer, a florist, and a saloon owner. Masonic Lodge 297 was led in 1881 by a printer, an advertising agent, a store owner, and three clerks.[31] We do not have membership lists of these lodges to count what proportion of the membership was working class, but most native and Canadian labor leaders for whom biographical information is available were active in native middle-class fraternal, political, temperance, or religious organizatons. A. M. Dewey, at various times president of the printer's union, president of the Trades Council, District Worthy Foreman (vice-president) of the Knights of Labor, and a national leader of the Knights, was typical. Born in Martinsburg, New York, a Republican, and an active prohibitionist, Dewey was grand secretary of the White Cross Reform Club and an officer in the Knights of Honor.[32]

Their residences, their club memberships, church affiliations, and political allegiances, as well as common Anglo-Saxon heritage made native, Canadian, and British workers a part of the cultural system of the native and Anglo-Saxon middle class. They were part of the world out of which the city's overwhelmingly Anglo-Saxon industrial elite had come. Over half of the 115 leading industrialists in Detroit were natives; over 80 percent, native, Canadian, or British; 71 percent were Republicans, 87 percent Protestants. Most still lived in native, middle-class neighborhoods. This Anglo-Saxon world ruled Detroit; the industrialists ran the big factories and along with middle-class allies provided much of the city's political leadership. There was opposition, but the Anglo-Saxon world usually got its way in local politics. The allocation of city services reflected their dominance. New sewer lines, street lights, or street railways were built to serve their neighborhoods on the center and West Side or the unoccupied sectors on the city's fringes that real estate promoters were developing, often entirely bypassing the more densely populated working-class East Side.[33] As the bottom layer of this world, native workers were in a contradictory situation. Compared to the Polish or Irish street laborers, the German workmen of the East Side, or black servants, they were part of a preferred caste. But within a cultural system in which economic success, and above all economic independence, were the measures not only of status and power, but also the evidence of virtuous behavior, they were dependent—wage earners.

The intellectual traditions of native workers were similarly contradictory. Nativism, republicanism, and evangelical Protestantism were intertwined in the Free Labor ideology that dominated the thinking of native workers. In America, as labor leader Richard Trevellick, one of the veteran exponents of this world view, explained in 1881, workers did not express their grievances "with the knife of the assassin or the torch of the incendiary. These were spurned by American workmen. They did not come to intimidate or offer threats, not with drums or banners, nor to destroy property; but they came in the name and authority of law." In America, argued another correspondent to the Detroit labor paper, a worker needed only to "show by his calm determination that he is in America and not in Russia."[34]

America, the republican ark, was different. American workers were guaranteed equal rights before the law by the Constitution, the Bill of Rights, the history of American patriots struggling to preserve these liberties. If workers' American rights were being violated, and certainly these labor leaders felt that in many ways they were, then they argued workers did not stand in opposition to society—rather they had to be the moral guardians of society who would guarantee that the traditions of American liberty, equal rights, and equal opportunity were preserved from the new threats of monopolistic corruption.

Workers did need to organize, but they "organized for a more worthy object" than mere wage increases—"to secure every man his liberty as a citizen." There was no "antagonism . . . between labor and employed capital," argued a union printer. "Capital employed in manufactures . . . in any of the thousand and one ways that it may be used to furnish work to the laborer must of necesssity be a BENEFIT TO THE WORKINGMEN." And "working men should not feel enmity toward such a one simply because he is rich." After all, capital was nothing more than the product of "the man who has the wisdom to save his dimes until they become dollars." The legitimate manufacturer was a laborer just as much as the artisan. Workers should not blame "the active and brainy manufacturer or businessman" for the problems caused by "that kind of Shylock" who demands "such a rate of usuance" that the employer is compelled to do "injustice against his employees in order to yield the pound of flesh."[35] What American liberty was all about, according to this view of the world, was insuring to every deserving worker the equal opportunity to do just as the "active and brainy manufacturer" had done. As an 1884 campaign circular of Detroit's Independent Labor party concluded, "Equality of Chances! Equality of Chances!! Equality of Chances!!! is his [the American worker's] cry."[36]

As David Montgomery, Alan Dawley, Bruce Laurie, and many other scholars have demonstrated, this equal rights tradition offered the basis for a powerful critique of the conditions American workers faced. But as the arguments of these Detroit workers show, it could also lead to an understanding of those conditions which saw them as aberrations from a naturally harmonious relationship between classes.[37] This world view could lead in very different directions. On the one hand, the democratic and egalitarian parts of the tradition led some native workers to an increasingly radical critique of their society. On the other hand, the ideology also led many native workers into alliances with their middle-class neighbors against immigrant workers whom they saw as the tools of monopolistic corrupters plotting to undermine American liberty. Some of the most radical and some of the most reactionary workers in Detroit were natives coming out of the same intellectual tradition.

The consequences of these conflicting interpretations of the equal rights tradition can be seen in the behavior of Detroit's native workers.

A disproportionate share of the city's most important labor leaders were natives. Among forty-five top labor leaders (top officers of the Trades Council, the Knights of Labor, Central Labor Union, and the largest union locals) for whom biographical information is available, fourteen were natives (i.e., double the native proportion of the working class) and an additional eight were Canadian and seven British. Thus, Anglo-Saxon Detroit provided two-thirds of the top labor leaders.[38] We do not have individual membership figures for the labor movement as a whole, but scattered data suggest that native workers also made up a larger than proportional share of rank and file union membership. Trades with exceptionally high percentages of native workers were among the most highly unionized. Over half of the members of Detroit railway unions were natives. The printing industry, which was 22 percent native in 1890, was over 60 percent unionized. The street railway workers, 27 percent native, won a union shop agreement in 1892.[39] Yet while perhaps a larger proportion of native workers than immigrants were unionized, the city's Independent Labor party in the mid-1880s ran poorest in the precincts where native white workers lived. And native workers provided the mass base for nativist organizations that disrupted union efforts in many key industries.[40] Native workers occupied key positions within the skilled sector that was the base of union efforts. They provided many of the movement's ablest and most dynamic leaders. But if Detroit's workers were to function as a class there had to be close cooperation between native and immigrant workers. Immigrant workers, however, lived within very different cultural systems from that of native white workers.

Germans

> The loving wife America lets us do the dirtiest jobs, and we must drink our little bit of Sunday beer in the cellar or the junkroom. But today she has granted us full freedom of speech; for this great day she has promised us a General Pardon in advance; we have permission to tramp about freely in the street and set off firecrackers, as much as we want . . . And should a crazy anarchist or socialist want to disturb us, then we will simply call the police.
>
> Robert Reitzel, *Der Arme Teufel*
> September 13, 1890

On Monday, October 6, 1890, Detroit's Germans turned out in force for the first celebration of a newly created German-American holiday: German Day. In honor of the occasion the city council ordered all city offices closed for the afternoon. The city clerk rented carriages to carry dignitaries, and many factories and businesses gave their employees the afternoon off. The official pretext for the holiday was the anniversary of the landing of the first Germans in Pennsylvania in 1683, but German Americans had never considered that event worthy of commemoration until a Philadelphia German newspaper had suggested the idea the year before. German Day had far more to do with the recent experiences of Detroit's German immigrants than it had to do with remembering German pioneers.[41]

One-quarter of the city's German population, over 10,000 people, marched in the parade, according to the *Evening News*. Seventy-six German societies were represented, and the official order of march reads like a catalog of German Detroit: German bands, drum corps, and singing societies; German policemen, master brewers, and master bakers; German GAR members, Odd Fellows, Foresters, United Friends, Knights of Honor, and Knights of Pythias; German shooting societies and militia units; Catholic, Lutheran, and Evangelical church societies; regional organizations for Bavarians, Westphalians, Hessians, Swabians, and other provinces. There was only one glaring omission: not a single German labor organization joined the line of march. Yet German Detroit was overwhelmingly working class, and Detroit's German working class was well organized in 1890 with its own unions, its own singing and athletic clubs, its own city labor federation, its own daily and weekly press. German labor organizations normally directed a major part of the city's German cultural life with festivals, plays, concerts, meetings, and balls that catered to a much wider audience than their own members.[42]

The *Evening News* had noted that local German socialists opposed the idea of the holiday, but offered no explanation. The *News* reported only one incident on the day of the parade that gave any hint of this opposition, and the editorial treatment of the event was designed to make it appear comical. "ANARCHIST FLAG OUT" was the subheading on one short paragraph. A saloon owner along the parade route had hung a giant red flag from the front of his building. Parade organizers protested and the police ordered him to take it down.[43]

Perhaps such reporting reflected more than an editor's antiradical biases. To Anglo-Saxon Detroit the non-English-speaking ethnic communities in their midst were like foreign lands—strange and unknown worlds described in the Sunday supplement sections of newspapers like travelogues to exotic and colorful places. They had little understanding

44

of the internal structures of these communities, of the vigorous debates and conflicts that divided ethnic groups. And, unfortunately, many modern historians, emphasizing the autonomy of separate immigrant worlds, have also tended to treat them as homogeneous ethnic cultures. The struggle over the creation of Detroit's German Day gives us an entrance through which we can look within the German community at the nature of ethnic feelings, the complex relationships between ethnicity and class, and the nature of ethnic working-class culture. Only by understanding the ways in which ethnic and class consciousness were combined in ethnic working-class cultures can we understand the possibilities and problems of cooperation between workers of different nationalities and workers of different cultural traditions within a single nationality.

In 1890, Germans were by far the largest ethnic group in Detroit, German immigrants and their children making up 27 percent of the city's population, outnumbering native white Americans by three to two, and far outdistancing all other immigrant groups; 43 percent of all immigrants were German. The proportion of Germans in Detroit had been steadily increasing since mid-century. In 1860, Germans already outnumbered the Irish, the early leaders; by 1890, the ratio of Germans to Irish was nearly five to one.[44]

Yet Germans did not enjoy a corresponding increase in their influence in city affairs. There had been no German mayors, and while Germans had increased their representation on the city council to seven of twenty-six aldermen in 1884, even at the ward level German political victories depended on their ability to win nominations at caucuses and city conventions controlled by natives and Irish Americans. In 1887, for example, the Irish captured all but two of the positions on the Democratic slate, and the sole German Democrat was defeated in the general election. Germans complained that they were similarly discriminated against in the apportionment of patronage jobs, and the German East Side received a much smaller share of the appropriations for new city services than its proportion of the city's population.[45]

In part, German political disappointments were the product of divisions within the German community. Germans did not function as a politically cohesive group. Two-thirds of German church members were Protestant, one-third Catholic, while a vocal minority of freethinkers attacked Catholics and Protestants alike. These religious splits had important political, social, and ideological consequences. Catholics voted Democratic and vigorously opposed prohibition and other legislative restrictions of personal behavior. Many had fled Bismarck's *Kulturkampf* against German Catholicism, and, still smarting from the experience, they viewed native and Protestant campaigns against corruption and immorality as veiled attacks against them.[46] German Lutherans generally fit into what Paul Kleppner has called the ritualists—Protestant sects who mirrored Catholic objections to extending state power over individual morality. Detroit Republicans actively courted German Lutherans in the late 1880s, and by the early 1890s some appear to have joined other German protestants in the Republican Party. But in 1892 the *Evening News* estimated that the German vote split 65 percent Democratic, 35 percent Republican.[47]

A variety of institutions supported these divisions in German Detroit. Catholics maintained parochial schools, a variety of church societies and religious fraternal organizations (with a total membership of 3,400 in 1892), and a weekly German Catholic newspaper, *Die Stimme der Wahrheit* (Catholic and Democrat, circulation 5,000 in 1883). Many also read the *Volksblatt*, an independent Democratic daily (circulation 3,460 in 1890). Lutherans supported twenty-one private schools. The German Republican *Abend-Post* had a daily circulation of 5,600 in 1890. Religious radicals and agnostics supported a full range of radical counterparts.[48]

But while the divisive power of Old World religious traditions was still very much alive, their experiences as German Americans brought Germans together. Germans of all traditions felt abused by non-German politicians, threatened by the increasingly vicious and vocal nativist movement, angered by the day-to-day indignities of dealing with people who ridiculed their language and culture.

Much of their ire was directed against the Irish, their most immediate antagonists in the Democratic party and the Catholic church hierarchy. German radicals, Republicans, and Democrats all delighted in anti-Irish attacks often thinly disguised as humor. The *Abend-Post* sarcastically reported the jailing of an Irish maid "from Erin's green shores" on drunk and disorderly charges. The *Volksblatt* denounced "Ireland uber Alles!" in the Democratic party when the 1894 Democratic ticket failed to include a single name with "a German ring." The guests at a Turnerverein masked ball gleefuly greeted a couple dressed as an Irish policeman and an Irish washerwoman laden with many babies.[49]

Repeated prohibition campaigns by native Republicans also unified the Germans. The beer garden played a central role in German family recreation quite different from the largely male saloon culture of other nationalities. Unions, fraternal societies, and athletic clubs built much of their social life around Sunday family picnics where members and families gathered around beer kegs to enjoy the band, play games, or listen to speeches. While native reformers viewed prohibition as a defense of family life, to most Germans it seemed like a dangerous precedent which could lead to more sinister attempts at forced assimilation, a direct attack on a whole way of life.[50]

German Day had been conceived by its organizers as a way of countering these threats with a public display of German strength and unity. The Irish have their St. Patrick's Day every year; Germans must have a similar occasion to make their presence felt. But when a committee led by August Marxhausen, the publisher of the *Abend-Post*, and several prominent brewery owners called a planning meeting at Arbeiter Hall in late August of 1890, they were outraged when many in the audience vigorously denounced the idea. When opponents returned to the next meeting a week later, organizers tried to order them from the hall.[51] The anger of the confrontation was not caused simply by the exasperation of enthusiasts unprepared to entertain criticism of a pet project. The two sides were old antagonists. The opponents were representatives of German working-class radicalism who had fought many of these same businessmen for the leadership of Detroit "Deutschtum" through most of the previous decade. The debate about German Day was another round in a continuing struggle over who was to speak for Detroit's Germans.

Robert Reitzel was the spokesman for the opposition. A former minister of an independent congregation, a poet, and polemicist for radical causes, Reitzel had come to Detroit in 1884 to edit *Der Arme Teufel*, a leftist literary journal which combined free-thought philosophy with literary analysis and radical politics. He had quickly become a fixture on the podiums of Detroit German working-class gatherings, the featured speaker at Paine festivals, Paris Commune commemorations, and memorial meetings for the anarchists convicted of the Haymarket bombing.[52]

Bourgeois "Deutschtum" hated him. Herr Muller, the editor of the German Catholic *Die Stimme der Wahrheit*, attacked him and his "Freethinker garbage" every week. Reitzel responded with his own weekly "Stimmemuller" column sarcastically recounting this week's charges against the "god blasphemer Reitzel," or woefully chiding Muller for forgetting him when no anti-Reitzel material had appeared. "Is it pos-

sible that I have insulted friend Muller?" A respectable German politician attacked him on the street with a horsewhip, but Reitzel gleefully
described the gentleman's mortification when a policeman carted them
both off to jail. August Marxhausen had tangled with him two years
before when Reitzel had helped to found the German daily *Arbeiter
Zeitung* as a labor alternative to the *Abend-Post* and the *Volksblatt.*
Marxhausen, a liberal and radical Republican who had always covered
labor news sympathetically, had offered to establish a workers' page in
the *Abend-Post*, and he considered the founding of the new paper a personal insult. "Such unthankful workers," mocked Reitzel. "They say
we want to have one newspaper in the whole bunch that breathes the
spirit of justice on every line . . . August can pack it up." [53]

August was the chief spokesman for the German Day planners,
and it was his explanation of the reasons for German Day that provoked
the sharpest exchanges with the opposition. "Germany was our Mother,
but America our wife," Marxhausen had said. And while Germans had
some complaints, they did not want to seem like less than patriotic
Americans: America had been good to them. [54]

Yes, a loving wife, Reitzel mocked with more than a touch of bitterness, a "loving wife" who "lets us do the dirtiest jobs." What right
do these businessmen have to represent themselves as the Germans of
Detroit? What about us? he asked his radical and working-class compatriots. "German Days will be appropriate when the humane ideals
that were driven out of Germany in 1849 can be returned." Demonstrations should be for protesting the destruction of human freedom in Germany and in America. These people are only concerned with making
money, and their German Day is only a ploy to help them make more. [55]

Thus, the debate over German Day was much more than a tactical
or factional dispute. It went to the heart of the question of German-
American identity. Were German Americans to view themselves as a
group much like other Americans, concerned about preserving something of their language and culture, but ultimately demanding their full
share in a patriotic consensus? Or were they to remain true to a working-class vision of human liberation, to democratic traditions that radicals argued both Americans and bourgeois Germans were all too quick
to abandon. Reitzel and most German-American working-class radicals, in correct socialist fashion, vigorously proclaimed their internationalism and denounced all forms of nationalism and patriotism. But
their arguments unconsciously revealed some ultimately very nationalistic assumptions. Being American, to them, meant being bourgeois,

and the German Day organizers were traitors to true German ideals of human freedom because they were too anxious to be accepted as full-fledged Americans.[56]

The same debate had surfaced two years before in Detroit's Turnerverein. The Turners had originally been a movement of working-class athletic clubs in which sport and gymnastics were philosophically integrated into a liberal rationalist world view which saw sound bodies as the basis of a healthful, enquiring citizenry who could intelligently combat the superstitions of traditional religion and undemocratic politics. But by the 1880s Detroit's Turnerverein, like most Turner clubs, included a substantial middle-class membership. A new governing board, elected in 1888 and made up largely of German businessmen, decided it was time to shed some of the organization's radical image. They fired an old radical who had been the club's director and spokesman for many years. And when the Turners' Women's Circle invited Reitzel to be the featured speaker at the club's annual Paine Festival, the board refused to let them use the Turner Hall. After the temporary secession of the Women's Circle, two rival Paine festivals organized by each faction, and a series of boisterous meetings, the new board was overturned and several of the prominent conservatives resigned from the organization. The issue, according to Reitzel, had been whether "their program should be a comfortable abode for freer culture . . . in the enormous social struggle of our time, should the Turners take the side of capital or the side of human rights demanded by the workers?" Once again Reitzel equated the side of capital with assimilation to American values. The crisis in Turnerdom had come about because too much of "the cunning and intrigue . . . the Americans excuse with the word 'smartness'" had found entrance.[57]

The German Day organizers had their parade, protests notwithstanding, and certainly many German workers marched. In such an overwhelmingly proletarian community any large crowd would be mainly working class. But bourgeois Deutschtum had not necessarily won the contest. Every German labor organization honored the boycott. When planning meetings began the following summer for the next parade, the German labor movement renewed its attack. Apparently once the novelty of a new idea had passed, popular support dwindled, and the *Volksblatt* reported that "the parade was a colossal washout . . . a disgrace." After 1891 German Day parades were discussed no more. The opponents won in the end.[58]

The influence of the radical opponents of German Day rested on two organizational pillars: the German labor movement and the network of German cultural institutions dedicated to the propagation of free thought. Organized socialists and anarchists were a small group: the Detroit branch of the Socialist Labor party had fewer than a hundred members in the late 1880s, and the anarchist Social Revolutionary movement had dwindled to less than twenty by 1890.[59] But the German labor and radical cultural organizations were much larger. The avowedly socialist German Central Labor Union had nine affiliated locals with an estimated 500 members in the early 1890s, while many other primarily German unions affiliated with the Trades Council or the Building Trades Council were also sympathetic to socialist ideas.[60] The CLU contingent at Labor Day parades, habitually shunted to the rear because native organizers disapproved of their red flags, averaged between 500 and 1,000 in the late 1880s and 1890s, while other German unions (300–500 most years) like the cigarmakers, metal polishers, and German carpenters also carried red flags.[61]

German labor gatherings drew large crowds: 1,000 people attended the *Arbeiter Zeitung*'s first birthday party in June 1889; in November 2,000 came to a memorial service for the Haymarket anarchists.[62] We do not have circulation figures for the *Arbeiter Zeitung*, but *Der Herold*, a weekly German labor paper in the late 1890s, had a circulation of 4,800 in 1900, about two-thirds as large as the Catholic *Die Stimme der Wahrheit* and about 60 percent as large as the *Abend-Post*, the largest German daily. The secretary of the Turnerverein reported that 367 people took part in club activities in one month. Radical plays like *The Nihilist* or *Captain Dreyfus* and musical presentations routinely filled the largest East Side theaters and lecture halls.[63]

German working-class families who were sympathetic to radical thought could do more than read a weekly paper or attend an occasional lecture. Labor and cultural organizations combined to create a radical German-American working-class culture much like the separate world German Social Democrats had created for workers in Germany by the turn of the century.[64] Their children could go to Tobias Sigel's Turner Sunday school, where they were taught scientific and logical explanations for natural phenomena to free them from "the dogmas of religion." Families could gather together at union and Turner excursions like the one in 1888 to a rural beer garden where the parents proudly looked on as the little "Turnerschuler und schulerin" marched in together under the tutelage of their teacher. Many children also attended Herr Herrman's Seminary School, a day school with a full curriculum of world history, cultural history, and natural science, where Herr Herrman above all else "tries to develop in the children . . . understanding . . . for the most serious struggles." Graduates of the Seminary School included Otto Zoll and John Heges, president and financial secretary of the Cigarmakers' Union in 1891. Radical Detroit Deutschtum had its own calendar of holidays and festivals beginning with the annual Paine Festival in January, a celebration of Tom Paine's democratic and anticlerical ideals; Fasching masked balls in late February (a German equivalent of Mardi Gras); the Commune Festival in March, commemorating the beginning of the Paris Commune; May Day; Labor Day (although many German socialists considered Labor Day a bourgeois copy of May Day); and the annual November memorial of the execution of the Haymarket anarchists.[65]

This culture was radical, working-class, but also above all else German, and despite their insistent professions of internationalism, German labor leaders never completely resolved how being German and being working class were connected. The Central Labor Union claimed to be the federation of Detroit's "progressive" unions, but in practice it was the federation of the city's German-speaking unions. Repeated jurisdictional disputes suggest that ethnicity, not politics, determined affiliation. The CLU rarely attempted to recruit radical unions of other nationalities, but if a newly organized union with a German membership applied for Trades Council affiliation without joining the Central Labor Union, the CLU protested jurisdictional violation.[66]

"The German-American proletariat doesn't believe in a fatherland," declared the editor of *Der Herold*, "for them there are no frontiers, they are internationalists." But his own editorial practices belied the claim. Most of his coverage was of events in Germany, and the majority of the remainder dealt with German activities in other American cities. Except for German labor activities there was virtually no reporting of national news or local events. Robert Reitzel's *Der Arme Teufel* similarly gave overwhelming emphasis to German and German-American news. This ethnic emphasis contrasted sharply with the English-language labor press and was far more pronounced than in the bourgeois German papers, the Detroit *Abend-Post* and the *Michigan Volksblatt*. German labor activists were seriously concerned about the preservation of German language and culture. When Robert Reitzel pleaded with his readers to send their children to the German seminary school, he outlined the political character of the curriculum but concluded by urging parents not to let their children forget the German language. A worker who wrote Reitzel to criticize one of the paper's columns displayed similar concerns. After rigorously dissecting Reitzel's argument to demonstrate its ideological errors, he angrily concluded by pointing out grammatical errors in one of Reitzel's paragraphs. "At least you could write correct German!"[67]

The anticlerical and religious nonconformist tinge of German working-class radicalism offended many Catholic and Lutheran workers, but not so seriously that it undermined the capacity of German labor leaders to mobilize a substantial proportion of Detroit's German workers. Throughout the 1880s and 1890s Detroit's German workers provided the most dependable source of mass support for the city's labor movement, but the relationship between German and non-German labor leaders was always uneasy. German workers were active in such multi-ethnic labor organizations as the Knights of Labor. They were the most consistent supporters of the citywide Independent Labor party in the mid-1880s.[68] One-third of the city's German workers voted for ILP candidates in 1886, more than double the party's citywide average. The Germans' formal expressions of labor solidarity were always rigorously correct: German unions were usually among the first and most generous to respond to other unions' appeals for strike funds. Boycotters could always depend on the support of the German East Side.

Native labor organizers recognized the central role of German workers in Detroit's labor movement. Most citywide labor gatherings organized by natives or Germans convened in Arbeiter Hall, and organizers always scheduled German and English speakers for mass meetings. Despite the Anglo-Saxon cast of the Trades Council, German labor leaders were repeatedly elected to Trades Council offices even when the majority of delegates opposed their socialist ideas.

But the relations between German and Anglo-Saxon labor always included tensions. That should not surprise us. To nativist workers, the Germans were the largest component of the immigrant hordes. And to Germans, native workers were, after all, Americans.

Poles

> [The Bishop] urged all Poles to follow the true church, and not be led astray by a hireling shepherd actuated by malice against the church and playing the part of the hypocrite.
>
> Bishop Foley at the dedication of St. Casimir Church, 1890
> *Evening News*, December 22, 1890

As Polish migration to Detroit accelerated in the 1880s, Detroit's East Side Polonia grew to be the city's second largest immigrant community.

By 1892 the *Evening News* estimated that between one-seventh and one-eighth of Detroit's population was Polish. In a three-week series of Sunday feature articles, "Poland to America," *News* reporters explained the origins of this community by following one Polish immigrant from Straszkowo, his village in Prussian Poland, to Detroit. Vavrsin Jastrzembovski, a landless agricultural laborer, could not support his wife and three children on his wages of ten cents a day. One day he returned home to announce to his wife that he had borrowed the money for a ticket to America. "The Poles in America eat meat every day . . . and have houses and lands of their own, and get rich and fat." He would send for her.[69]

At the Peninsular Car Works he made $1.10 per day. Boarding with another family for $3 a week, he saved more than half of his wages. Soon he had saved enough to go down to Zoltowski's grocery, where Mr. Zoltowski helped him arrange an international money order to send the ship passage money to his wife. Now, only a few years later, Vavrsin was reunited with his family, a proud home owner with money in the bank.[70]

At the conclusion of their story, the *News* reporters admitted that there was no Vavrsin Jastrzembovski. They had created him as a composite from the stories of several families they had interviewed. Vavrsin, they argued, was a typical Polish immigrant. Like him, Detroit's Poles were simple, superstitious folk, hardworking, and thankful for the bounty of America. Many workers had come alone, but now most families lived together in their own small homes. They did much of the city's hardest physical labor for wages that most natives would consider unacceptable, but they rarely complained, rarely got into trouble. Far fewer Poles showed up in police arrest statistics than their proportion of the population, and hardly any Poles were on the city's welfare roles.[71]

Parts of this story were accurate. Most Detroit Poles had come from Prussian Poland; most had been peasants in Poland. Half the Polish work force were unskilled day laborers and unskilled factory hands at the very bottom of the wage hierarchy; 95 percent were working class. Most had little education. Many families built their own small homes, and a higher proportion of Poles were home owners than among the rest of the city's population.[72]

But simple, docile, hardworking Vavrsin was a classic ethnic stereotype, a stereotype many Anglo-Saxon Detroiters accepted with few questions. Some of the city's leading employers based their hiring practices on it. The Michigan-Peninsular Car Company, for example, apparently convinced that Poles would make a more tractable work force, began a concerted policy of hiring Poles in the late 1880s, and by the late 1890s most of its work force was Polish. Nativist workers, using the same argument in reverse, directed much of their anger at Poles, whom they considered too ignorant to understand the need to fight to maintain "American" living standards. Modern scholars have only just begun to challenge this stereotype.[73]

But during the same years that much of Anglo-Saxon Detroit imagined Poles as ignorant, conservative, and docile folk impervious to doctrines of solidarity and class struggle, over 2,500 Polish families carried on an intense struggle which involved repeated, militant, direct actions, systematic self-organization, tremendous personal sacrifices, and a long-term loyalty to principle and group solidarity that should have been the envy of any labor organizer. In November 1885, the Catholic bishop of Detroit removed Father Dominik Kolasinski, the pastor of St. Albertus, the largest Polish parish in the city, and ordered him to leave the city. For nine years, Kolasinski's parishioners fought two bishops, most of the city's Catholic clergy, and much of the lay leadership of Detroit Polonia to have Kolasinski reinstated at the head of their own parish, free of the bishop's interference. They suffered excommunication, abuse, and ridicule; built a new church out of their own funds, the largest church in Michigan at that time, and ultimately emerged triumphant, the legitimacy of their new parish officially recognized by intercession of the Vatican, and the parish independent of the bishop's financial authority.[74]

The church played a far more central role in Polish community life than in ethnic communities which were religiously divided, like the Germans. The Polish church was a universal and unifying institution. There was virtually no rationalist or anticlerical tradition among Poles, and secular nationalism was also weak, so the church in Poland had been a primary focus for the national aspirations of a people who were politically divided between Germany, Russia, and Austria. The distinctive Polish church rituals and religious observances thus had far more than purely religious significance. In Detroit, where Polish immigrants faced the hostility of much of the rest of the city, these social and political functions were perhaps even more important than they had been in Poland.[75]

Dominik Kolasinski arrived in Detroit in 1882. A charismatic and flamboyant figure, a dramatic orator, Kolasinski immediately won the enthusiastic support of the parish and quickly became a symbol of their antagonism to church authorities. Kolasinski was a Polish nationalist.

He organized a parade in 1883 to celebrate the anniversary of the Polish victory over the Turks at the Battle of Vienna in 1683, the first demonstration ever held by Detroit Poles in which an estimated 15,000 people took part. He tried to overcome regional rivalries in the Polish community between Prussians, Galicians, Russians, and Kashubs, and he sponsored Paderewski concerts and lectures on Polish literature to stimulate national feeling. A former altar boy described him to an investigator in 1928 as "a Polish Patriot, first and foremost." [76]

Like each of his predecessors as pastor of the St. Albertus parish, Kolasinski eventually clashed with the bishop, but unlike the others Kolasinski was willing to challenge the bishop's authority. When Bishop Borgess ordered Father Kolasinski to turn over all parish financial records in November 1885, following a dispute over parish building plans, he refused. Borgess suspended him, but Kolasinski fought back, and his parishioners were ready to fight with him. He had built the impressive new church for them which the bishop had opposed, "the finest Polish church in America," and now "the 'German' bishop . . . had suspended 'their' priest." [77]

Parish members, led by a group of angry women, physically dragged Kolasinski's replacement from the altar the first time he tried to say mass, and crowds repeatedly battled police for a year and a half thereafter as parishioners prevented the replacement from entering the church. Bishop Borgess had to sue Kolasinski in civil court to get him to vacate the parish residence. But even when Kolasinski seemed to accept defeat, leaving the city for a new parish assignment in North Dakota in April 1886, his followers continued the fight. They staged repeated demonstrations against the bishop, including Saturday takeovers of Catholic churches in neighboring communities to show their continued solidarity. Kolasinski's advocates claimed that his parishioners even were willing to forego the sacraments rather than break ranks to go to the other Polish parishes recognized by the bishop. [78]

Finally, in December 1888, Kolasinski returned to take the leadership of what became a rebel parish of 2,800 families unsanctioned by the church. In January they began plans for a new Polish church, even grander than the one the bishop had taken away from them. Within a month and a half of Kolasinski's return, in a community of $1.10-a-day laborers, he had already raised $17,000 toward the new church. [79] Four years later, in December 1893, the Sweetest Heart of Mary Church was completed. The Kolasinskiites celebrated Christmas mass that year for the first time in nine years. Finally, in February 1894, after a compromise arranged by a representative of the Vatican, Kolasinski read a public apology and the bishop reluctantly agreed to accept the congregation back into the church.[80]

The remarkable story of Kolasinski and his rebel parish provides a window into Detroit's Polonia much like German Day revealed something of the internal struggles of Detroit's Deutschtum. For nine years these supposedly simple folk had split Detroit's Polonia (fifty years later a young sociologist found his East Side respondents still clearly identified as Kolachy, Kolasinskiites, or Dombrochy, adherents of Kolasinski's officially sanctioned replacement)[81] and defied legal and ecclesiastical authority to preserve something that was important to them. It suggests that the native labor organizers who despaired of ever organizing "the Polacks" seriously misunderstood the Polish working class.

Indeed, few Polish workers were active in the formal labor movement before the end of the 1890s. There were no Polish labor leaders of any consequence—not a single Trades Council, Central Labor Union, or Knights of Labor district official between 1880 and 1900. Even within the second echelon of labor activists—local union leadership— Poles were almost completely absent. Among a list of 383 Detroit labor activists (including lists of Trades Council delegates and relatively insignificant offices in small locals) between 1880 and 1892, there were only five Polish surnames. There were no identifiably Polish union locals. On at least four different occasions several hundred Polish workers joined general laborers' unions, but these organizations were always shortlived.[82]

Yet Polish workers, to a remarkable degree, displayed the same characteristics of solidarity and militance during labor struggles that they demonstrated in support of Father Kolasinski. Polish workers were in the forefront of 1886 and 1891 car-shop strikes, and in both cases stayed out longer than their Anglo counterparts when the strikes appeared to be broken. In 1886, after other workers had broken ranks, they wanted to stay out in behalf of the native Knights of Labor strike leader whom the company refused to rehire.[83]

Equally significantly, Polish workers responded positively to a class appeal: they identified themselves as working people. Polish precincts gave Independent Labor party candidates a higher percentage of their votes in 1886 than all but a handful of German precincts,[84] and Polish Democratic politicians employed more forthrightly prolabor rhetoric than other ethnic politicians.[85] Thus, the absence of Polish union membership may tell us more about the unions than about the Poles.

Polish workers, like Germans, were part of an ethnic working-class culture. Both halves of that label were crucial; Kolasinskiites and car-shop strikers were the same people.[86] Their actions demonstrated their willingness to cooperate with other workers. Polish workers could be part of a working-class culture of opposition, but only if its organizers understood and were willing to accept what being Polish meant to Polish workers. Poles who were saving to bring over family members they had left in Poland, who were struggling to maintain a Polish church in America, could not be expected to respond positively to labor organizers who championed immigration restriction or demanded adherence to American cultural values.

The Irish

There are no Irish in Detroit; they are all West Britons.
Daniel Tindall to the *Irish World*, February 9, 1878

In the late 1870s and early 1880s, Daniel Tindall was Detroit's most consistent supporter of the *Irish World*'s national fund-raising appeals. He contributed six times between 1878 and 1881: twice to the Skirmishers' Fund established by the Clan na Gael and former Fenians to finance guerrilla war in Ireland, three times to the Land League Fund of the American Land League, and once to the Spread the Light Fund *Irish World* editor Patrick Ford created to help circulate the paper among Irish tenant farmers and laborers. His contributions were generous, usually $2, a large sum for an unskilled worker who probably earned less than $1.50 per day.[87]

The *Irish World* was the most important exponent of the radical wing of Irish-American nationalism, which linked Irish nationalism with a wider range of reform issues, particularly the cause of labor. Patrick Ford and his columnists argued that Irish land struggles, the struggle for Irish political independence, and American labor conflicts were intimately related. Irish farmers had been driven off the land, dispossessed, starved, and forced into exile because of English monopolization of the land. As laborers in America, they were exploited by factory lords who monopolized American industry, depriving workers of the value they produced. As one columnist put it, "All Despotism Over Industry Entered Through the Same Door. Landlord and Factory Lord— One Monopolizes the Land, the Free Gift of God, and the Other the Whole Profit of Steam and Other Natural Wealth which belongs to All."[88]

We know very little about Daniel Tindall, but what little we can uncover suggests that he was typical of Ford disciples. He was an aging sailor who had left his birthplace in County Waterford in the late 1840s or early 1850s, a time when rural modernization was creating continuing social antagonisms following the great famine. He lived at 144 Humboldt Avenue, in the new industrial district along the Michigan Central Railroad tracks just west of Corktown, with his sons Patrick, Robert, and Daniel, Jr., all sailors, William, an iron molder, and an Irish housekeeper. Two of his sons also contributed to the Skirmishers' Fund.[89] Like the Tindalls, most of Detroit's contributors to the *Irish World*'s fund-raising appeals were Irish workers, usually laborers, factory hands, or metal workers living in the Irish neighborhoods of the West Side, often working in the same shops, boarding with one another, or related to each other. Of the fifty-seven contributors between 1876 and 1881, three were anonymous; occupations of forty of the remaining fifty-four have been identified. All but three were working class; sixteen were laborers or other unskilled workers like sailors, porters, or helpers in factories; twenty-one were skilled workers. Almost half (sixteen) were metal workers. Two-thirds lived either in Corktown, in the neighboring areas of the Tenth Ward along the Michigan Central Railroad, or in the factory district along the river just southwest of Corktown, several boarding in the same rooming houses close to Baugh's Steam Forge, where at least half the contributing metalworkers worked. Judging from surnames all but two were Irish.[90]

Yet while these workers might seem to be representative Irish workmen, their attachment to radical nationalism was hardly typical of Detroit's Irish workers. These contributors were only 2 percent of Detroit's Irish workers.[91] As Daniel Tindall's disgusted comment on his fellow Detroit Irish suggested, the flame of radical nationalism was exceptionally weak in Detroit. Over 200,000 people sent money to Patrick Ford for the Skirmisher's Fund or the Land League during these years, yet Detroit could count only fifty-seven contributors.[92] Ford collected over $150,000 for the Land League in 1880 and 1881, yet Detroit contributed only $41.25, and only half of that was collected by the weak local Land League chapter ($21; Tindall sent $6 on his own). In comparison, Cleveland Land League chapters sent nearly $1,000; Chicago chapters $1,800; the Tombstone, Arizona, Land League branch collected nearly twenty times as much as Detroit's Davitt Branch.[93]

It would be wrong, however, to conclude that Irish workers in Detroit did not identify with their heritage. Most Irish workers simply expressed ethnic identity in ways different from what radical nationalists like Daniel Tindall hoped—mainly through the church and the Democratic party. Somewhat higher ethnic intermarriage rates and more dispersed residential patterns among the Irish suggest that ethnic identity may not have been as strong as among Germans and Poles,[94] but Irish participation in nonradical ethnic organizations like the Hibernian Benevolent Society, the Ancient Order of Hibernians, church societies, Irish temperance lodges, and Democratic ward organizations was very high. The Hibernian Benevolent Society had 275 members in 1879. The AOH had 2,800 members in 1892. And Irish Catholics were probably more politically cohesive than any other major ethnic group in the city.[95]

Such organizations did not ignore the political and nationalistic aspirations of Irish workers. Irish church leaders, for example, gave qualified support to the American Land League at the same time that they expressed misgivings about the more socialistic parts of the Land League program and sharp disapproval of Ford and the *Irish World*. "Much good can be effected" by the Land League, argued the editor of the *Western Home Journal*, the organ of Detroit's Irish Catholics, but the *Irish World* was going "headlong to the Devil," and Ford and the Skirmishers would "only tear Ireland apart." The Hibernians probably attracted much of their membership for the mutual insurance programs and social events, but Hibernian leaders mobilized their growing ranks behind Irish Democratic politicians. The order issued blacklists of candidates believed to be anti-Catholic and held rallies for aspiring Irish politicians.[96]

Overwhelmingly working class, Detroit's Irish community certainly contributed to the city's labor movement. The district master workman of the Knights of Labor during the Knights' peak years was a Cork-born shoemaker. One of his successors as master workman was an Irish-born hatter. Both were active in the Independent Labor party as was Bernard O'Reilly, a shipcarpenter out of County Westmeath who helped organize the Knights of Labor shipcarpenters' assembly and then used his labor credentials to launch a career as a Democratic alderman and state senator.[97] But all three were among the first to desert the ILP for the regular Democratic organization as the Knights' fortunes waned.[98] In a community where most Irish workers supported the conservative church hierarchy and regular Democratic organization, Irish labor leaders would not be the most consistent supporters of labor radicalism or labor reform.

The wavering strength of radical nationalism was further compounded by the relative prosperity of Detroit's Irish working class.

Comparing the relative position of the Irish and the Germans in eighteen cities, JoEllen Vinyard found that Detroit's Irish ranked higher compared to Germans than in any other city. Relatively high on the ethnic hierarchy, situated in a city with an exceptionally high percentage of Catholics and a strong Catholic church but an exceptionally low percentage of Irish inhabitants, Detroit's Irish were able to maintain a privileged position within the immigrant working class through their hold on the church hierarchy, the Democratic party, and some sectors of the economy. A minority of Detroit's Irish workers supported radical nationalism, and the class-conscious strategy it implied. For the majority there seemed to be other ways to defend their culture and improve their status.[99]

The Working-Class Subculture of Opposition

Each for himself is the bosses plea.
Union for all will make you free.

Parade banner of Detroit Coopers' Union, 1880[100]

Ethnic cultural systems rested on generations-old traditions and consciousness. Initially, many immigrants may have had only weak attachments to a national identity, but as they confronted antagonism and discrimination and dealt with the new problems of living in industrial Detroit, even those who had not thought deeply before about their cultural heritage found strength in their national traditions and developed emotional commitments to language, religion, and daily cultural practices.

But for working people, ethnic identity was interwoven with class experience. They were not merely natives, Germans, Poles, or Irish, but native workers, German workers, Polish workers, Irish workers. Their cultures were ethnic working-class cultures, and people did not divide ethnic and class feelings into separate components in their minds. Much of the scholarly debate on ethnic versus class identity is thus quite artificial.

Yet there is a very real problem underlying such debates. As workers entered factories with multiethnic work forces, as they confronted citywide or national political issues, if their interests were to be defended, if there was to be an effective working-class presence, the separate threads of different ethnic working-class cultures had to come together into a working-class subculture of opposition which transcended ethnic identities.

Each of the ethnic working-class cultures included components of mutualism, solidarity, and egalitarian politics which provided the basis for a common ground on which they might come together, but a multi-ethnic working-class subculture of opposition had to be created in a way that competing ethnic cultural systems did not. New institutions had to be created, and a new moral code developed that convinced workers that they owed the same kinds of loyalties to workers of other nationalities that they owed to people of their own nationality. As the abundant evidence of ethnic conflict demonstrates, this was no simple process, but the logic of their situations led activists of many nationalities to believe that the effort was essential. Unless workers could cooperate with each other, they believed, all would suffer.

The Detroit coopers' banner summarized how such activists viewed workers' alternatives. The creed of individual success, according to the coopers, was a mirage advocated by the bosses. If workers really hoped to escape oppressive conditions, they must look to each other for support. Increasing numbers of workers did. The fines, searches, long hours, and callous treatment inspired a new ethic of rebellion and mutual support which competed with the opposing values of individual gain. The result was the beginning of a working-class subculture based on the coopers' second alternative: solidarity.

It was only a beginning. The notion of a subculture of opposition was not universally accepted by Detroit workers by any means nor did it completely take the place of native and ethnic cultural systems even for those who identified with it most strongly. Workers' allegiances were divided. It was a *sub*culture composed of people who also continued membership in ethnic cultural systems at the same time, and it was never able to maintain a fully developed range of institutional counterparts to ethnic cultural systems. It was a goal or ideal for dissatisfied workers who in practice spent much of their lives outside the subculture.

It was strong enough to produce and maintain a network of new institutions which transcended ethnicity and economic particularism to recruit workers on a class basis: unions, Knights of Labor assemblies, workingmen's club rooms, cooperative stores and factories, labor newspapers, singing societies, social clubs, political organizations, and a workers' militia. They drew occasional support from a much larger community than their actual members. Together, these organizations tried to satisfy as broad a range of needs as the ethnic cultures with which they competed.

But the subculture of opposition was far more than the sum of its formal institutions. It was more than the movement culture of its activist core. Grounded in the mutualism and democratic traditions of each of its ethnic working-class fragments and augmented by the patterns of cooperation which workers of all nationalities had evolved through their experiences in the industrial system, the subculture also included a wide range of informal practices and commonly understood moral precepts which were communicated to and accepted by a broad segment of the city's working population: setting stints and limiting output, honoring picket lines and boycotts, helping needy compatriots.

The ideological content of the subculture was largely negative: a reaction against prevailing conditions. Implicitly, its growth represented a questioning of the ideology of individual success. But doubts about the Horatio Alger myth were hardly a sufficient basis for overcoming the forces of fragmentation. Underlying the beginnings of this counterculture were changes in the character of industrial life. The growth of large firms in Detroit, the expansion of factories, and technological changes within the factory which changed the character of work shattered personal bonds with employers and brought workers of different nationalities together. Expansion of the city and development of new residential sections created new neighborhoods where workers of different nationalities mingled on a daily basis. By the 1880s larger factories were beginning to replace smaller workshops in some industries. The transformation was slow, and in 1890, only about a third of Detroit's industrial work force worked in factories of more than 200 people. But despite the continued development of small manufacturing firms in the 1880s (the total number of industrial establishments in Detroit increased from 919 to 1,746 in the decade), the mean number of employees per industrial establishment increased from 13.6 in 1880 to 21.9 in 1890. Thus, the growth of large firms had not destroyed the viability of small companies, but the relative importance of the larger factory was increasing.[101]

Strike activity was concentrated in the large firms and in the industries subject to technological change. Of the ninety-nine strikes recorded in Detroit by the U.S. Commissioner of Labor between 1881 and 1894, twenty-nine were in the tobacco industry and twenty-one were in the metal trades, both leading examples of industries in which the skill status and established work rules of craftsmen were threatened by technological change; in the metal trades, large firms predominated—most of the city's largest factories were in the metal trades. Nearly half the strikes (forty-five), affecting the overwhelming majority of all strikers, involved more than 100 individuals each. In the many small companies with only a handful of employees, a family-like atmosphere may have still prevailed. The continuing expansion of this small business sector of the economy is one more example of the way in which industrial growth also fostered new fragmentary influences, but for the increasing numbers of workers employed by large and impersonal corporations, or facing major changes in the role of their crafts in industry, the myth of an idyllic relationship between master and journeyman was obsolete. [102]

Instead, workers faced a new work discipline which drove them beyond normal endurance and a set of work rules which robbed them of basic dignity. Complaint was tantamount to rebellion. New machines magnified the level of production, but while employers grew rich, they used the labor surplus created by displaced workers to drive down the wage levels. As one worker argued, his employer was "conspiring with his fellow employers to bring about a lower rate of wages." [103]

So, formally or informally, workers combined, too, to raise wages, change work rules, and exert some control over the productive process. On the simplest level, they cooperated to find ways to make work easier or less boring. In the big cigar factories the cigarmakers took daily turns reading to the other workers. At the end of the day, each cigar-maker gave the day's reader some of the cigars he had made so that the reader received as many as he would have made in a day. Charles Erb, one of Detroit's socialist stalwarts, mused in later years that this system had been the source of his political conversion. A new man had chosen an excerpt from Marx as the day's reading, and Erb was so fascinated that he immediately went out and got a copy of *Das Kapital* to read for himself. [104]

Such cooperation depended on mutual trust and rigid attention to an ethic of equality. Employers and foremen fought against it and tried to use favoritism to pit workers against one another. The *Labor Leaf* reported how unscrupulous supervisors used their positions to squeeze extra income for themselves out of their workers by such devices as forced Christmas gifts or outright kickbacks in exchange for work. On the docks, job contractors who took out contracts from shipowners to load and unload maintained high incomes by this system of kickbacks. One of the primary benefits of organization for the longshoremen was the elimination of this system. The union took out the contracts itself and distributed work equally to its members without any cut. [105]

The printers faced a similar problem. Employers paid for type-setting on a piece rate basis per 1,000 ems. An *em* is a unit of measure, the space normally occupied by the letter *m*. Obviously headlines, display ads, other areas with white space, would be much less time-consuming to set than normal copy. The union members in each print shop formed a "chapel" and elected a "father of the chapel" who was responsible for seeing that the "fat" was evenly distributed. The *Labor Leaf* advised printers to "elect a 'father' who has moral courage enough to stand up for what is right." [106]

Informal self-organization of work and rewards led to a moral code which governed behavior in the workshop but extended beyond the workplace as well. Violating the workers' own commonly understood rules or working for less than the union wage scale (unless granted special dispensation by the local union) constituted *ratting*. A "rat" or "scab" suffered social ostracism if not direct physical attack. During the Pingree and Smith strike in 1885, John Lambert, who had helped organize the shoemakers into the Knights of Labor prior to the strike, deserted his fellow workers to return to work. "His former acquaintances refuse to recognize or associate with him in any way," the *Labor Leaf* reported. The names of scabs were published in banner headlines in the labor papers, and the unmarried strikebreakers slept in the factory rather than face the danger of crossing picket lines. [107]

Workers who had unwittingly been recruited as strikebreakers during a strike were expected to leave once they realized the true situation. Those who were legitimate artisans, and not professional strikebreakers, usually did so without coercion. In return for honoring the code of solidarity, a worker could expect temporary support and a ticket home or to the nearest likely source of work. [108] Such assistance to unemployed artisans was standard practice most of the time, not just during a strike. A union traveling card guaranteed a workingman a roof overhead, a meal, and either help finding a local job or the cost of transportation to the next stop. Some unions maintained a tramp fund for this purpose. The system benefitted both sides: the tramping artisan and the stably employed worker. The tramp could travel in search of work, even if he was penniless, and not be forced by fear of starvation into begging or degrading or underpaid labor. The employed worker could maintain existing wage levels without fear that the unemployed would be used to drive down wages.

A clear etiquette prevailed for both parties. The recipient of aid considered it a right, not a gift or a handout; in better times he or she would do the same for someone else. In turn, however, the wanderer could not overstay his welcome (not more than a few days if there were no prospects for work) or waste money on liquor or gambling. Cases of abuse were reported in the labor papers, and the names of offenders widely circulated. A Louisville printer warned the *Labor Leaf's* readers about one Oliver Davis, who "hails from London, Ont. He came here in very bad shape and received two week's board at the expense of my purse . . . tried to bust a faro bank and got broke."[109]

The doctrine of mutual assistance extended to the sick and injured, and to families left without support by the death of the wage earner. For example, when the doctor told one of the members of the Brassworkers' Local Assembly 2312, who had been sick for five months, that he could not return to work until spring, the assembly organized a raffle to support the man's family. Prizes, including a "finely executed bronze statue of Napoleon crossing the Alps," were contributed by members who made them in their spare time.[110]

These core values of cooperation, mutual trust, equality, and mutual assistance constituted the beginnings of the emerging working-class subculture. They conflicted with native middle-class values of competition, individualism, and personal success. As will be shown in succeeding chapters, the unions and the Knights of Labor assemblies formed the functional hubs of this moral code, and as much of their time was spent in administering it as in more commonly recognized union functions such as wage negotiations. Labor organizations fought to nurture this ethic, to enforce their code of conduct.

Union debates over strategy and policy reflected this desire and the difficulties of carrying it out. There were no obvious answers to the questions raised by industrialization, no easily agreed-upon set of tactics which would insure successful resolution of the crisis. For the entire decade prior to 1886, workers' organizations were torn by internal debates over ideals and strategies. To strike or not to strike? Both union and Knights of Labor officials feared rash action might destroy their organizations. Should we engage in politics? Would political action advance the movement or engulf it in petty partisan squabbles? Such questions could not be avoided. But until 1886, the drift of events served to reinforce the ideals of cooperation and equality, and the search for a better way of organizing the industrial system.

The realities of more and more trades contradicted even modest dreams of status and mobility as entire categories of skills were mechanized out of existence. Such pressures did not automatically produce greater solidarity. The very threat seemed to make some skilled workers even more conscious of the need to set themselves off from the mass, to salvage crumbling realities with homage to respectability. Such games could have gone on forever had not the pressure of wage cuts, speed-ups, unemployment, and poverty continued unrelenting. Kicking and screaming, perhaps, squabbling with one another, backsliding and sidestepping, dragged forward by their more farsighted compatriots, by the mid-1880s many Detroit workers seemed to have realized that they faced a personal and group crisis. The evolution of workers' thinking was slow and difficult. People were separated by their economic and cultural differences, caught up in the day-to-day struggle for survival. They were afraid of getting into trouble, losing their jobs.

Such fear and deference is hard to document. Nineteenth-century celebrants of industry denied the existence of so European a phenomenon; the victims rarely acknowledged their fears, even to themselves. But appeals to manliness and courage are such a common theme of the nineteenth-century labor agitator that they must suggest widespread existence of timidness and acceptance. We might like to find evidence of rebellious thousands singing the *Internationale*. Social reality was often much more bleak.[111]

A few examples are suggestive. In 1885, the director of the State Bureau of Labor Statistics noted that fifty to one hundred men showed up every day at the front steps of Detroit's City Hall on the chance that there might be work. There were no protests or demonstrations; the men stood around for a while and then went home. A compassionate manufacturer explained to the Labor Bureau that five to fifteen men applied for work every day at his factory although he had not advertised for help. Those already employed, seeing the numbers who were desperate enough to work for almost any amount, "really overworked themselves fearing that otherwise they would be discharged."[112]

In December 1883, the Detroit House of Corrections recorded eighty-five voluntary commitments in one month. A few were habitual criminals or drunks; most were simply unemployed workers with nowhere else to go. Only twenty-five of the eighty-five had ever been in jail before, including ten arrested for drunkenness; men explained they had "no work, no money, were sick" or "hungry," and just "wanted to get some place to stay out of the cold." Nearly half (thirty-six) had been out of work more than a month.[113] These people certainly had grievances against the industrial system, but people who begged for work or voluntarily turned themselves into prison were not likely to become soldiers of the class war.

There was a hidden dimension of fear that may have been even more decisive than these obvious kinds of submissiveness. We can find many examples of courageous workers who refused to be bullied, who demanded that employers respect long-standing work rules that gave the worker some control over the pace of work. How much were they, even the courageous, inhibited by an employer's display of power? When a trade unionist was fired and left town in search of work, what happened to the spirit of rebellion in the friends he left behind? In 1886, painter John Goldring was driven out of town after defending the Haymarket anarchists and the right of workers to use force to defend themselves from police attack. He was unable to get work, the daily newspapers attacked him by name from their editorial columns, and his partner asked him to leave. The Detroit *Labor Leaf* defended Goldring and bitterly denounced his critics, but Goldring left. What did other revolutionaries in the city conclude about speaking out in public? [114]

Such questions are inherently unanswerable. Even the participants could not really know exactly how much of their behavior was dictated by the almost instinctive caution that such experiences produce. But if we are to understand the tensions underlying working-class behavior in Detroit, we must recognize the existence of fear, the process of self-restraint that takes place when people say to themselves: "What will happen to me if I do this?" Consciousness exists in a concrete reality of power. People do not develop their ideas, their political consciousness out of pure reflection. When the propertyless defend property rights, or the oppressed seem to meekly submit, we cannot assume that such belief or such action represents a freely given consent in any meaningful sense. What seems possible always limits a sense of what is just.

The development of a working-class subculture of opposition was a partial process. Yet such a process did take place. If we are to understand it, we must recreate the tensions which existed between cooperative ideas emerging from workers' experiences and the hope of individual escape, between faith in a different future and despondency over any chance for change, between ethnic suspicions and the recognition of the need to work together. Detroit's workers were groping toward a new group consciousness, attempting to bridge the gulfs that separated them. To understand that process we must begin by examining the development and internal conflicts of the organizations workers created to fulfill their needs for group action.

NOTES

1. *Der Arme Teufel*, February 21, 1885.

2. *Der Arme Teufel*, May 2, 1885.

3. Detroit *Evening Journal* clipping, September 1, 1885, in Knights of Labor Scrapbook, LC; *Labor Leaf*, December 12, 1885. For an extended discussion of union membership trends in the early 1880s, see chap. 4.

4. *Labor Leaf*, January 28, 1885; *The Spectator*, November 17, 1883; *SBLS*, 1903, p. 325; *SBLS*, 1908, p. 350.

5. Several works by sociologists and anthropologists have been suggestive to me, including Barrington Moore's two books, *Social Origins of Dictatorship and Democracy* (Boston, 1976), and *Injustice, the Social Bases of Obedience and Revolt* (White Plains, New York, 1972), Eric Wolf's *Peasant Wars of the Twentieth Century* (New York, 1973), and Ted Robert Gurr's *Why Men Rebel* (Princeton, 1974).

6. Alan Dawley, *Class and Community, the Industrial Revolution in Lynn* (Cambridge, 1976); Paul Faler, *Mechanics and Manufacturers in the Early Industrial Revolution, Lynn, Massachusetts, 1780–1860* (Albany, 1981); Daniel Walkowitz, *Worker City, Company Town, Iron and Cotton-Worker Protest in Troy and Cohoes, New York, 1855–84* (Urbana, 1978); John T. Cumbler, *Working-Class Community in Industrial America: Work, Leisure, and Struggle in Two Industrial Cities, 1880–1930* (Westport, Conn. 1979).

7. Dawley, *Class and Community*; Faler, *Mechanics and Manufacturers*; Cumbler, *Working-Class Community*.

8. *Eleventh Census*, 1890, vol. 1, pt. 11, pp. 664–65. Most of the "other immigrants" were Poles. These results are probably not completely reliable. The census only recorded parents' birthplace, not always a reliable guide to ethnicity. Moreover, many Poles were counted as Germans since they came from Prussian Poland.

9. *Eleventh Census*, 1890, vol. 1, pt. 1, p. 897; pt. 2, pp. 664–65; Olivier Zunz, *The Changing Face of Inequality, Detroit from 1880 to 1920* (Chicago, 1982), table 1.5, p. 37, table 9.1, p. 221. "Native" will hereafter refer to native born of native parents. A notable exception to the native job profile is the overrepresentation of native women among the domestic servants, probably a result of employer preferences for English speakers.

10. JoEllen Vinyard, *The Irish on the Urban Frontier: Nineteenth Century Detroit, 1850–1880* (New York, 1975), pp. 404–8. As the recent econometric study by Joan Hannon ("The Immigrant Worker in the Promised Land: Human Capital and Ethnic Discrimination in the Michigan Labor Market, 1888–1890," Ph.D. dissertation, University of Wisconsin, 1978) demonstrates, this native advantage cannot be explained by superior skills, education, or resources. Hannon demonstrates that immigrant workers with comparable skills or other resources fared worse than natives.

11. *Eleventh Census*, 1890, vol. 1, pt. 2, pp. 664–65; *SBLS*, 1891, p. 431; Zunz, *The Changing Face of Inequality*, vol. 2, tables 1.5 and 9.1. For a general discussion of the characteristics of British workers see Rowland Berthoff, *British Immigrants in Industrial America* (Cambridge, Mass., 1953).

12. Ibid. The notable exception to the generally high profile of Canadian workers is the large number of female domestic servants, a result of the ability of Detroit's middle class to draw on Windsor to satisfy its preference for English-speaking domestics.

13. *Eleventh Census*, 1890, vol. 1, pt. 2, pp. 664–65. For a discussion of the changing position of German artisans in Chicago's economy, see Hartmut Keil and Heinz Ickstadt, "Elemente einer deutscher Arbeiterkultur im Chicago Zwischen 1880 und 1890," *Geschichte und Gesellschaft* 5 (1979), Heft 1: 106–10, and *German Workers in Industrial Chicago, 1850–1910: A Comparative Perspective* (DeKalb, 1983), especially the papers by John Jentz, "German Workers in Chicago's Manufacturing Industries: 1880–1900," and Hartmut Keil, "The German Working Class of Chicago in 1900."

14. *Tenth Census*, 1880, vol. 1, p. 876; *Eleventh Census*, 1890, vol.1, pt. 2, pp. 664–65, and vol. 1, pt. 1, p. 672; Sister Mary Remigia Napolska, *The Polish Immigrant in Detroit to 1914* (Chicago, 1946), p. 30; Peter A. Ostafin, "The Polish Peasant in Transition: A Study of Group Integration as a Function of Symbiosis and Common Definitions" (Ph.D. dissertation, University of Michigan, 1948), pp. 76–78. The 1890 Census reported only 5,351 Poles in Detroit, but several authorities argue most Poles were counted as Germans, Austrians or Russians because Poland was divided between those countries. The *Evening News* claimed in 1892 that Poles made up one-seventh to one-eighth of Detroit's population. This figure probably included the second generation. Numerous descriptions of Polish activities also suggest a Polish population much larger than the census figure.

15. *Eleventh Census*, 1890, vol. 1, pt. 2, pp. 664–65; Zunz, tables 1.5 and 9.1; Ostafin, p. 251. Among forty-six first-generation family heads, Ostafin found eight men who had been skilled workers in Poland.

16. Zunz, table 1.5; Vinyard, chaps. 2, 5, Appendix C.

17. *Eleventh Census*, 1890, vol. 1, pt. 2, pp. 664–65; Zunz, table 9.1; *SBLS*, 1891, pp. 430–31. The relative prosperity of Detroit's Irish is the main theme of Vinyard's book.

18. David Katzman, *Before the Ghetto, Black Detroit in the Nineteenth Century* (Urbana, 1975), pp. 62–63; *Eleventh Census*, 1890, vol. 1, pt. 2, pp. 664–65.

19. Katzman, pp. 107–8, 110–11, 115–17.

20. *SBLS*, 1886, pp. 158, 163.

21. Melvin G. Holli, *Reform in Detroit, Hazen S. Pingree and Urban Politics* (New York, 1969), pp. 65–68.

22. Olivier Zunz, "The Organization of the American City in the Late

Nineteenth Century: Ethnic Structure and Spatial Arrangement in Detroit," *Journal of Urban History*, 3 (August 1977): 453, 463. Zunz's arguments are more fully developed in his book. JoEllen Vinyard argues that the presence of some highly visible ethnic neighborhoods blinded contemporary Detroiters and later scholars to the dispersed nature of Detroit immigrant residences. Her case is strongest for Detroit's Irish, her main focus, but Zunz shows that some dispersal is not inconsistent with ethnic clustering. For Zunz's discussion of the concept of ethnic dominance in mixed neighborhoods, see *The Changing Face of Inequality*, pp. 46–47.

23. Zunz, "The Organization of the American City," p. 457, and *The Changing Face of Inequality*; *Eleventh Census*, vol. 1, pt. 2, pp. lxxi, lxxii; Holli, p. 11.

24. Katzman, p. 58; George P. Groff, *The People of Michigan* (Lansing, 1974), p. 83; *Eleventh Census*, 1890, vol. 4, pt. 2, pp. 219–27; Lawrence D. Orton, *Polish Detroit and the Kolasinski Affair* (Detroit, 1981), chap. 1.

25. Vinyard, pp. 182–83, 190–91.

26. Ralph Janis, "The Brave New World that Failed: Patterns of Parish Social Structure in Detroit, 1880–1940," (Ph.D. dissertation, University of Michigan, Ann Arbor, 1972), pp. 37, 39; Zunz, *The Changing Face of Inequality*, p. 68.

27. Ostafin, pp. 251–53.

28. Vinyard, pp. 191–92, 416–17.

29. British and Canadian workers were more numerous than the Irish by the end of the century, but they did not develop a full counterpart to the cultural systems of the other major groups (although British workers did carry with them some important traditions about work and workers' rights). Blacks did develop a separate cultural system, but they made up only 2 percent of Detroit's working class in 1890. No other immigrant group made up more than 2 percent of Detroit's working class in 1890. Children of immigrants are treated as part of the cultural system of their parents.

30. *Eleventh Census*, 1890, vol. 1, pt. 2, pp. 897, 664–65; Zunz, *The Changing Face of Inequality*, pp. 16–17, 85–86, 105–9, 131–35.

31. Detroit *City Directory* (Detroit, 1881).

32. *Labor Leaf*, September 29, 1886, April 15, 1885, October 27, 1886, April 1, 1885, December 31, 1887; *Detroit Times*, April 17, 1881; *Evening News*, June 22, 1890, January 18, 1891; Grenell, "Autobiography," pp. 1–3, 26–27, 44–46; Ross Scrapbooks, vol. 1, pp. 17–20, clipping, "The Labor Champions," Burton Historical Collections, Detroit Public Library.

33. Zunz, *The Changing Face of Inequality*, pp. 204–7, chap. 5.

34. *Detroit Times*, April 10, 1881. The nature and origins of the Free Labor ideology is explored by Eric Foner, *Free Soil, Free Labor, Free Men* (New York, 1970), and David Montgomery, *Beyond Equality* (New York, 1972).

35. *Detroit Times*, April 17, 24, 1881.

36. "Circular no. 2" of the Independent Labor party (Detroit, 1884), Burton Historical Collection, Detroit Public Library.

37. Montgomery; Dawley; Bruce Laurie, *Working People of Philadelphia, 1800–1850* (Philadelphia, 1980).

38. I created an information file on Detroit labor leaders by combining data from all available sources. This ethnic profile of Detroit labor leaders is drawn from that file. Sources include daily and labor presses; personal correspondence, clippings and other documents in the Labadie Collection, Burton Historical Collection, and Powderly Papers; city directories; State Bureau of Labor Statistics Reports; and county histories. Hereafter cited DLL.

39. Zunz, *The Changing Face of Inequality*, pp. 225–26; *Eleventh Census*, 1890, vol. 1, pt. 2, pp. 664–65.

40. Wayne County Election Records, 1884, 1886, Burton Historical Collection, Detroit Public Library. Ethnic composition of precincts determined from Zunz, *The Changing Face of Inequality; Eleventh Census*, 1890, vol. 4, pt. 2, pp. 219–27; Manuscript Census, 1880; and a series of articles describing the ethnic composition of precincts in the *Sunday News* in 1892. For a fuller description of voting behavior see chap. 4, pt. 3.

41. *Evening News*, October 1, 3, 5, 1890.

42. *Evening News*, October 5, 6, 1890.

43. *Evening News*, October 5, 6, 12, 1890.

44. Census 1850–1900, published *Population* volumes.

45. Holli, pp. 10–11; Zunz, *The Changing Face of Inequality*, pp. 114–16, 123–28.

46. Zunz, *The Changing Face of Inequality*, p. 107; Holli, pp. 10–21; *Evening News*, June 5, 1892. One percent of Detroit's Germans were Jewish.

47. Paul Kleppner, *The Cross of Culture* (New York, 1970); *Evening News*, July 4, 1892.

48. *Evening News*, October 31, 1892, November 2, 1892; N. W. Ayers and Sons, *American Newspaper Annual* (Philadelphia, 1883); Karl J. R. Arndt and May E. Olson, *German-American Newspapers and Periodicals, 1732–1935* (Heidelberg, 1961), pp. 211–15; *City Directory*, 1890.

49. *Detroiter Abend-Post*, June 29, 1880; *Michigan Volksblatt*, January 16, 1894; *Evening News*, February 28, 1893.

50. Holli, pp. 13–14; Zunz, *The Changing Face of Inequality*, chap. 5, p. 13. The list of delegates and organizations to the Detroit Anti-Prohibition Association convention published in the *Labor Leaf*, March 26, 1887, gives a good sense of the preponderant role of Germans in antiprohibitionism and the range of Germans opposed to prohibition.

51. *Evening News*, August 1, 1891; *Der Arme Teufel*, August 30, 1890, September 6, 1890.

52. Adolph Eduard Zucker, *Robert Reitzel* (Philadelphia, 1917), pp. 9–18.

53. Zucker, pp. 31–36, 39; *Der Arme Teufel*, December 6, 1884, February 25, March 3, 1888.

54. *Der Arme Teufel*, September 13, 1890.

55. Ibid.

56. *Der Arme Teufel*, September 13, 1890, January 16, April 24, June 5, 1886, June 11, 1887; *Der Herold*, July 22, 1898.

57. William Frederic Kamman, *Socialism in German American Literature* (Philadelphia, 1917), pp. 58–63; *Der Arme Teufel*, January 28, February 4, July 28, 1888.

58. *Evening News*, October 5, 1890, August 24, 1891; *Der Arme Teufel*, October 5, 1891; *Michigan Volksblatt*, October 7, 1891.

59. *Evening News*, September 5, 1887, February 1, 1891.

60. "Labor Day Review," 1892, p. 37, LC. *Evening News*, August 31, 1890. The membership estimate is a newspaper estimate of the number marching under the CLU banner in the 1890 Labor Day Parade, probably an underestimate of dues-paying members.

61. *Evening News*, August 31, September 14, 1890; *Der Arme Teufel*, September 11, 1886, September 10, 1887; *Der Herold*, September 8, 1899.

62. *Der Arme Teufel*, June 1, November 9, 1889.

63. Arndt and Olson, pp. 211–15; N. W. Ayers, *American Newspaper Annual* (Philadelphia, 1902); *Der Herold*, April 14, 1889, March 10, 1899; *Der Arme Teufel*, December 12, 1885.

64. Carl Schorske, *German Social Democracy* (Cambridge, Mass., 1955).

65. *Der Arme Teufel*, December 15, August 11, 1888, September 7, 1889; *Evening News*, July 19, 1891.

66. *Der Herold*, May 27, November 25, 1898, March 31, 1899. The only notable exception to the CLU's exclusively German emphasis were several attempts to organize Polish laborers, many of whom spoke German.

67. *Der Herold*, July 22, 1898; *Der Arme Teufel*, September 7, 1889, May 5, 1888.

68. Wayne County Election Records, 1884, 1886, Burton Historical Collection, Detroit Public Library. Ethnic composition of precincts determined from Zunz, *The Changing Face of Inequality; Eleventh Census*, 1890, vol. 4, pt. 2, pp. 219–27; Manuscript Census, 1880; and a series of articles describing the ethnic composition of precincts in the *Sunday News* in 1891. For a fuller description of voting behavior see chap. 4, pt. 3.

69. *Evening News*, March 20, 27, April 3, 1892.

70. Ibid.

71. *Evening News*, April 3, 1892.

72. Ostafin, pp. 16, 251, 262; Zunz, *The Changing Face of Inequality*, pp. 157–59, 171–74, 188–89, 221. According to Zunz, 86 percent of Poles in Detroit came from Prussian Poland.

73. Napolska, pp. 39–41; *Advance and Labor Leaf*, February 11, 1888. Victor Greene and David Brody have documented the militance and solidarity of Slavic workers in coal and steel: Victor Greene, *The Slavic Community on Strike: Immigrant Labor in Pennsylvania Anthracite* (Notre Dame, Indiana, 1968); David Brody, *Steelworkers in America: The Non-union Era* (New York, 1969). James Barrett shows that Polish stockyard laborers were integrated into the Chicago labor movement in the early 1900s, and by the World War I era had assumed leadership roles. Employers then *avoided* hiring Poles because they were believed to be too solidly pro-union. See James Barrett, "Work and Community in the Jungle: Chicago's Packing House Workers, 1894–1922" (Ph.D. dissertation, University of Pittsburgh, 1981).

74. Orton, *Polish Detroit and the Kolasinski Affair*.

75. Orton, pp. 28–31, 137–59; Ostafin, "The Polish Peasant in Transition." Orton notes but does not emphasize the political role of the church, suggesting that Kolasinski followers who spoke to Ostafin in the 1930s had let their memories color the events. Ostafin tends to see the Kolasinski affair as an example of deviant behavior, indicative of the maladjustment of peasant folk to a difficult urban environment.

76. Orton, pp. 25–27; Ostafin, pp. 98–100.

77. Orton, p. 41; Ostafin, pp. 105–6.

78. Orton, pp. 43–62. Leslie Woodcock Tentler challenges these claims of foregoing sacraments. As evidence of their contention, Kolasinski and his supporters asserted that he had performed hundreds of baptisms, first communions, and marriages in the first months after his return in 1888, but Tentler demonstrates by an examination of parish records that this was not the case. Leslie Woodcock Tentler, "Who Is the Church? Conflict in a Polish Immigrant Parish in Late Nineteenth-Century Detroit," *Comparative Studies in Society and History*, 25 (April 1983): 261–64.

79. Orton, pp. 79–80, 94–95; Ostafin, pp. 112–14.

80. Orton, pp. 123–24, 126, 131–44; Ostafin, pp. 114–23.

81. Ostafin, pp. 98–102.

82. DLL; *Labor Leaf*, December 10, 1884; *Evening News*, April 30, 1891; *Industrial Gazette*, February 15, 22, March 8, 22, 1895; Holli, p. 67; *Der Herold*, November 25, 1898; *Detroit Sentinel*, May 22, 1897. By the late 1890s, however, some Poles had been recruited into the Socialist Labor party. The 1898 SLP city ticket included several Polish surnames.

83. *Evening News*, May 22, 1886.

84. See note 68. For a fuller description of voting behavior, see chap. 4, pt. 3. The four precincts with the highest proportion of Poles (each with Polish majorities by 1891) had a mean ILP vote in 1886 of 23.5 percent, compared to a city wide average of 14.0 percent.

85. See for example the campaign speech of Martin Kulwicki, Democratic legislative candidate, Detroit *News-Tribune*, October 31, 1900.

86. Tentler found that the Kolasinskiites were close to a cross section of Detroit's Polonia, but the rebel parish was slightly more proletarian than the St. Albertus parish, which remained loyal to the bishop: 60 percent of the bridegrooms in Kolasinski's parish were laborers compared to 51 percent at St. Albertus, while St. Albertus had somewhat higher proportions of skilled workers and small businessmen. See Tentler, "Who Is the Church?" p. 253.

87. *Irish World*, February 9, 1878, January 10, December 25, 1880, April 9, July 23, 1881; Eric Foner, "Class, Ethnicity, and Radicalism in the Gilded Age: The Land League and Irish America," *Marxist Perspectives*, 1 (Summer 1978): 9–11, 14; Detroit *City Directory*, 1878, 1881.

88. Foner, "Class, Ethnicity, and Radicalism," 11–15, 22–30. See also Daniel Walkowitz, *Worker City, Company Town*; David Montgomery, *Beyond Equality*, pp. 120, 126–34, 377–78; Michael Allen Gordon, "Studies in Irish and Irish-American Thought and Behavior in Gilded Age New York City," (Ph.D. dissertation, University of Rochester, 1977) for discussions of the relationship between Irish attitudes and Irish participation in the labor movement. For a typical reference to the *Irish World* in the labor press, see the *Detroit Unionist*, June 12, 1882; *Irish World*, May 7, 1881.

89. *Irish World*, February 9, 1878; Detroit *City Directory*, 1878, p. 188; Victor Walsh, "'A Fanatic Heart': The Case of Irish-American Nationalism in Pittsburgh during the Gilded Age," *Journal of Social History*, 15 (Winter 1981): 6–9.

90. *Irish World*, February 9, July 6, August 10, 1878, January 10, November 3, December 25, 1880, January 8, 15, February 12, 26, March 12, April 2, 9, June 25, July 23, 1881; Vinyard, p. 197; Detroit *City Directory*, 1878, 1879, 1880, 1881. Two of the anonymous contributors were also identified as non-Irish: an American and an Australian.

91. *Tenth Census*, 1880, vol. 1, p. 876; Zunz, table 1.5.

92. *Irish World*, May 24, 1879, September 24, 1881. Number of contributors based on calculations of average size of contributions in a sample of four issues divided into total reported contributions.

93. *Irish World*, September 24, 1881, November 13, December 25, 1880, January 8, April 4, June 25, July 23, April 9, 1881.

94. Vinyard, pp. 383, 416–18; Zunz, *The Changing Face of Inequality*, p. 246; Zunz, "The Organization of the American City."

95. Detroit *City Directory*, 1879; *Evening News*, November 2, 1892.

96. Vinyard, pp. 33–36. Theoretically the *Western Home Journal* was the organ of all Michigan Catholics; in practice it was written and edited by Detroit Irish Catholics and directed to an Irish audience. Vinyard, pp. 291–93, 424.

97. "The Labor Champions," Ross Scrapbooks, vol. 1, pp. 17–20, Burton Historical Collection, Detroit Public Library; *Advance and Labor Leaf*, April 21, 1888; Wayne County Historical and Pioneer Society, *Chronology of Notable Events* (Detroit, 1890), p. 419.

98. For the demise of the ILP, see chap. 6.

99. Vinyard, chap. 9.

100. *Labor Review*, October 23, 1880.

101. Holli, pp. 5–7; George N. Fuller, ed., *Michigan—A Centennial History of the State and its People* (Chicago, 1939), pp. 536–40; Silas Farmer, *History of Detroit and Wayne County and Early Michigan* (Detroit, 1890), pp. 801–36; *Evening News*, May 4, 1886; *Tribune*, May 8, 1886; clipping, "Among the Molders," June 16, 1889, LC; *Evening News*, May 5, 1892; Michigan Factory Inspectors, *First Annual Report of Factories in Michigan* (Lansing, 1894), pp. 9–25; *Tenth Census*, 1880, vol. 2, pp. 399–400; *Eleventh Census*, 1890, Compendium, pp. 802–5.

102. *Third Annual Report of the Commissioner of Labor: Strikes and Lockouts, 1887* (Washington, D.C., 1896), pp. 474–87.

103. *SBLS*, 1886, p. 150.

104. "Rubbing Elbows with People Worth-While—XXVI—Charles Erb," undated clipping in Detroit Labor Leaders File, LC; *Evening News*, March 8, December 6, 1891.

105. *Labor Leaf*, December 31, 1884, September 6, 1891.

106. *Labor Leaf*, November 18, 1885. Unequal distribution of "the fat" was an issue for many trades, and the cause of several strikes. See the *Labor Review*, May 1880, for example, where the question was cited one of the key issues in an iron molders' strike.

107. *Labor Leaf*, June 10, 17, 1885.

108. Strikebreakers recruited by employers during the 1892 bakers' strike, for example, left on this basis. The practice was so widely accepted that in 1887 striking Detroit ship carpenters sued several men who accepted traveling money and then stayed on. They seemed genuinely surprised when the court failed to grant redress for what they considered a clear breach of an accepted code of behavior. The judge ruled that the attempt to persuade the strikebreakers not to work was a violation of conspiracy laws.

109. *Labor Leaf*, February 25, 1885. For a study of tramping carpenters during this period see Jules Tygiel, "Tramping Artisans: The Case of the Carpenters in Industrial America," *Labor History*, 22 (Summer 1981): 348–76.

110. *Labor Leaf*, January 28, 1885.

111. For a typical appeal to manliness, see the Preamble to the Constitution of Detroit Bricklayers and Masons' Union No. 2, *SBLS*, 1884, pp. 62–63.

112. *SBLS*, 1885, p. 116.

113. *SBLS*, 1884, pp. 190–91, 56–57.

114. *Labor Leaf*, June 30, July 7, 1886. For a general discussion of workers' struggles to maintain work rules during this era, and the importance of appeals to courage, see David Montgomery, "Workers' Control of Machine Production in the Nineteenth Century," *Labor History*, 17 (Fall 1976).

3

THE ORGANIZATION OF A SUBCULTURE OF OPPOSITION: Craft Unions, Socialists, and Knights of Labor

A subculture of opposition began to emerge as a series of informal responses to immediate conditions and problems, but confronted with the fragmenting influences of the diverse economic and cultural environment in Detroit, such spontaneity needed more formal organization and group commitment to develop and sustain itself. Organization provides courage, resources, and support. As people begin to look to an organization as a focus for activity and group loyalty, the organization can also become a unifying symbol which strengthens commitment and provides a group myth, an elaboration of the abstractions on which class consciousness is based.

Craft Unions in the Late 1870s

Although by the late 1870s the local labor movement was a generation old, the city's unions did not play this unifying role. They lacked the strength, and in some cases the inclination, to represent anyone beyond their own small membership.[1] Union membership fluctuated wildly from year to year; locals lapsed and reorganized frequently; only six local unions had an uninterrupted existence throughout the 1870s. When the Detroit Trades Council was organized, its constituent unions reported a total membership of only 432, a startling revelation of the lack of organization in a city of over 100,000 people.[2]

The inability of the trade unions to serve as a unifying symbol for the city's workers was based on more than their weakness. Many of the unions failed to honor even the most minimal concepts of solidarity. Detroit Local No. 2 of the Machinists and Blacksmiths' Union refused, for example, to aid a striking Scranton, Pennsylvania, local. Terence Powderly, the secretary of the Scranton machinists' union, had written asking for assistance for his group, but the Detroit union declined aid on the grounds that the Scranton local had not followed proper constitutional procedure in issuing its strike call. This petty legalism evaded the very essence of a code of solidarity. Such unions reflected, rather than superceded, the spirit of fragmentation and competition. While union activists and some union locals as a whole did attempt to maintain a spirit of mutual cooperation and support, they often found their efforts frustrated by their more recalcitrant associates.[3]

Judson Grenell, a member of the Typographical Union No. 18 and one of the leaders of the English-speaking branch of the local Socialist Labor party, lamented in 1878 that the printers were "almost fossilized," they were so conservative. The printers had recently received an ultimatum from local employers threatening them with a lockout unless they voluntarily accepted a 6¼ percent pay reduction. Grenell hoped the threat might finally bring the printers to life. It did not. The union meekly complied with the wage cuts and a month later rejected the proposed constitution of the Detroit Labor League. The constitution included provisions for a mutual defense system for situations like that the printers had just faced, but the printers wanted no part of it. Some denounced the threat of communism; others, as Grenell put it, were simply too "high tone" to associate with the likes of carpenters, shoemakers, or cigarmakers.[4]

Much of this caution and conservatism may have been induced by the experiences of the previous decade. Union membership had declined drastically in Detroit since the late 1860s, and few unions, locally or nationally, had survived the depression of the mid-1870s with more than a token membership intact.[5] Unions began to revive in Detroit in 1877. Between 1877 and 1879, seven unions were chartered or reorganized. The nonunionized majority of the city's workers began to display far greater interest in labor organization and social reform, but many unionists who had been active in the 1860s and 1870s seem to have been unable to overcome the spirit of caution and insularity they had learned in earlier years. By the early 1880s, the character of the city's trade union movement changed, but only after an influx of less cautious new members.[6]

Pressure for change came mainly from discontented unionists and other activists who had formed local branches of the Socialist Labor party and the Knights of Labor. Young activists in the Socialist Labor party tried hard to convince trade unionists of the need for an aggressive program of "trade amalgamation" and organization of the "unorganized laborers." The socialists converted many, but even when union representatives agreed to the principle of mutual aid, their organizations did not respond to appeals for help. In 1878, union delegates to the Detroit Labor League, a loose city union federation, voted in favor of the socialist proposal for mutual aid which the printers rejected. Member unions then ratified the mutual aid proposal, but many refused to forward funds when asked. The organization split over the question of emergency assessments and collapsed. When the Detroit Trades Council was formed in 1880, the treasurer of the defunct Labor League turned over the league's entire assets: $4.07.[7]

The Trades Council, like the Labor League, was a product of agitation by activists in the Knights of Labor and Socialist Labor party. It proved to be more resilient than the Labor League but faced similar bickering and shortsightedness. Several unions refused to support the council's programs. The question of mutual assistance was still a critical problem. The plasterers, for example, refused to support striking ironmolders because the council had not provided aid for them during their seasonal layoffs. The plasterers had missed the point. It was beyond the scope of an organization as weak as the Trades Council to provide regular unemployment relief, but mutual aid against employer attack was central to the survival of both the Trades Council and individual unions. The plasterers were not alone, however. Several other unions maintained only token affiliation, rarely participating in Trades Council activities. The editors of the local labor paper complained that council delegates were failing to attend meetings.[8]

Yet by 1880, there was a clear sense of ferment among Detroit workers. That fall the Trades Council held a public demonstration in which 1,500 local workers marched. In fall elections, the socialist president of the carpenters' union was elected alderman. Persistent agitation by the socialists and the Knights of Labor was beginning to pay off.[9] It is not clear whether they had convinced many veteran trade unionists. A systematic comparison of names of individuals known to be members of the Knights of Labor or the Socialist Labor party with a similar listing of known union leaders active prior to 1875 reveals that only three veteran union leaders had joined either the Knights or the SLP. There seems to have been little direct leadership carryover from the pre-1875 unions to the more active organizations after 1880.[10] The activists had convinced enough people, however, to promote a vigorous ideological and strategic debate within the labor movement and among workers in general. At union meetings, public forums, and in the columns of the labor press, advocates of various points of view discussed both practical programs and fundamental questions about the nature of industrial progress, the roles of labor and capital, or alternative economic and political systems.

A process had begun which would transform not only the labor movement but also the most basic attitudes of a broad section of the city's workers. Throughout the early 1880s a continually ascending level of activity among Detroit workers produced new organizations and stimulated old ones. The conservative craft unions of the 1870s were carried along in the process, sometimes reluctantly, but often with a growing enthusiasm as well. Some crafts, under pressure of mechanization, responded to the growing sense of solidarity with a move away from earlier craft conservatism. The keys to this unity were the socialists and the Knights of Labor.

Labadie, Grenell, and American Socialism

In the fall of 1879, Joseph Labadie wrote to Terence Powderly, the grand master workman of the Knights of Labor: "I believe that by force alone can be removed the societary wrongs which have fastened themselves upon the people. But first must come agitation, organization, intelligence, and then the demand!"[11] Labadie was then master workman of the Detroit Knights of Labor. His career is important because it illustrates the interconnections between trade unionism, socialism, and the Knights of Labor in Detroit. As a printer Labadie was active in the typographical union and a founder of the Detroit Trades Council. After joining the Socialist Labor party, he became a local and then national leader in the socialist movement. He founded the first assembly of the Knights in Detroit, and together with a group of similar radical activists used the Knights as a basis for mass education, union organizing, and labor politics. Labadie and many of his associates ultimately abandoned the SLP, but not socialism or labor radicalism, for the Knights. The local SLP section stagnated, but as the Knights prospered, a powerful vision of workers' solidarity was communicated to thousands of Detroit workers.[12]

Scholars have emphasized the conflict between the Knights of Labor and the American Federation of Labor while the socialists have often been viewed as a disruptive influence in both. But in Detroit in the early 1880s, the most serious ideological debates were all more clearly reproduced within organizations rather than between them. Activists of all persuasions were part of a single movement. Socialists played crucial roles as organizers of the Knights of Labor and the trade unions; activists combined forces quite readily despite ideological differences. In Detroit, trade unionism, socialism, and the Knights of Labor had common roots: they emerged together out of the subculture of opposition.[13]

Labadie was born in Paw Paw, Michigan, in 1850. At fourteen, he went to work in his uncle's jewelry store as an apprentice watchmaker, but apparently he did not like the trade, and he went on the tramp. He learned printing in a newspaper office in South Bend, Indiana, and then began more extensive wanderings: Kalamazoo, Grand Rapids, Saginaw, Cleveland, Rochester, Syracuse, New York City, and Detroit in 1872. He had joined the printers' union in 1868 or 1869 but only became active in union affairs in 1876. Once he did, he was immediately prominent in the Detroit Typographical Union but decided nearly as quickly that the trade union was not a permanent solution to the labor problem. In 1877, Labadie joined the socialists.[14]

Socialism had come to Detroit in 1874, three years before Labadie's conversion. A local cigar manufacturer had unwittingly helped to introduce it to Detroit's workers. He had wanted to begin production of a new line of the most expensive hand-rolled cigars and had not trusted the skills of any of the local cigarmakers. Instead he recruited two top-quality German cigarmakers in New York and paid their fare to Detroit. Gustav Herzig and Henry Kummerfeldt proved to be all he had hoped for and more. They were indeed superb craftsmen, but their employer had opened a Pandora's box which he and other Detroit employers must have regretted in the following years. Herzig and Kummerfeldt were also veteran union organizers and experienced socialist agitators.[15]

They began socialist agitation in Detroit's German community almost immediately. They had arrived in the midst of a depression; many of the German workers they met had also had prior experience with unions in Germany, and German working-class culture already included a tradition of political radicalism. Working conditions and relations with employers in Detroit substantiated the prior convictions of German-born artisans who expected to find class struggle. Herzig and Kummerfeldt found their fellow workers and neighbors receptive and soon formed a local socialist group which affiliated with the Working-men's Party of the United States in 1876 or 1877.[16]

By 1877 the Workingmen's party appeared to be thriving in Detroit's German neighborhoods. While party membership was still small, the party's public forums were neighborhood social events which drew crowds of several hundred. The organization tapped a wide base of potential converts for whom socialism was a fraternal and cultural affair as well as a political movement. A network of subsidiary and related groups such as the Socialist Mannerchor, (men's choir), provided contact with people who considered themselves part of the movement but did not necessarily pay party dues or participate regularly in the party's political activities.

But despite this apparent success, party leaders recognized that cultural events, largely confined to the German community, were not the path to success. For practical as well as ideological reasons, they began to look for ways to attract English-speaking, especially native-born, workers. Many party meetings had drawn two or three hundred people, and the party was beginning to attract enough attention to merit some coverage in the daily newspapers, but the socialists had no funds or other resources with which to mount an effective citywide propaganda campaign. They decided to expand their program of public meetings to include agitation meetings in various parts of the city. Labadie and Judson Grenell, another young printer, were the first native-born converts. [17]

Grenell later described his introduction to socialism in some detail. He was already disillusioned with pure and simple trade unionism: "while the trade union was needed in order that employers and employees might be placed on an equal footing in bargaining . . . it was . . . just a palliative." Grenell had already had considerable experience as a union official in New Haven, Connecticut, as well as in Detroit. [18] One evening, as he was walking along a downtown street, he saw a building draped with large red banners. "SOCIAL DEMOCRATS MEET HERE," the signs said. "Walk In—Admission Free." Well, why not? [19] The slogans at the front of the room read, "To everyone according to his deeds," and "He who will not work, neither shall he eat." Grenell took a seat at the back of the room. As the speaker began, Grenell relates that he was fascinated: for the first time, "Here I saw . . . an effort to explain the *cause* of poverty in the midst of plenty . . ."

> Wage workers, these Social Democrats insisted, were continually creating surplus wealth which became the property of the employing class . . . the workers not receiving as much as they were creating, gluts in the market occurred,

when work slackened and willing workers were idle until this surplus wealth had been absorbed by consumers—the workingman who had created the surplus . . . The way to avoid this . . . was to create a cooperative commonwealth, with workingmen their own employers, and in which the compensation to each worker would be in proportion to individual production. Society collectively would be the only employer, and the employing class . . . would melt into the mass, with their compensation measured by their ability to create wealth. Profit in business would be eliminated. The cost of production would govern prices.[20]

Labadie and Grenell had much in common: both were printers, both were disillusioned with existing trade union practices, both reacted emotionally to the poverty and degradation of labor. Together they instigated a variety of new programs to spread socialism beyond the German community. In late 1877 they started the *Socialist*, a weekly newspaper which served both as the city's labor newspaper and as a forum for English-speaking socialists in other cities. It was one of the few socialist newspapers in English in the United States. Grenell was editor, Labadie chief columnist. They worked without pay in the evenings and on Sundays after sixty hours a week on their regular jobs. Along with a few other comrades, they wrote it, printed it, and distributed it themselves. "After working all day," Grenell wrote, "it requires considerable *grit* and determination to take the only time we can call our own and hie to a dusty garret and set type by the light of a kerosene lamp."[21]

Their determination paid off. In December, the *Socialist* reported to its readers that it was doing well financially. The newspaper was received enthusiastically by sympathizers in many parts of the country and soon reported regular distribution in Chicago, Boston, Brooklyn, Cincinnati, Evansville, Indiana, Allegheny City, Pennsylvania, and Grand Rapids, Michigan. By the summer of 1878, national party leaders moved the paper to Chicago, where the growing socialist movement could provide wider circulation. Grenell was offered the editorship but decided to stay in Detroit.[22]

Grenell and Labadie turned their efforts to pamphleteering. Grenell's father and brother were Baptist preachers. He had a bit of the preacher in himself as well, but "my missionary activities have ever been in the direction of political economy, rather than religion, though with not a few political economy is religion." They started a socialist tract society modeled after the Christian counterparts of Grenell's Baptist relatives.[23] The idea was to produce simple cheap pamphlets which explained socialism and which comrades and local branches could afford to buy and distribute free to fellow workers, sympathizers, or passers-by on street corners. With all labor donated free by party comrades, the tract society was able to sell their pamphlets to socialist organizers at $1.12 per thousand. Labadie and Grenell personally handed out thousands of them on Detroit streets and shipped thousands more all over the country. In April of 1880, Grenell reported that they had sold over 140,000 pamphlets since the previous July.[24]

The pamphlets were designed to attract "those curious to know something about the 'left' or 'radical' side of the labor movement." Grenell's approach to propaganda was pragmatic. He and Labadie tried many ways to attract members and "learned by 'trial and error' especially error." They came into conflict with the party's German leaders, who argued they must circulate "pure socialistic literature." Their German critics argued that new recruits were not "homogeneous" or "properly drilled and disciplined . . . the virus of the present social system must be eliminated from their minds."[25] Grenell ridiculed such critics as unnecessarily rigid. They "walked so straight they leaned backward." His propaganda efforts were successful, he pointed out. Despite strong competition from "the greenback hobby-riders" who offer "the workingman . . . immediate relief through cheap money," Labadie and Grenell had attracted enough English-speaking members to form an American branch of the Detroit section of the party. By the fall of 1877, there were three branches: German, American, and Bohemian. The American branch included several important local union officials besides Labadie and Grenell, including Thomas Dolan of the cigarmakers, E. W. Simpson, president of the carpenters' union, and Charles Bell, another printer.[26]

That fall the socialists staged their first electoral campaign. A report of their nominating convention gives some idea of the character of the group. Approximately 100 members were present at Lafayette Hall on Gratiot Avenue, in the heart of the working-class East Side. The meeting's chairman, Charles Stuermer (probably the brother of Adam Stuermer, secretary of the cigarmakers' union and of the Labor League) was a German, but the choice of candidates indicates the party's desire to broaden its appeal. Simpson was nominated for mayor, Dolan for city clerk, and Charles Erb, a second-generation German cigarmaker, for director of the poor.[27]

The socialists entered the campaign enthusiastically, but they faced tremendous handicaps. Part of their constituency could not vote. Some immigrants who could have qualified did not speak English and did not understand the political system. In 1884, only 38 percent of Polish workers surveyed by the Michigan State Bureau of Labor Statistics were voters. The party did not have enough money to mount an effective campaign, or the type of ward organization to bring voters to the polls, help them deal with the election officials, and make sure that their votes were counted.[28]

Their lack of financial resources and precinct-level organization was compounded by the hostility of the electoral bureaucracy. The socialists complained about corruption and false counts, a repeated charge of labor candidates throughout the 1880s. Their poll watchers were denied entrance to polling places, their voters were harassed, and ballot boxes were stuffed. Legal challenges to such practices were not only expensive but faced a bench controlled by members of the local political machines.[29]

Election officials initially credited Simpson with 825 votes for mayor, then threw out forty-seven socialist votes after a supposed recount in one precinct. The socialist vote, predictably, was heaviest in the German precincts of the East Side, but the scattering of votes in all city precincts suggests that the socialists had made some headway in expanding their support beyond the German community. Simpson's initial count represented 6 percent of the total vote, a fair showing considering the party's lack of organization, but party members were convinced that the actual vote had been much higher. Grenell claimed to have witnessed wholesale ballot stuffing, and Labadie, describing the next year's campaign, charged "in one precinct where we are certain we polled at least 15 or 20 votes, they graciously gave us 2."[30]

When Simpson ran for Eleventh Ward alderman in 1880, the evidence of corruption was even clearer. The votes were counted, Simpson was declared the winner by a narrow margin of nineteen votes, and the sealed ballot boxes were delivered to the city clerk. The defeated Democrat, recognizing that the city clerk was also a good Democrat, contested the election, and a recount produced a Democratic majority of eighty votes. Simpson protested and, after an investigating committee found that the ballot box seals had all been altered, removed, or destroyed, refused to surrender his seat on the Detroit Common Council.[31]

While electoral corruption disillusioned some socialists with politics, these campaigns helped the Socialist Labor party attract attention in Detroit. Local politicians recognized that socialist votes were concentrated enough in the working-class precincts that the party might determine the outcome for several legislative and city council seats. The Democratic and Republican machines were closely enough matched in Detroit that the socialists might hold the balance of power, and some machine politicians were sufficiently antagonized with their major party opponents to consider endorsing socialist or other independent labor candidates in wards controlled by the opposing party. In succeeding elections, socialist and independent labor candidates were able to take advantage of this situation. Simpson's 1880 victory, for example, in the normally Democratic Eleventh Ward, was partially the result of a tacit Republican endorsement (he refused outright nomination, but the Republicans did not nominate another candidate and notified supporters of their approval of Simpson).

As a result of the socialist electoral campaigns, the daily newspapers began to expand their previous token coverage of socialist rallies to include more thorough reports of party activities. Party speakers, apparently aware of this wider scrutiny, tried to assuage public fears. At a meeting of about 200 people in May 1878, Simpson strongly emphasized that the party was not a secret organization but a political party like any other, "the main object of which was to conserve the interests of the industrial class without making war on any other class."[32] Although some members argued for a more openly revolutionary image, officially the party steadfastly attempted to retain a public posture of peacefulness and even quite bourgeois respectability. "The Socialist Labor Party is a peace party, a law-abiding party," the *Socialist* declared. "Socialism is not a destructive and plundering outbreak of the poor against the rich . . . but is merely a scheme for a better and more equitable social system than that which now prevails." In 1881, the Detroit *Labor Review*, one of several local successors to the *Socialist*, asserted its loyalty to private property: "We believe in private property. What a man produces by his own labor is his own property, and we are opposed to the system that robs him of it." In the same year, in the ultimate gesture to respectability, Philip Van Patten, the party's national secretary, urged all sections to meet publicly and express their regrets at President Garfield's assassination.[33]

J. F. Bray, the widely respected elderly Pontiac socialist, summarized the party's radical goals but moderate tactics. Bray denounced attempts to alter hours and wages without altering "the relations between labor and capital . . . Labor can accomplish nothing until it had achieved its independence from the control of capital," he argued. "Absolute liberty is the thing to be contended for . . . Labor must control capital." The path to success was "political victory . . . The capture of Federal, State, and municipal governments by votes is the only way for a final settlement of the Labor question."[34]

Socialist Activities

Socialists recognized that in order to succeed they had to educate and organize the majority of American workers. In addition to their newspapers, pamphlets, and leaflets, the Detroit section sponsored an active program of agitation meetings, public rallies, and social gatherings. Ward clubs, organized during the 1877 elections, continued to hold regular educational meetings in members' homes. The Eighth Ward Club W.P.U.S., for example, announced an agitation meeting for Monday, February 11, 1878, at "J. Johnson's, 3311 Grand River Ave., between 4th and 5th streets." "Workingmen!" the *Socialist* admonished, "It is to your own interest to attend these meetings, for it is high time for you to take consideration of your condition."[35]

Social events combined agitation with fund raising. Tickets for the party's Grand Ball on Christmas Evening 1877 cost twenty-five cents, "admitting gentleman and lady." The *Socialist* reported that the section cleared nearly seventy-five dollars from the ball. Another ball was given a month later to raise money to support striking New York City cigarmakers, while proceeds of a similar affair in March 1878 went for "Agitation purposes." The singing section of the SLP gave a "Comic Concert" later that month. These concerts and balls usually charged twenty-five cents admission, although advertisements for the balls added "Ladies Admitted Free." Membership of the party appears to have been overwhelmingly male.[36]

In September 1878, a formal agitation fund was established, and proceeds from such social events were channeled into it. Although this fund-raising system did produce regular revenues, it was inadequate to support an active educational program. In May 1879, for example, the German branch of the Detroit section reported receipts for the agitation fund of $11.66, but Grenell reported a month later that the party would have liked to hold agitation meetings every night of the week but did not have enough funds to do so.[37]

On national holidays such as July 4th, the party staged major gatherings which included both speech making and socializing. The *Trades*, the semiofficial national organ of the Knights of Labor, described the July 4, 1879, eight-hour demonstration sponsored by the Socialist Labor party in Detroit as a "complete success," while the *Socialist* argued that the large crowds, over 2,000 workers and their families, were evidence of the movement's growth. Afternoon speakers read the Declaration of Independence and compared it to the SLP platform. J. F. Bray addressed the crowds in English, and Gustav Herzig spoke in German. Bray argued that under socialism "it would not be necessary to work more than six hours a day. As more machines were invented the hours would be reduced perhaps to five or even four." A public resolution, adopted by a vote of the gathering, summarized Bray's arguments: "Resolved, that we condemn not the use, but the abuse of forces which ought to conserve; that 'labor saving' machinery, to be truly such should save—not starve—the producing classes; then machinery would redound to the benefit of society by reducing the hours of toil and lightening the burden of those who are now compelled to produce wealth for other's enjoyment." The day's celebration ended with an evening ball attended by 600 couples.[38]

Participation in socialist-sponsored activities became a regular part of community life. Concerts, balls, public debates, and educational lectures were primary forms of entertainment and self-improvement, as well as political events. This cultural life promoted a vision of solidarity and class unity. Activists constantly sought ways to increase social contact and a sense of community among workers, to expand upon existing tendencies toward informal cooperation and mutual support.

In 1880, various labor groups rented several rooms on the third floor of a building in Hilsendengen's block, on the edge of downtown, to serve as a Workingman's Club Room, "all workingmen having a few hours of spare time either in day time or in the evening, can go and amuse themselves in reading, games, or conversation."[39] The Workingman's Club Room had a kitchen and a dining and reading room. Workers could have a good meal for a dime or a cup of coffee or tea for three cents. Labor papers were free. Typical events included a solidarity meeting for J. P. McDonnell, the socialist editor of the Paterson, New Jersey, *Labor Standard*, jailed for publishing a letter denouncing conditions in a local brickyard, and a "Bread and Water Beecher Banquet," a reference to Rev. Henry Ward Beecher's alleged assertion that "a man who cannot live on bread and water is not fit to live."[40]

As the labor movement grew in scope and significance, the number of meetings, debates, dances, dinners, recitals, and dramatic presentations grew correspondingly. Wider circles of people looked to these events for amusement and fellowship. But socialists recognized that work was still the central fact of working-class life. Organization around the issues growing directly out of work—that is, trade-union activity—would have to be central to any effort to reach large numbers of workers with their message.

Socialists were ambivalent toward the existing trade unions. On the one hand, a writer in the *Socialist* agreed that "Trade Unionists comprise the intelligent element of the laboring classes." A columnist in the Detroit *Times* (another of the successors of the *Socialist* started by Grenell, Labadie, and others) argued even more positively that "the trade union is the school of the mechanic in the sciences of government fitting him for leadership in the army of unskilled labor . . . Out of the trade unions of America the party of the future [i.e., the SLP] is being nursed and fostered, preparatory to the coming conflict between the many poor and the rich few." But despite their value, unions had limited potential. Only "SOCIALISM strikes at the very root of the labor troubles, while trade unions are merely designed to be ameliorative in their character . . . When the truths of Socialism have once permeated our trade union organizations, then—and not till then—will labor be able to enforce its demands." [41]

The socialists' solution to the limitations of trade unions was what they called "Trade Amalgamation . . . the combining of all trades into one gigantic union." In this way isolated crafts would begin to recognize the interdependence of all trades. The spirit of class solidarity would be strengthened as workers developed greater loyalty to each other and participated in common struggles, sympathetic strikes, or united political activity. One big union would be like a single army—first a training ground, then the basis for united action. [42]

The party's first national venture in trade amalgamation was the International Labor Union, an alliance of Marxist socialists and other labor radicals. The International Labor Union was designed to be a mass organization uniting skilled and unskilled workers around a program of immediate demands and an ultimate goal of abolition of the wage system. The organization stressed shorter hours and universal organization. Socialists hoped that workers would come to understand the need for socialism as a result of the International Labor Union's trade union struggles. The central committee included two members from Detroit, and the *Socialist* devoted considerable space to the union's program and organizing appeals. [43]

However, the International Labor Union failed to attract large numbers of workers except in a few eastern textile centers. It was not mentioned in the Detroit labor press after 1878. But the one big union concept did appeal, not only to socialists but also to a wide variety of reform-oriented workers and trade unionists who found their craft unions too weak to stand alone against employers. Where the International Labor Union failed, the Knights of Labor succeeded, ultimately so well that it dwarfed the socialists and caused many Detroit activists to conclude that the SLP was no longer relevant.[44]

Beyond the SLP: The Knights of Labor

The Knights of Labor began in Philadelphia in 1869 as a secret society of local garment cutters who sought a new form of organization to supercede the failing Philadelphia Garment Cutters Association. The idea came from Uriah S. Stephens, a veteran garment cutter and trade unionist. Stephens was convinced that the old-style craft union was obsolete: the isolated craft union was weak and unstable; a wider basis of solidarity was needed. Stephens stressed the "benefits of amalgamation" in a "great brotherhood." Only in this way could "the complete emancipation of the wealth producers from the thraldom and loss of wage slavery . . ." be realized. His arguments were remarkably similar to socialist justifications for the International Labor Union, but the roots of Stephens' beliefs were in evangelical religion and Masonic fraternalism. He had trained to be a Baptist minister, but after his family went broke in the panic of 1837, he was apprenticed to a tailor. His belief in Christian brotherhood led him to the antislavery movement, and he campaigned for both Frémont and Lincoln. Stephens was a Mason, Odd Fellow, and a Knight of Pythias. He was impressed with the stability of fraternal organizations compared with most labor unions, and the capacity of Masonic ritual to command the respect and even awe of its followers. A working-class fraternity, based on the spirit of Christian brotherhood, united by strict secrecy, bound by oath to a secret ritual, could not only perform all of the functions of unions but also educate its members and inculcate the kind of loyalty and comradeship which was necessary for solidarity.[45]

It is possible that some Detroit socialists were already aware of the existence of the Knights of Labor when Charles Litchman, grand scribe of the Knights of St. Crispin (shoemakers) and grand secretary of the Knights of Labor, came to Detroit in October or November 1878 to campaign for the Greenback-Labor ticket and organize the local Crispins into the Knights of Labor. Grenell was impressed with Litchman's speech on "Labor and Finance." It sounded "socialistic" and Litchman advocated a system of universal cooperation to do away with the wage system. Grenell argued that Litchman had failed to show how Greenbacks would produce cooperation, but he took Litchman's plea for cooperation as a de facto endorsement of socialism. The speech was very successful and would help the SLP's recruiting.[46]

Labadie was invited to meet Litchman at the house of Otis C. Hodgson, a shoemaker. He must have been impressed. Here was the labor army the socialists were seeking: a secret brotherhood based on the slogans "An injury to one is the concern of all" and "Abolition of the wage system." Hodgson, Litchman, Labadie, and another shoemaker named Miller organized Knights of Labor Assembly 901 with Labadie as master workman and organizer.[47]

By December 1878, Local Assembly 901 was meeting regularly. Meeting rooms were rented and meeting dates announced under the name Washington Literary Society. The name Knights of Labor was not written or spoken. When Labadie and Grenell started another labor paper in January 1880 to replace the *Socialist*, they carried the policy of secrecy into the newspaper's title—in its masthead appeared only ***. Secrecy provided some measure of safety from the very real danger of dismissal. Hodgson, for example, was fired for union activities in 1880 when he was nominated on the Greenback-Labor ticket for county clerk. Secrecy also allowed the organizers and activists of the local movement to move at a measured pace. Premature action would be dangerous. An army must be recruited, trained, disciplined.[48]

The Knights' program and ritual impressed other socialists and activists as well. The shoemaker named Miller who had helped to found the local assembly was probably the same Charles Miller who was a member of the central committee of the International Labor Union. Within weeks, more than a dozen prominent socialists were initiated, particularly those from the American branch. The religious and quasi-masonic character of the ritual was not so distant from the spirit of many socialists. Labadie had insisted in a letter to the *Socialist* only a month before that the basis of communism was simply the desire to "help one another . . . it is that soul and mind destroying selfishness that keeps us from that ideal system." The image of Christ as one of the first agitators was common in socialist and other labor literature. "Not a Section or a trade union," wrote the editor of the Detroit *Labor Review*, "but has among the members true followers of the meek and lowly

Galileean who went about doing good. They read his word reverently; they follow his teachings conscientiously."[49]

The Knights appealed to the same spirit of noble self-sacrifice. Universal organization was an ultimate goal, but until the influx of members in the mid-eighties, the Detroit Knights functioned somewhat like an elite, the leadership of labor's army who would educate the masses through agitation and example. They approached their task in a systematic manner; they would build the Knights as a cadre of "the most reliable material" out of the general labor movement. At the same time, they organized mass organizations to serve as a recruiting ground for the Knights and a preliminary level of organization for the masses of workers. One pioneer knight related how they organized the Detroit Trades Council for those reasons: "Some scheme had to be devised by which . . . recruits to the K of L . . . could be . . . got . . . a central body, composed of delegates from the several trade unions, should be formed. It was thought in this way the members of the K of L would come in contact with representative trade unionists and use the trades council as a feeder to the K of L by picking out the most desirable ones for membership in the order."[50]

The influence of the socialists in the early activities of the Knights in Detroit was decisive. Of the thirty-eight men known to have been initiated into the Washington Literary Society in its first few months, seventeen are identified as SLP members in the socialist press or other sources. Included in the list of party members in addition to Master Workman Labadie were Grenell and all three of the party's 1877 electoral candidates: Simpson, Dolan, and Erb. The composition of both organizations was very similar. The SLP's members were "principally cigarmakers, shoemakers, molders, and musicians—no lawyers or ministers." The thirty-eight Knights included eleven cigarmakers and nine shoemakers. All but one was a skilled worker.[51]

The relationship between members of the two organizations is clearly evident in the portions of the minute books of the Washington Literary Society which have been preserved. The Knights had decided to read and discuss an educational paper at each meeting. At the January 6, 1879, meeting Master Workman Labadie, a prominent SLP member and member of the SLP national executive board the following year, appointed Charles Bell, another prominent party member, to deliver the next paper. Two weeks later, when Charles Erb, 1877 SLP electoral candidate, was appointed to give the next paper, Adam Stirmer, secretary of the cigarmakers' union and a frequent reporter of socialist activities in the *Socialist*, nominated A. Poder, secretary of the Bohemian branch of the SLP for membership; A. Reinke, secretary of the German branch, was also nominated by Stuermer (same fellow—spelling was haphazard in the minutes). Erb's paper at the next meeting was titled with the slogan that had introduced Judson Grenell to socialism, "He who will not work shall not eat." The next paper reader was Brother Corville, secretary of the socialists' Eighth Ward Club.[52]

The relationship between the Knights and the SLP, nationally as well as locally, became even clearer in 1880, when the national executive board of the SLP was moved to Detroit. The members of the SLP national executive board formed interlocking directorates with both Local Assembly 901 and the general (i.e., national) executive board of the Knights of Labor. Philip Van Patten of LA 901 was national secretary of both the SLP and the Knights general executive board. E. A. Stevens of LA 901 was an SLP organizer who traveled extensively around the country for the party and a member of the Knights of Labor general executive board. Labadie was a member of the SLP national executive board, master workman of 901, and president of the Detroit Trades Council. Grenell, also a member of the SLP national executive board, was an officer both in LA 901 and the Trades Council. Finally, on the national level, Terence Powderly, grand master workman of the Knights of Labor, was a party member.[53]

Not all the Detroit Knights of Labor were socialists. A few were philosophically conservative, but nearly all the Knights' future Detroit leaders were closely associated with leading socialists in Local Assembly 901 for several years. When Lyman Brant or Hugh McClelland later became candidates of Detroit's Independent Labor party, they had not been converted to socialism, but they had spent four years addressing men like Labadie and Grenell, Dolan, Simpson, and Erb as "Brother Knight." They had been intimately exposed to socialist arguments and had adopted concepts like the labor theory of value or the producer cooperative even if they had not accepted socialist theory as a whole.[54]

The SLP thus exercised an influence within the Knights of Labor, both locally and nationally, far out of proportion to its numbers. This was not the result of any conspiracy to take over the organization, as Powderly charged later after he had repudiated radicalism. The Knights and the SLP drew on the same constituency. Activists were attracted to both organizations because both addressed themselves to the fundamental issues that had moved them to action. Nonsocialist labor reformers bore no particular malice toward socialists in the early 1880s. They respected socialists as honest, courageous, and sincere labor reformers whose major error was a bit too much idealism. As one Detroit advocate of cooperation explained, "the ulterior objectives" of the SLP would be "a work of time." He supported the party's platform but the "efforts of the party should be directed to some more practical object than seems at present to be aimed at." Socialists saw the Knights of Labor as the embodiment of their vision of labor solidarity. Many, particularly among the American branch, had come to socialism through a humanitarianism much like that of the founders of the Knights. Their orientation was moral and practical, not ideological.[55]

Indeed, as the Knights prospered, many of the key socialist agitators in Detroit began to wonder whether the Knights more closely reflected their socialist vision than the SLP did. By 1881, just as Knights of Labor was multiplying in Michigan (K. of L. membership in Michigan increased from seventy-three in 1881 to 1,023 in 1882), many party members were questioning the future of the SLP. A correspondent to the Detroit *Labor Review* feared that socialism was dead in America. The *Labor Review* admitted that the "party may have spent its force" and that it was "an insignificant minority as yet."[56] The problem, according to *Labor Review* correspondents critical of the party, was that it had become impractical, so absorbed in internal debates over political economy and strategy that it ignored the masses of workers who faced immediate problems and sought effective solutions. "The Socialist Labor Party must become practical in its methods," the *Labor Review* said. "It needs *body* and *strength* as well as purity . . . Principles cannot be spread effectively unless the members quit dreaming and disputing among themselves, and go actively to work in making converts . . . We are in danger of becoming a mutual admiration society. Let us pay some attention to the outside majority."

The blame, according to critics, lay with the Germans, who treated politics more as a matter of theology than a process of practical change. A letter from a rural Michigan woman to the party's executive board symbolized how the overwhelmingly German character of the party separated it from "the outside majority." The woman wanted to learn about socialism: "There is a profound ignorance in this section of the subject . . . I do not understand any language but the English and have looked almost in vain for help . . . a seeker after truth." It is certainly ironic testimony to the party's image that such a seeker felt the need to apologize for speaking English in an English-speaking country.[57] "The movement was too purely German," wrote a Cincinnati correspondent. "It must be Americanized."

One way to do this, according to the editor of the *Labor Review* (Labadie or Grenell), was to address the immediate demands of Detroit workers: "Let us be practical. Let present conditions engage our attention. The 'Ameliorative Measures' some of our comrades denounce are directly in the line of progress from barbarism to socialism. It is natural that these subjects should engage the attention of workingmen, they are wrongs easily discernable and their solution is not difficult. State Prison Convict Contract Labor has no such bad effect on the labor market as many imagine; but that it does effect wages to the detriment of free labor is undeniable. Eight hours is no panacea for all our ills; but it will be an excellent thing to obtain. The same may be said of the inspection of workshops, food and dwelling—all will do good."[58] But whenever these issues were raised, German stalwarts denounced them as reformist palliatives and accused their advocates of weakness and desertion of principle. Labadie and Grenell had already encountered this attitude when some of the pamphlets published by their Socialist Tract Society were criticized for ideological wavering. The issue surfaced again in 1880 when the party's American branch enthusiastically supported the Greenback ticket of Weaver and Chambers. The supporters of the alliance saw it as a means of winning over potential sympathizers, but local "kickers," as the critics were called, denounced socialists who worked in the Greenback campaign.[59]

Advocates for endorsing Weaver pointed out that working-class Greenbackers supported labor organization and denounced monopoly in language almost identical with the socialist platform. These working-class Greenbackers would eventually come in conflict with middle-class leaders in the Greenback party. As Van Patten, one of the instigators of the alliance, explained to Powderly, "The Greenback Party is rapidly approaching its own crisis when the middle class conservatives will object to the ascendancy of the Labor Movement in general." Until then, they must support the Greenbackers.[60] Van Patten campaigned for the Weaver ticket in Detroit; Labadie and Grenell expanded the *Labor Review* from a monthly to a weekly during the campaign. When a rally of 1,000 Weaver supporters was broken up by police and the speakers arrested, Van Patten led a protest meeting of 1,500 on the same spot and dared city authorities to arrest him as well. Henry Poole and John Goldring, SLP members, were placed on the local Greenback slate. Supporters of the alliance were convinced that these crowds demonstrated mass support for the Greenback ticket and confirmed the wisdom of Greenback-Socialist cooperation.[61]

Yet the kickers went so far in their opposition to the alliance that Van Patten feared a split in the SLP and threatened to resign as national secretary of the party, if it came to that. The Germans opposed the alliance, Van Patten told Powderly, but "the English speaking Socialists are enthusiastic to support Weaver and Chambers. . . . I fear we will have a split—and I shall feel strongly inclined to resign. Certainly I cannot as a consistent Socialist oppose the Greenback Party when their Platform enunciates the foundation principles of Social Democracy— 'That it is the duty of government to guarantee to the man of labor the full result of his toil.'" Who exactly was kicking and why they objected is not completely clear; we have no surviving local sources from the German point of view. Van Patten wrote Powderly that the kickers were Germans who "were afraid that the Greenback Party is managed by men who care more for political success than for the Labor Movement." Probably German stalwarts viewed the whole Greenback movement as just another example of American craziness. Van Patten also reported that the Germans were suspicious of the Knights. Emotions clearly ran high on both sides.[62]

In September 1880, the Detroit kickers started a rival labor paper, the *Bulletin*, in competition with the *Labor Review* because of the *Review*'s support for Greenbackism. The *Labor Review* bitterly denounced the kickers: "There is a class in the Social Labor Party so pure (?) immaculate (?) and perfect (?) that if a person deviates in the least particular from the path they have laid out as the only true, correct, and regular one . . . he is at once denounced as a traitor and one who has 'sold out.'"[63]

The experiences of the 1880 campaign reinforced earlier tensions between German- and English-speaking labor radicals. To the Germans the poor showing of the Greenback ticket—only 597 votes countywide and only 249 in the city of Detroit, far fewer than the socialists had polled by themselves in 1877 and 1878—vindicated their suspicions of alliances with middle-class reformers. To the English-speaking radicals, German conduct during the campaign showed that the Germans were more concerned with doctrinal purity than results. Labadie, Grenell, and the other socialists who went into the Knights of Labor were far removed from the talmudic spirit they found in SLP ideologues. Grenell felt such "stiff-backed socialists . . . have closed their eyes to all the experiences of the world. Only step by step has the human race made advances." While the "stiff backs" argued that reform would diminish class consciousness, Grenell believed that just the opposite was the case: "The ignorant and down-trodden are far less liable to demand their rights than the intelligent and more prosperous. Every law and custom that will tend to a more equitable division of the joint products of labor and capital will help to create a desire for still greater justice, until finally . . . profits can be entirely eliminated."[64]

Gradually the Knights of Labor socialists, like Labadie and Grenell, began to reduce their participation in party activities. They continued socialist agitation, but within the Knights. The party lost its most energetic and capable organizers. In 1883, the party's national leaders repeatedly addressed inquiries to the Detroit section, but apparently received no replies. The national executive board wanted to know what was wrong: "Not having received any official communication yet from Section Detroit . . . asking the comrades in Detroit why they remain in a constant silence, though Detroit has hitherto been considered one of our best standing sections . . . We therefore hope that the Detroit comrades will not stand back in the struggle for our cause."[65] They were not standing back, but the men who had made Detroit one of the party's most active sections were now devoting their energies to the Knights of Labor. The party may be dead, the *Labor Review* speculated, "but *socialism* is a living idea, and can never die!"[66]

The SLP survived, maintaining some influence in the German neighborhoods, but it never regained the dynamism or following it had had in the late 1870s. In 1887, the party reportedly had eighty to 100 members. By 1883, in contrast, Detroit had sixteen functioning Knights of Labor assemblies with 797 members, and in July 1886, Knights of Labor Detroit District Assembly reported 4,679 members. The Knights of Labor had produced the labor army the socialists had hoped for, but in the process the SLP was reduced to a peripheral role. The Knights of Labor assemblies, growing in both size and number, took over most of the educational and cultural activities the SLP had directed in earlier days. But although the SLP suffered, the socialist ideal of class solidarity did not. Labadie, Grenell, and the other SLP activists who left the party helped to transmit its beliefs to a far wider audience. For a time the Knights of Labor looked as though it might make socialist dreams become reality.[67]

NOTES

1. Detroit's first union, Typographical Union No. 18, was organized as a local body in 1848 and joined the International in 1852. By the mid-1860s, there were more than a dozen trade unions and a Trades Assembly with a reported membership of 5,000, which intervened successfully in local politics. The movement declined rapidly in the late 1860s and the Trades Assembly disbanded around 1870. Supporters were unable to reorganize it and several attempts to replace it with similar city labor federations also failed. See *SBLS*, 1884, p. 74, *Labor Day Gazette*, 1891, LC; Thomas M. Dolan to David Boyd, July 9, 1900, LC; Detroit Labor Leaders File, "Looking Backward," by John Drew, LC; *Labor Day Review*, 1892, LC.

2. Detroit Trades Council File, LC; Joseph Labadie to T. V. Powderly, December 7, 1879, Terence V. Powderly Papers, Catholic University, Washington, D.C.; hereafter cited as TVP.

3. James B. McFeely to Terence V. Powderly, November (?) (illegible), 1876, TVP.

4. *The Socialist* (Chicago), December 7, 1878, January 11, 1879.

5. The effects of the 1870s depression on national union membership are discussed in Foster Rhea Dulles, *Labor in America* (New York, 1968), p. 112, and Philip S. Foner, *History of the Labor Movement in the United States* (New York, 1947), 1: 439–40.

6. *Michigan Federation of Labor 1915 Yearbook*; *Labor Day Review*, 1892, LC; Detroit Trades Council File, LC.

7. *The Socialist*, December 8, 1877, January 5, 12, 19, December 7, 1878, January 11, 1879; "Constitution of the Detroit Labor League," LC; Detroit *Evening News*, September 5, 1887.

8. Detroit Trades Council File, LC; Knights of Labor-Michigan File, LC.

9. *Labor Review*, October 23, 1880.

10. Detroit Labor Leaders File.

11. Joseph Labadie to T.V. Powderly, December 7, 1879, TVP.

12. *Michigan Federation of Labor Yearbook*, 1896, pp. 16–17; "The Labor Champions," newspaper clipping, c. 1886, *Ross Scrapbooks*, vol. 1, pp. 17–20, Burton Historical Collections, Detroit Public Library; undated clipping c. 1889 in AFL-History File, LC; clipping from Detroit *Evening News*, September 6, 1891, in Detroit Trades Council File, LC; clipping from Detroit *Post and Tribune*, October 17, 1880, in Detroit Trades Council File, LC; Sidney Fine, "The Ely-Labadie Letters," *Michigan History*, 36, no. 1, pp. 1–32. For a discussion of a similar figure, Joseph P. McDonnell, see Herbert Gutman, "Class, Status, and the Gilded Age Radical: A Reconsideration," in *Work, Culture, and Society in Industrializing America* (New York, 1977), pp. 260–92.

13. Conflict between the Knights of Labor and the AFL was the central theme of the Wisconsin School of labor historians (followers of John R. Commons), notably Selig Perlman, author of the section in Commons' *History of Labor in the United States* (New York, 1918) on the Knights and the origins of the AFL. Works by such historians as Gerald Grob (*Workers and Utopia*, Chicago, 1969) and Philip Taft closely follow the Commons-Perlman perspective. Norman Ware (*The Labor Movement in the United States*, New York, 1929) does not accept Perlman's prejudice in favor of the AFL but also structures his discussion of the period around the conflict between the Knights and the trade unions. Ware generally concurs in the negative assessment of the Socialists, placing central blame for Knights of Labor policies he feels were incorrect on a group of Socialists in the Home Club centered in New York. Philip Foner (*History of the Labor Movement in the United States*, vols. 1 and 2, New York, 1947, 1955) gives a much fuller and more sympathetic description of the socialists, but despite criticisms of Gompers and craft conservatism, generally accepts the most important part of the Commons-Perlman thesis, e.g., that trade unionism was more progressive than the Knights of Labor.

14. Labadie to Judson Grenell, undated c. 1920s, LC; *Michigan Federation of Labor Yearbook*, 1896, pp. 16–17; "The Labor Champions," Burton Historical Collections.

15. Detroit *Evening News*, September 5, 1887.

16. Ibid.; Detroit Labor Leaders File, LC.

17. Judson Grenell, "Autobiography," unpublished manuscript (Clearwater, Florida, 1930), Michigan State University Archives and Historical Collections, pp. 30–31. "Rubbing Elbows with People Worthwhile—XXVI— Charles Erb," by Grenell, undated clipping, c. 1905, in Detroit Labor Leaders File, LC; Detroit *Evening News*, September 5, 1887.

18. Grenell, "Autobiography," pp. 23, 28–29, 31.

19. Grenell, "Rubbing Elbows with People Worthwhile."

20. Grenell, "Autobiography," p. 30.

21. Grenell, "Autobiography," p. 32; *The Socialist*, June 14, 1879.

22. *The Socialist*, June 14, 1879; Socialist Labor Party of America Records (microfilm edition), State Historical Society of Wisconsin, 1970: outgoing correspondence, September 19, 1883, and October 10, 1883; flyer c. 1880 advertising Socialist Tract Society; *The Trades*, April 10, 1880.

23. Grenell, "Autobiography," pp. 1, 32.

24. *The Socialist*, June 14, 1879; Socialist Labor Party of America Records (microfilm edition), State Historical Society of Wisconsin, 1970: outgoing correspondence, September 19, 1883, and October 10, 1883; flyer c. 1880 advertising Socialist Tract Society; *The Trades*, April 10, 1880.

25. Grenell, "Autobiography," p. 32; *The Socialist*, April 20, 1878.

26. Grenell, "Autobiography," p. 32; *The Socialist*, September 28, 1878, December 8, 1877.

27. Detroit *Free Press*, September 28, 1877. Erb was born in Detroit of foreign parents. The newspaper described him as Dutch, but this was probably slang for German.

28. *SBLS*, 1884, p. 143. Stephen Thernstrom estimates that 25 percent of Boston's workers could not vote in this period because they had not been in the city long enough to meet residency requirements. "Socialism and Social Mobility" in Laslett and Lipset, *Failure of a Dream?* (Garden City, N. Y., 1974), p. 516.

29. Grenell, "Autobiography," p. 33.

30. Detroit *Free Press*, November 7, 8, 1877; Grenell, "Autobiography," p. 33; Labadie to T. V. Powderly, December 7, 1879, TVP.

31. *Bulletin of the Social Labor Movement*, vol. 1, no. 14, December and January, 1881.

32. Detroit *Free Press*, May 23, 1878.

33. *The Socialist*, May 11, 1879, June 8, 1878; *Labor Review*, August, September, 1881.

34. *The Socialist*, February 16, 1878.

35. *The Socialist*, February 9, 1878.

36. *The Socialist*, December 8, 1877, January 12, February 16, March 23, 1878. The only reference to female SLP members in Detroit is a report of a Christmas Ball in the January 12, 1878, issue of the *Socialist*. The tone suggests that this women's section was an unofficial women's auxiliary of "wives, sisters, and sweethearts."

37. *The Socialist*, September 28, 1878, May 3, June 14, 1879.

38. *The Trades*, July 12, 1879; *The Socialist*, July 12, 1879.

39. *Three Stars*, January, February 1880.

40. *Labor Review*, March 1880; David Montgomery, *Beyond Equality* (New York, 1972), p. 230.

41. *The Socialist*, March 16, 1878; Detroit *Times*, April 10, 1881; *The Socialist*, January 12, 1878.

42. *The Socialist*, January 12, 19, 1878; Detroit *Times*, May 8, 1881.

43. Foner, 1:500–502; *The National Socialist*, June 15, 1878; *The Socialist*, February 16, 1878, January 19, 1878.

44. Foner, 1:503–4.

45. Ware, pp. 22–23, 26–9, 74; Foner, 1:435–37.

46. *The Socialist*, October 19, 1878; Knights of Labor-Michigan File, LC, especially 1926 typewritten account of Joseph Labadie. There is some confusion about when Litchman came to Detroit and the details of his visit. Grenell described the October 1878 speech but said nothing about the Knights of Labor. This is not surprising since the Knights were secret, and Grenell may not yet have been initiated. Labadie's 1926 account (he was seventy-six) puts the meeting with the Crispins in November 1879, a lapse of memory clearly contradicted by other evidence. An account published in 1887 puts Litchman's

meeting and the founding of the K. of L. LA 901 in November 1878. Anne Inglis, curator of the Labadie Collection in the 1920s, believed that Litchman came to Detroit several times and that Labadie had combined the visits in his memory.

47. Knights of Labor-Michigan File, LC.

48. Minutes of the Washington Literary Society, LC; ***, LC; *Labor Review*, October 2, 9, 1880.

49. *The National Socialist*, June 15, 1878; Minutes of the Washington Literary Society, LC; *The Socialist*, October 19, 1878; *Labor Review*, March 1882. Grenell's Baptist heritage should be recalled. He came to Detroit to work on the *Michigan Christian Herald*, which his minister brother had helped organize, and was employed there from 1876 to 1879. See also Herbert Gutman, "Protestantism and the American Labor Movement: The Christian Spirit in the Gilded Age," in *Work, Culture and Society in Industrializing America*, pp. 79–117.

50. Reminiscence of George W. Duncan, Knights of Labor-Michigan File, LC. Labadie argued that Duncan exaggerated the feeder role of the Trades Council. It had other functions as well.

51. *The Socialist*, May 18, 1878; Detroit Labor Leaders File.

52. Minutes of the Washington Literary Society, LC.

53. *Proceedings of the Knights of Labor General Assembly*, 1879; Detroit Labor Leaders File, LC; Detroit Trades Council File, LC; Minutes of the Washington Literary Society, LC. Powderly was given an SLP red card by Van Patten at the 1880 Weaver convention at which a formal alliance between the SLP and the Greenbackers was arranged. By 1887, Powderly had repudiated socialism and labor radicalism. After Haymarket, he redbaited radicals within the Knights, hoping thereby to maintain the Knights' image of respectability. Labadie and other radicals recalled Powderly's earlier socialist membership. Powderly claimed that he had accepted the card simply as a gift out of personal courtesy to Van Patten, and he had never really been a socialist. Ware and others have accepted Powderly's story, but he was clearly lying. A number of Detroit SLP members testified to Powderly's active participation between 1880 and 1882. The evidence is clear: Van Patten to Powderly, August 13, 1880: "From your letter I judge that you wish to remain a member of the SLP." Detroit *Evening News*, September 16, 1887: Henry Kummerfeldt, who was treasurer of the SLP national executive when it was in Detroit, ridiculed Powderly's story. He personally remembered opening Powderly's letters with one dollar dues. Powderly was a member from 1880 to 1882. Herzig, Labadie, Grenell, and P. C. Christiansen, all SLP officers at the time, corroborated Kummerfeldt's account. The exact nature of Powderly's socialism is unclear, but his participation is not. The kind of utopian socialism accepted by many labor leaders would be quite consistent with Powderly's reform agitation.

54. Lyman Brant was the president of Detroit Typographical Union 18, a leader in the International Typographical Union, and one of the founders of the 1881 Federation of Trades that became the AFL. He was elected to the Michigan legislature in 1882 and 1884. McClelland was a cigarmaker and was also elected to the state legislature in 1884. Both joined LA 901 in January 1879.

55. *Labor Review*, August 1881.

56. Ibid., August, November 1881; Jonathan Garlock and N. C. Bilder, "Knights of Labor Data Bank," Inter-University Consortium for Political Research, Ann Arbor, hereafter cited *KLDB*.

57. *Labor Review*, November 1881; Socialist Labor Party of America Records, letter from Adelia Marger, December 5, 1880. A number of contemporary and modern scholars have emphasized the Germanness of the SLP as a major source of weakness, among them Friedrich Sorge, *Labor Movement in the United States*, ed. Philip S. Foner (Westport, Ct., 1977). Sorge notes that after 1878 the anti-Socialist laws in Germany produced an influx of German socialists who were more interested in Germany and factional disputes within the German SPD than in events in the U.S. One indicator of German dominance in the SLP is that the SLP, although habitually short of funds itself, collected funds in the U.S. for the SPD. Sorge's argument is confirmed for Detroit by a note in the *Bulletin of the Social Labor Movement*, December-January 1881: "Comrades Koennecke and Keitel, two exiles from Germany, are with us, and addressed mass meetings which were largely attended."

58. *Labor Review*, August 1881, March 1882.

59. Grenell, "Autobiography," p. 32.

60. Philip Van Patten to T. V. Powderly, July 15, 1880, TVP.

61. *Labor Review*, October 2, 9, 1880.

62. Van Patten to Powderly, July 15, 1880, TVP.

63. *Labor Review*, September 3, 11, 1880. I have, unfortunately, only been able to locate one issue of the *Bulletin*, published after the Weaver campaign, which casts little light on the identity of the kickers.

64. Detroit *Post and Tribune*, November 4, 1880; Judson Grenell, *Economic Tangles*, pp. 132–35, LC.

65. Emil Kreis to Section Detroit, June ?, 1883 (illegible), also, July 27, October 10, December 5, 1883; SLP Records, State Historical Society of Wisconsin.

66. *Labor Review*, August 1881.

67. Detroit *Evening News*, September 5, 1887; *KLDB*; *Proceedings of the Knights of Labor General Assembly*, 1886, pp. 326–28. The SLP was further weakened by defection of members to the anarchist IWPA. It is not clear exactly when this began in Detroit, but Detroit had two IWPA sections in 1885. This split is described in Henry David, *The History of the Haymarket Affair* (New York, 1958). It probably postdated the withdrawal of Labadie,

Grenell, et al, which does not seem to be directly related to the IWPA defection. Labadie described himself as an anarchist by the mid-1880s, but his anarchism was philosophical, based on arguments gleaned from Benjamin Tucker's *Liberty*. Labadie carefully disassociated himself from "Most, Schwab, '*The Alarm*,' and that class of people" in a letter to Prof. Ely in 1885 (Sidney Fine, "The Ely-Labadie Letters," *Michigan History*, 36 [March 1952]: 1–32).

Detroit Stove Works, 1880: with 625 employees in 1880 and more than 1000 by the end of the decade, one of the largest of the many factories lining the Detroit waterfront. [Archives of Labor and Urban Affairs, Wayne State University, Detroit, Michigan]

Shipcarpenters at work at the Detroit Dry Dock Company in suburban Springwell, ca. 1890. The strike here in the spring of 1886 helped stimulate the eight-hour-day movement. [Burton Historical Collection, Detroit Public Library]

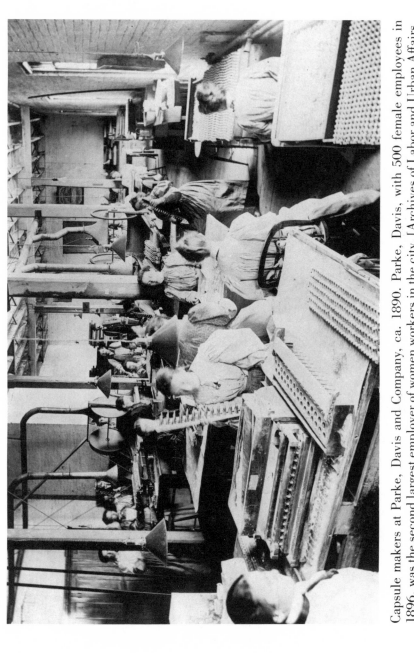

Capsule makers at Parke, Davis and Company, ca. 1890. Parke, Davis, with 500 female employees in 1896, was the second largest employer of women workers in the city. [Archives of Labor and Urban Affairs, Wayne State University, Detroit, Michigan]

Judson Grenell, ca. 1885. [Labadie Collection, Department of Rare Books and Special Collections, University of Michigan Library]

Joseph Labadie, ca. 1885. [Labadie Collection, Department of Rare Books and Special Collections, University of Michigan Library]

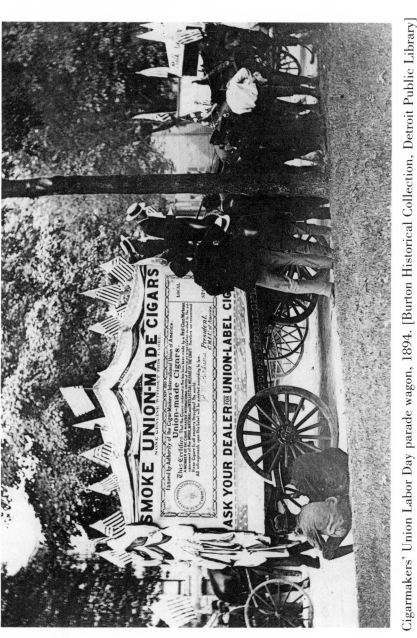

Cigarmakers' Union Labor Day parade wagon, 1894. [Burton Historical Collection, Detroit Public Library]

Knights of Labor parade ribbon. Local Assembly 619, organized by employees of the Michigan Stove Company in 1888, claimed several hundred members by the following year. [Original in author's possession]

4

THE GROWTH OF WORKING-CLASS INSTITUTIONS IN DETROIT, 1880–86

The SLP's political campaigns and social events, the party's recruitment of English-speaking people, the founding of Knights of Labor Assembly 901, and the organization of the Trades Council were the first stages in the creation of the infrastructure of a revitalized labor movement based on values of solidarity and opposition to the existing industrial system. The scope, complexity, and range of workers' organizations increased throughout the early 1880s, so that by 1885 there was a network of interrelated institutions which recruited workers on a class basis and provided for a wide enough variety of workers' needs that activists and supporters could function much like participants in a counterculture—working, agitating, learning, socializing, shopping, and relaxing within a cultural milieu that was consistent with their convictions. This pattern of broad concurrent participation in a variety of organizations whose functions went far beyond collective bargaining is the best evidence for the existence of what I have called the subculture of opposition. While the number of active participants was never more than a fraction of the city's wage workers, that proportion grew steadily in the early 1880s, and the increasing numbers of participants exercised wider and wider influence beyond their own ranks, thus laying the basis for an explosive expansion of the movement in 1886.

Unions

The unions formed the initial base from which this network of subsidiary organizations was launched. The Independent Labor party, the workingmen's militia, the labor press, the cooperatives depended upon union support for their survival. As union membership expanded and the unions were increasingly influenced by the growing spirit of reform, they were willing and able to provide such support. At the same time union participation in a broader range of activities accelerated the process of internal change within the unions. Unions became more ready to assist each other, more aggressive in organizing their own trades, more interested in organizing other crafts, and more willing to expend time and energy on member education.

The Detroit Trades Council, for example, started small in March 1880, amidst some of the same bickering which had destroyed the Labor League,[1] but when ironmolders at the Detroit Stove Works struck in May, the Trades Council endorsed the strike and was able to raise $88.70 in strike support from the other unions within the first week of the strike. Even unions like the typographical union, which had refused to endorse the Labor League constitution a year and a half earlier because of opposition to the principle of strike support for other unions, voted money for the ironmolders. A benefit picnic held by the Trades Council at the beginning of July raised more money, and a few days later, the ironmolders returned to work victorious with a 5 percent wage increase.[2] The Trades Council's ability to mobilize support for the ironmolders contrasted sharply with the failure of the Labor League. Membership in the ironmolders' union tripled from fifty to 150 as a result of the success and reached 250 by October.[3]

Other unions reported similar increases in 1880: the cigarmakers from fifteen in February to 250 in October; the painters from eighty-five in April to 150 in October; the cabinetmakers, organized in February, 170 in October. The Trades Council had thirteen affiliated unions (out of sixteen in the city) in October—up from six in April—and by January 1881, Philip Van Patten and Thomas Dolan of the SLP had organized seven more new unions and the Trades Council had twenty-four member unions. By April 1881, Francis Egan of the printers, new president of the Trades Council, reported thirty-one member unions and claimed a membership of 4,000.[4]

Local socialists were the most energetic advocates of the Trades Council and helped to organize many of the constituent unions. Officers rotated frequently, but about half of the officers elected during the council's first year were SLP members. E. W. Simpson became the first recording secretary, Labadie served as both corresponding secretary and president, Philip Van Patten was also elected corresponding secretary, and Adam Stuermer was treasurer. The organization was not, however, simply a party front. The first president, Francis Egan, was a Republican. The council expressed its independence of the SLP when it denied the party's request to march in the council's public demonstration in October 1880, although it encouraged individual party members to march with their unions. The council thus sought to be a broad-based representative of all the city's organized workers.[5]

In October 1880, the Trades Council staged a public demonstration as a show of its strength. The parade drew 1,500 participants.[6] The Detroit *Post and Tribune* found the display of union power disconcerting. "To the outsider there is something mysterious in the movement."[7] Perhaps as a gesture of defiance, leading the parade as grand marshall was William Kydd, who had been fired from Fales Brothers, paper dealers, for union activities three weeks before.[8] Each of the Trades Council's member unions joined the parade along with four marching bands, a contingent of Detroit Stove Works laborers expressing gratitude for the council's support in their recent strike, and another contingent of unorganized laborers and tradesmen. Banners and transparencies carried by various unions indicated the range of social reforms the unions sought. The Knights of Crispin (shoemakers) declared "Children Belong in Schools Not in the Factories" and suggested an anticapitalist perspective with the slogan "Stop the Robbery. Labor Must Have All Its Products!" The machinery molders urged "Bread and Water for Idle Speculation, Not for Mechanics," a reference to Henry Ward Beecher's sermon. The ironmolders expressed opposition to contract labor by prisoners with a banner reading "Free Labor, No Convict Labor." Several unions argued that higher wages would benefit society in general, not just the workers receiving the higher pay. The machinery molders, for example, linked general prosperity with workers' wages: "Prosperity Means Fair Wages." The ironmolders thought that improvements in the workers' conditions were the measure of progress: "Human Progress Requires the Elevation of Labor." The painters argued the converse, that "Low Wages Mean Degradation and Crime." The typographical union indicated its acceptance of the doctrine of solidarity: "The Trades Council is the Workingman's Legislature," "Mutual Aid," "Amalgamate." The cigarmakers defended the eight-hour day: "8 Hours A Day Means an Increase in Pay."[9]

The typographical union's description of the Trades Council as a workers' legislature suggests the scope of the council's activities. The council was supported by dues from its constituent unions based on their membership, one cent per member per month. Each union was allowed to send six delegates to the biweekly meetings,[10] which typically included each local's report of its activities and the state of its trade, practical questions of immediate concern to the council as a whole, and theoretical discussions or educational presentations. In 1880, in addition to writing and ratifying its constitution, expanding its organizing efforts, aiding the ironmolders, and staging the fall demonstration, the council passed a resolution supporting California Workingmen's party leader Denis Kearney, made plans to welcome Charles Litchman on his next speaking tour, discussed the importation of Canadian workers by local employers, and heard lectures on cooperation (i.e., formation of producers' cooperatives).[11] Particularly striking was the continuing emphasis on educational lectures; meetings were not simply bureaucratic affairs. In December 1884, the *Labor Leaf* listed recent discussion questions including the "Malthusian Theory of population, tariff, hours of labor, employment of children in workshops, and prison management."[12]

The character of the Trades Council reflected the temperaments of the individual delegates. With six delegates per union, council meetings were large affairs including a cross section of the labor movement and almost all ideological viewpoints, but the more militant and committed activists were disproportionately represented. In most unions, competition for election as council delegate was less intense than for other important union offices. Many delegates were volunteers enthusiastic about the ideas of trade amalgamation and solidarity.

Individual union attitudes toward the concept of trade amalgamation or the Trades Council programs varied from those of extremely conservative unions which rejected the whole concept of solidarity and refused to affiliate in any way with other unions, to those of revolutionary unions which considered the Trades Council far too cautious and conciliatory. While the overall ideological balance within the labor movement was shifting to the left during the early 1880s, this ideological spectrum continued.

At one extreme, the Brotherhood of Locomotive Engineers rejected not only Trades Council affiliation but almost all alliances with other organizations, practiced exclusionary membership policies, and campaigned in favor of political candidates opposed by the other unions. Membership was limited to white men over twenty-one years of age who could read and write and were "of good moral character" and "temperate habits." Members had to be employed as engineers at the time of application and have at least one year's experience as an engineer.[13] The conservative character of the Detroit BLE was perhaps best illustrated by its conduct during the 1884 elections. Detroit Typographical

Union 18 had undertaken a vigorous campaign against General Alger, the Republican candidate for governor, because Alger, owner of the Detroit *Post and Tribune*, refused to hire union printers and forbade any printer in his employ from joining the union. The Trades Council endorsed the typographers' campaign, and unions all over the state wrote the *Labor Leaf* pledging to help defeat Alger, but the BLE campaigned for Alger. Most trade unionists considered his opponent, Greenback-Democratic incumbent Josiah Begole, the most prolabor governor in the state's history, but Begole had angered the engineers when he failed to seek the brotherhood's endorsement for an appointment to the state's railroad commission.[14]

The Progressive Cigarmakers Union No. 21 was representative of the other end of the ideological spectrum. In order to insure internal democracy, the Progressives rotated leadership duties with a new chairman at every meeting. The only regular officer, secretary Henry Schulte, an active member of the revolutionary anarchist International Working People's Association, helped organize the Central Labor Union in 1886, the forthrightly anticapitalist German city labor federation. Schulte chaired the CLU's first agitation meeting, which discussed "the brutal acts of the capitalistic class against labor organizations."[15] The radical posture of the Progressives did not isolate them from other unions. Schulte had occupied all of the offices from corresponding secretary to president in Cigarmakers Union No. 22 prior to the formation of the Progressives, and was subsequently elected recording secretary, financial secretary, and president of the Trades Council, master workman of Knights of Labor Local Assembly 2348, and recording secretary of Knights of Labor District Assembly 50.[16] Schulte's acceptance by the Trades Council was one indication of the radicalization of the Detroit labor movement. In 1885 the Trades Council seated him as a delegate of the IWPA, a reversal of the earlier policy forbidding representation or independent participation for socialist political organizations. In the same year the Trades Council staged another demonstration and allowed SLP members to march under the party's banner rather than just as union members.[17]

The 1885 march indicated the movement's progress. The demonstration drew an estimated 3,000 marchers, twice the estimate of the 1880 march, although there were widespread rumors (which later proved to be true) that employers had hired spotters to record names of union supporters. The unions, the socialists, and the Knights of Labor had combined forces in an impressive display of unity. Leading the parade were large portraits of Henry George, Tom Barry (the radical leader of the recent Saginaw Valley lumber mill strike and recently elected Knights of Labor general executive board member), Terence Powderly, and Richard Trevellick.[18]

By 1884 and 1885, both the unions and the Knights of Labor were making more serious attempts to counteract the fragmenting effects of ethnic, craft, and skill differences. As early as 1883 the English-language labor press began publishing announcements in German and occasionally in Polish. Editorials repeated a refrain of worker solidarity. Workers would progress together; they must resist employers' offers of opportunities for individual gain which were at the expense of fellow workers. Otherwise, competition among the workers would eventually drive down wages to the detriment of all. The *Labor Leaf* cited the demise of the horsecollar makers' union as a lesson in the effects of competition among workers. Some horsecollar makers had taken extra work home at night while many other horsecollar makers were unemployed. They would regret such temporary gains, the *Labor Leaf* argued. Work should be shared in times of scarcity, and there would be less downward pressure on wages as a result.[19] Some of the most highly paid crafts in the city accepted the logic of the *Labor Leaf*'s argument. The bricklayers' union, for example, took the initiative in organizing other building trades workers—first the carpenters and then the primarily Polish laborers and hod carriers.[20]

Yet despite these efforts, the local labor movement did not grow dramatically between 1881 and 1885. By 1885, the movement was more sophisticated and more radical, performed a wider range of functions, and included more auxiliary and supportive institutions. However, in December of 1885, Judson Grenell estimated union membership in Detroit at 5,000, 1,000 more than in 1881, but still only one-sixth of his estimate of the number of wage workers in the city.[21] Union organizers considered this modest growth disappointing and attributed it to worker apathy, but the causes were more complex. Some workers consciously rejected collective action in favor of the ethic of individual achievement. Others may not have understood union appeals or considered economic concerns less pressing than cultural issues. Ethnic barriers between workers were very real.

But as the rapid influx of members the following year suggests, many more workers had been influenced by the labor movement than those who actually paid union dues. A substantial proportion of the nonunionized workers were neither opposed to unionism nor indifferent to it. While unable or afraid to organize, they sympathized with union doctrines. It is impossible to measure the number of such unorganized supporters precisely, but two types of evidence suggest that prior to 1886 the number was at least as large as the number of union members. First there is the extraordinary growth in membership in 1886. Just nine months after Grenell's estimate of 5,000 members, one of the daily newspapers estimated the combined membership of the unions and the Knights of Labor at 13,000.[22] Unless we assume overnight conversions for some 8,000 people, we must believe that many of them had been sympathetic before but had hesitated to join a labor organization until a period of unprecedented union power.

This interpretation gains credibility when we examine union activities which depended on nonunion support for success, especially boycotts. Few boycotts could have been successful if they had been observed by only the four or five thousand union members present in Detroit before 1886. There are no systematic records of boycotts to measure the success rates, but scattered reports suggest much more substantial declines in sales of boycotted firms than could have been accomplished by union members alone. In 1881, for example, the Trades Council reported a drop of one-third in the circulation of the Sunday edition of the Detroit *Free Press* as a result of a boycott called by the typographical union. Thus, union membership was not the only indication of union support. The effects of boycotts, successful political activities, strikes by nonunionized workers, and the growth of a wider range of working-class social, cultural, and educational institutions all indicate that between 1881 and 1886 sympathy with the movement's objectives and at least a low level of class consciousness were increasing more rapidly than union membership.

Perhaps slow growth in formal membership resulted from the movement's inability to protect its members from harassment. The labor press regularly reported firings of union activists, and beginning about 1881 employer antiunionism started to become more systematic and organized. In 1881, for example, vessel owners organized (unsuccessfully) to destroy the seamen's union. The owners' association taxed each vessel owner at the rate of five cents per ton of cargo in order to accumulate a contingency fund with which to fight the union.[23] In the same year, the Michigan Stove Company nearly destroyed the ironmolders' union that had won the previous year's strike. At the end of March, the company closed temporarily, ostensibly because of a shortage of coke. When the company reopened a few days later, it announced that all previous agreements with the workers' shop committee were void, that such workers' shop committees would not be permitted in the future, and that the factory was now a "new shop." Each former employee must apply for work as if the factory were opening for the first time. To soften the blow of this attack on the union, the company announced a pay increase of 10 percent for molders who would comply with the new regime. Sixty union molders who would not were discharged. The workers received extensive financial support from other unions as they had the year before, but this time the company was determined, and its power was greater. Probusiness priests recruited scabs for the company in their Sunday sermons. Union molders who found work at other area companies were fired as the Michigan Stove Company circulated a blacklist of union members. Once the union was driven out, workers complained that the wage increase was not honored, and the company even refused to publish a price list of the piece rate it would pay. Employees would not know the rate of pay until they received their pay envelopes. Other companies followed the Michigan Stove Works' example. Baugh's Steam Forge fired its union molders and stood firm against the union despite apparent efforts by sympathizers still employed to sabotage production. The Peninsular Stove Company followed suit in October of 1882. Local manufacturers sought assistance from the National Stove Founders Defense Association formed in 1882. By the mid-1880s, membership in the ironmolders' union had been reduced to "a mere handful."[24]

The experience of the ironmolders was duplicated in many other trades. Against such stiff opposition many unions folded. When the broommakers' union collapsed in 1884 after a long strike, the *Labor Leaf* advised workers to "prepare for war in time of peace." Workers should sacrifice to maintain high union dues, in order to accumulate large enough strike funds to last through protracted strikes.[25] Many unions and Knights of Labor assemblies resorted to secrecy to protect their members from reprisal, but employers hired spies to report the names of union supporters. In 1885, in preparation for the Trades Council demonstration, employers hired thirteen Pinkerton agents to infiltrate local unions and Knights of Labor assemblies. Once accepted as members, the agents marched freely in the parade and recorded names of marchers for their employers. A number of workers were fired as a result, including five shoemakers at Pingree and Smith.[26]

Union membership trends must be evaluated with this level of employer opposition in mind. In the face of concerted efforts to suppress unionism entirely, even the moderate membership increase between 1881 and 1885 was a relative success. Unions had survived tough opposition, established stable organizations, grown slightly, dramatically increased their political influence and community stature. Even where antiunion drives succeeded, as in the case of the ironmolders, widespread support for organization remained. Following their defeats in the early 1880s, a core of ironmolders, resorting to the secrecy of the Knights of Labor, formed a molders' assembly within the Knights. By the late 1880s, the result, Garland Assembly 619, had organized skilled and unskilled iron workers on an industrial basis into the city's largest Knights of Labor assembly with a reported membership of 800. Unionism had become a part of the mass culture of workers that transcended the fortunes of a particular union local.[27]

But trade union consciousness is not class consciousness. The spirit and practice of the city's unions in the early 1880s reflected the complex and conflicting trends in workers' attitudes. While the growing radicalization of unions, the expansion of union functions, the increased support for political and educational activities reflected the tendency toward class consciousness, the structure and some of the practices of unions perpetuated craft and ethnic differences among workers. Many unions recruited membership on the basis of narrow craft specialization, ethnicity, or both. Technological changes within industry produced new subcrafts who demanded autonomous organization.

At the same time that radical activists were preaching the doctrine of trade amalgamation, many crafts were subdividing and disamalgamating. Printers, for example, had three separate unions: Typographical Union No. 18, the German Printers Union, and the Pressman's Union. Although the defeats of the early 1880s might have suggested a need for unity, molders divided into three unions in addition to the Knights of Labor assembly: Iron Molders' Union No. 31, Machine Molders No. 244, and the Brotherhood of Brass Molders (which affiliated with the Knights of Labor in 1882 and disaffiliated again in 1891). Stove company workers formed a wide array of craft unions in the early 1880s, in addition to the molders' unions, for nearly every step in the production process from stovemounting to metal polishing. Even such self-consciously socialist unions as the Progressive Cigarmakers depended as much on ethnicity as ideology for support. All of its spokesmen were Germans. The Central Labor Union organized with a good deal of revolutionary fanfare and Marxist rhetoric, but its *raison d'etre* was the desire for a German union federation: for German unionists, a certain amount of socialist phraseology was accepted cultural practice.[28]

The implications of union growth were thus contradictory. Union success was possible in part because of class consciousness, yet unions defined themselves in ways which reflected the very forces which prevented the development of class consciousness. Advocates of class-conscious organization were divided on how to respond. Some, like the Progressive Cigarmakers, seemed to feel that forthright allegiance to socialism qualitatively changed the character of unionism. Some SLP members, following the Lasallean tradition in German Social Democracy, were openly hostile to trade unionism, arguing for the supremacy of politics and the party. Men like Joseph Labadie and Judson Grenell tried to strike a middle ground. On the one hand they energetically supported trade union organization on the grounds that any organization was better than none at all. At the same time, they tried to convince unionists of the need for a broader, more social definition of goals and a more comprehensive form of organization. Eventually, they hoped, all of the unions could be convinced to join the Knights of Labor.

Knights of Labor

The initial progress of the Knights of Labor in Detroit hardly justified the central role that its organizers envisioned. After rapidly initiating three dozen men in four months, Local Assembly 901 ceased to grow. Apparently the small circle of the founders' acquaintances quickly reached its limits. The assembly stagnated for the next two years, some members lost interest, and the membership dropped to twenty-three.[29]

The assembly functioned primarily as a biweekly study group and collective strategy session for a group of organizers and active reformers. The sessions brought together socialists, single taxers, cooperators, and Greenbackers for necessary ideological debate. Among the city's most important union organizers and working-class political activists, they needed to talk out their differences in an amicable private atmosphere. Despite differences, they still had to work together. The minutes of the Washington Literary Society suggest a friendly spirit, a sharp contrast to the factional strife within the SLP. But the Knights did not grow. Labadie and Van Patten wrote Powderly glowing letters about future prospects, but Local Assembly 901 remained a cadre, not a mass organization.[30]

Perhaps they were too busy with the Weaver campaign, the Trades

Council, and the SLP. Labadie organized a small group of coal miners near Jackson, Michigan, at the end of 1879, but when new assemblies finally began to appear in Detroit at the beginning of 1882, the reports mention a new organizer, David Barry. Secrecy also interfered with organizing efforts. Since the name of the order could not be spoken or written, not to mention its program or goals, there was no way to publicize the Knights. Prospective members could not even be approached directly since the organization's existence could not be revealed to nonmembers. Candidates who had previously been approved (without their knowledge) had to be recruited without being told exactly what they were joining until after they were initiated.[31]

Finally, at the 1881 general assembly the Knights abandoned extreme secrecy,[32] and the fortunes of the Detroit Knights improved. Local Assembly 901 initiated more than 100 new members in the first six months of 1882. Members of various crafts then began to leave LA 901 for their own assemblies, first a trunkmakers' assembly and then Peninsular Assembly 1733, the remnants of the old Crispins (shoemakers') lodge. By late April, assemblies of painters (mostly for the railroad car shops), bootmakers, and forgemen had been added, and in June, five assemblies applied for a district charter. Others followed quickly: tailors, shipcarpenters and caulkers, telegraphers, plasterers, brass workers, and one mixed assembly—a total of twelve by the end of the year with a membership of 397.[33]

District Assembly 50 was still much smaller than the Trades Council, but for the first time, the Knights suggested their future potential as a mass organization. The new district assembly, with its vision of class solidarity, had attracted some of the city's trade unions and had organized several previously unorganized crafts. A brochure published by DA 50 explained its purpose.

> The alarming development and aggressiveness of great capitalists and corporations, unless checked, will inevitably lead to the pauperization and hopeless degradation of the toiling masses.
>
> It is imperative, if we desire to enjoy the full blessings of life, that a check be put upon unjust accumulation, and the powers of evil of aggregated wealth.
>
> This much desired object can be accomplished only by the united efforts of those who obey the divine injunction, "In the sweat of thy brow shalt thou eat bread."
>
> Therefore, we have formed the Order of the Knights of

Labor, for the purpose of organizing and directing the power
of the industrial masses . . .[34]

The Detroit Knights continued to grow throughout 1883 as membership reached 797. Organizing efforts lagged in Detroit in 1884, with
several assemblies disbanding and others in financial distress, but Detroit organizers had begun to crisscross the state, literally rushing from
one speaking engagement to another, leaving trails of new assemblies
behind them. In July 1882, the *Unionist* reported that "the Saginaw
Valley is being honeycombed with Assemblies of Knights of Labor.
Muskegon and Grand Haven are getting down to business. Calls from
all over the state are pouring in for organizers to come and organize
them." Richard Trevellick wrote Powderly that month describing "8 or
10" recent speaking engagements and reporting on David Barry's activities as well. Barry had established four new assemblies in one week.[35]

In 1882, Michigan membership topped 1,000; by the end of 1883,
it reached 3,297; and in 1884, it doubled again.[36] In January of 1884,
the Knights' first state assembly met in Detroit in response to a convention call by the Detroit Knights. Joseph Labadie presided as fifty delegates passed resolutions demanding a federal law prohibiting the importation of foreign contract labor, pledging solidarity to other labor
organizations, asking members and sympathizers to boycott the Detroit
Free Press and the Detroit *Post and Tribune* because both papers refused
to hire union men or Knights of Labor, and urging local assemblies to
establish programs for "educating members in the principles necessary
to the success of our cause." The delegates elected John Devlin state
master workman and Labadie chairman of the state executive board.
Although membership had not increased as rapidly in Detroit as in
some areas in the state, Detroit Knights could see themselves as leaders of a burgeoning statewide movement.[37]

Equally important, while the unions had formed the initial mass
base for most workers' independent cultural, educational, and political
activities in Detroit, by 1883 or 1884 these functions were being taken
over by the Knights of Labor. Despite a much smaller membership than
the trade unions, the Knights dominated the Independent Labor party,
the labor press, and the various educational forums and social events.
In 1882, for example, of the nine men nominated by the Independent
Labor party, at least six were Knights. Three aldermen elected by the
ILP in 1883 belonged to the Knights, while six of the seven state representative candidates in 1884 were Knights. Between 1882 and 1889,

all of the editors and regular columnists in the English-language labor press were Knights. The Knights had an aura of growing power; they were closely linked to a dynamic national movement while national trade union ties were weak, and the national trade union federation, the Federation of Trades and Labor Unions, was practically nonexistent.[38]

For these reasons, as well as the Knights' abstract doctrines, activists had high hopes for the future of the order in the city. Finally in 1886, their dreams seemed to come true. As a tidal wave of previously unorganized workers joined by the thousands, organizers recognized that apparently apathetic workers had been listening all along. Many of the trade unions, caught up in the excitement, left the Trades Council to become Knights of Labor assemblies, and at one 1886 meeting delegates from only seven unions remained. DA 50 paid per capita tax on 4,679 members on July 1, 1886, and claimed 8,000 members in fifty-one local assemblies by that fall. The possibilities seemed limitless.[39]

The Knights' success was based on the organization's ability to draw together the major trends within the labor movement and merge them with a groundswell of popular protest that went well beyond the ranks of organized workers. Its ideology was inspiring but vague, perhaps purposely so. Slogans like "An injury to one is the concern of all" could be interpreted as a euphemism for socialism by radicals and as a much more limited observation by craft conservatives. In a city like Detroit, with its ethnic and economic diversity, any movement which hoped to unify all workers had to create common bonds that ignored real differences and antagonisms. The Knights of Labor had this capacity. Their millenarian and reformist rhetoric could appeal to a wide variety of workers: to radicals it was the embodiment of class solidarity; to reformers it was a vehicle for their political goals; to unionists in isolated or tactically weak crafts it was a source of mutual assistance; to moralists it was a model of Christian brotherhood and moral uplift; to feminists it was a universalist vindication of their own ideals; to demoralized and proletarianized artisans it was a hope for escape from the wage system.[40]

In some ways, this unity was artificial. The order had not overcome the underlying fragmentation either in its own ranks or in the majority of the city's workers, but had provided a rhetoric and a form of organization that could partially supersede it. But merely enrolling a large number of people in an organization pledged to an ideal of solidarity did not mean that all of them were willing or able to act on that ideal. The influx of 1886 revealed tendencies in the mass culture of the city's workers responsive to a class appeal, but in their enthusiasm and excitement, most of the Knights' leaders overestimated how widespread a change had taken place. As the struggles of the next few years would reveal, conflicting forces still pulled in other directions.

It is easy to understand this overenthusiasm. The Knights seemed to be able to accomplish what the trade unions could not. They could provide effective support for crafts with weak or nonexistent national unions. Antiunion employers seemed to buckle under pressure from the Knights. Knights of Labor organizers could point to a series of successes around the state and around the country.[41]

Detroit trunkmakers were typical of trades without a national union. They organized as Trunkmakers' Assembly 1767 in 1882. When a local trunk manufacturer fired Knights of Labor trunkmakers for membership in the order, all the firm's trunkmakers went out on strike. The district assembly assessed its members ten cents per week to support the strikers. Representatives of the district executive board negotiated with the manufacturer. The owner capitulated, rehired the Knights, and agreed to restrict apprenticeships and appoint a Knight as shop foreman.[42]

In part, the Knights' power flowed from their national structure. With support from the Knights, weak craft unions were no longer dependent only on local assistance in struggles against employers with national markets. For example, when the Knights of Labor shoemakers struck Pingree and Smith in April 1885, they apparently faced the same hopeless situation that had destroyed shoemakers' unions across the country for more than a decade. Within the memory of middle-aged shoemakers, shoemaking had been a highly respected hand craft, but modern firms like Pingree and Smith were mechanized and most machine workers were easy to replace. Pingree and Smith refused to bargain, hired scabs, and continued their operations without interruption.[43]

The shoemakers appealed to Detroit District Assembly 50; the DA issued a national boycott order. Announcements went out to regional labor papers and the Knights' national *Journal of United Labor*. By 1885, the Knights had penetrated nearly every city or large town in the entire country. This was the significance of national organization: activists in hundreds of other cities could immediately be recruited to spread the boycott order. Few unions were effectively enough organized on a national scale to function this way.

In the meantime, the district assembly helped unemployed shoemakers organize their own Cooperative Shoe Company with capital raised through a stock subscription system. Local unions bought stock; at the Michigan state assembly in June, local assemblies around the state were urged to support the boycott and to buy stock in the Cooperative Shoe Company. The board of directors included representatives of the shoemakers and prominent leaders of the DA. Profits, after deductions for depreciation, a contingency fund, and 5 percent for labor organization, were to be equally divided between the workers and stock subscribers.

In June and July, the *Labor Leaf* began to report cases of scabs giving up after systematic harassment by local unionists. The local assembly in Filer City, Michigan, reported that two merchants who normally carried Pingree and Smith's shoes had agreed not to reorder when their current stocks ran out. A Muskegon local assembly told *Labor Leaf* readers that all shoe dealers in the city were honoring the boycott. By August, the boycott appeared to be having the desired effects; Pingree and Smith were faltering and they announced a 25 percent wage reduction. In December, the Boot and Shoe Cooperative Association reported on its second quarter of operation. Finally, in March 1886, District Master Workman J. D. Long announced victory over Pingree and Smith in the *Journal of United Labor.*[44]

Such impressive local results combined with widespread publicity of national victories by the Knights, most notably the victory over Jay Gould's Southwestern railroad system in 1885, produced a public image of strength and power. Activists were quick to suggest that this success vindicated their conception of trade amalgamation. Power followed organization. As a speaker at an 1885 Knights of Labor social explained, "the power of concentrated capital" allowed businessmen to "coerce labor." If employers could combine in trade associations, monopolies, pools, and mergers, then "only by combination could labor protect itself."[45]

The Knights of Labor were designed to be such a combination both to win immediate demands like those of the Detroit trunkmakers and shoemakers, and to educate workers toward more long-range goals and inculcate the spirit of class solidarity. The rituals, structure, and rhetoric of the order were all geared to producing a spirit that could overcome craft, ethnic, regional, and other divisions. The passwords, secret signs, symbols, ceremonies have struck many modern scholars as so much mumbo jumbo, and indeed, some of the activists of the 1880s frequently lost patience with the amount of time consumed by rituals at the beginning of every meeting. District and state assemblies

117

(that is leadership bodies) often passed resolutions to simplify or elimi-
nate observations of ritual. But organizers (and scholars) who lost patience with ceremony really misunderstood something about the role of
ritual as group affirmation and as a social glue. The Knights produced
an impressive array of regalia in vast quantities: buttons, banners,
badges, ribbons, drinking mugs, flags, trivets, cigar boxes, all with appropriate symbolism. The rituals and the physical accouterments that
went with them all stressed themes of universal brotherhood—globes
suggested universality, shaking hands meant solidarity. By 1886, transient workers could move almost interchangeably from one to any of
thousands of other assemblies and be readily accepted among people
who spoke of common themes and used identical phrases. Fraternalism
was a far more prevalent American phenomenon during most of the
1880s and 1890s than unionism. It has been little studied, but clearly
the Knights had drawn on something in popular culture that people understood and liked. Their ritual was not egregious, but quite functional
in promoting loyalty and identification with the order.[46]

The organizational structure promoted the same themes as the ritual. While actual practice often ignored strict constitutional forms, in
theory the organization was a pyramid running from the local assembly,
to the district, then to the general assembly, and finally to the executive
board and the grand (later general) master workman. Each Knight theoretically acknowledged the supremacy of the same central leadership.
Local assemblies in Detroit were mainly organized on a craft basis not
fundamentally different from the trade unions (many assemblies had
started as trade unions). Ten of the first eleven local assemblies in Detroit were craft locals (the sole exception was Pioneer Assembly 901),
and fifty-one of seventy assemblies organized in Detroit and vicinity
between 1878 and 1888 had some occupational concentration (including industrial unions which included multiple crafts). There were
also seven German assemblies. Yet each assembly recognized the central authority of the district executive board in far more fundamental ways than the trade unions accepted direction from the Trades
Council. Trade unions stressed craft autonomy; if they obeyed any outside authority, it was usually their national or international craft union.
Knights of Labor assemblies regularly received orders and advice not
only from the district but also from Powderly, including assessments,
rulings on internal disputes, special dispensations on a wide variety of
matters. Assemblies needed permission from the district executive
board to strike.[47]

In practice, the Knights operated far more flexibly than this centralized authority structure suggests. Locals frequently acted and then sought endorsement after the fact; even when they disapproved, officers usually felt compelled to agree in order to maintain the public appearance of unity.[48] But the psychological significance of acknowledging common leaders who had nominal authority cutting across craft and ethnic lines should not be overlooked, nor can the pressure of group conformity be underestimated as a force for bringing together locals of different crafts. Unions frequently supported members of other crafts financially and through boycotts and sympathetic strikes, but such support was always voluntary, and therefore even minimal contributions could be viewed as magnanimous acts. Knights of Labor assemblies, in contrast, were under moral and constitutional compulsion to support fellow Knights if their officers had endorsed the action.

Both the spirit and the structure of the Knights also stimulated creation of industrial unions for whole factories or even entire industries. It is not coincidental that the two most prominent industrial unions in the American Federation of Labor, the miners and the brewery workers, had come out of the Knights of Labor and maintained dual affiliation with the Knights into the mid-1890s. In Detroit, industrial or semiindustrial unions formed the largest local assemblies. George Washington Assembly 8775 organized streetcar employees in all job categories and had 307 members in 1888; Garland Assembly 619 reportedly included 800 metal workers at the Michigan Stove Works, while Devlin Assembly 3954 organized a similar number of metal workers in the railroad car shops.[49]

The common ritual, centralized structure, spirit of solidarity, and industrial character of some assemblies all lent themselves to the broader definitions of union functions sought by radical activists. With the rise of the Knights came a flourishing of political, social, educational, and cultural activities. The labor movement had transcended the framework of an economic bargaining agent into wider realms that involved all facets of workers' lives.

Political Action

One of the first manifestations of this broader outlook was the politicization of the labor movement. Indeed, the Socialist and Greenback electoral campaigns of the late 1870s had preceded union growth and had stimulated both union expansion and radicalization. After the abortive Greenback-Socialist fusion in 1880, activists looked for a new vehicle to mobilize the growing labor movement into a political organization with a broader base than the SLP. Finally, in 1882 the Trades Council, Knights of Labor, and SLP joined forces in an Independent Labor party which drew an average of 2,106 votes for its legislative ticket in 1882—about 10 percent of the total vote, a substantial improvement over the 1880 Greenback campaign and the SLP campaigns of the late 1870s.[50] By 1886 the ILP vote topped 3,600—14 percent.[51]

Labor candidates characteristically combined a formal written platform of specific legislative reforms with a broad, ideological appeal to the rights of labor. The 1882 platform included eight planks: reservation of public land "for actual settlers, not . . . railroads or speculators," factory and mine safety inspection, abolition of convict contract labor, abolition of the contract system for municipal work, prohibition of child labor to age fourteen, eight-hour day, establishment of a state bureau of labor statistics, and compulsory education for children under fourteen.[52] This issue-oriented ideological appeal did not break party identification and ethnocultural voting patterns among the majority of the city's workers.[53] Even the minority who did vote for the labor party reflected varying ethnic loyalties: German workers provided more than half the labor votes in 1884, while the ILP ran poorly in working-class precincts where most workers were native, British, Canadian, or Irish.[54] But by the mid-1880s, the ILP did establish the labor movement as a recognizable political force capable of mobilizing a tenth of the city's voters and able to do much better in some races at the ward level.

No fully independent labor candidate was ever able to poll over 20 percent on a citywide basis, but the party's demonstrated vote-drawing capacity gave it a balance-of-power position in local politics. Both major parties had large and dependable constituencies; the outcome of elections hinged on the minority of swing voters who might be induced to shift parties from one election to the next. The machines sought to accomplish such shifts by varying their ethnic coalitions through intricate ticket-balancing schemes. The Independent Labor party had found a new basis for motivating a swing vote. If ILP leaders were willing to cooperate with the major parties on some levels, they might exact significant concessions: major party endorsements for labor candidates, support for key labor reform legislation, nominations of labor leaders to patronage appointments. In some cases, the machines were anxious enough to secure labor cooperation that they might demand very little in return for labor support. This was particularly true in the state legislative races because the legislature chose United States senators, and senators controlled much of the federal patronage which helped

Table 8. Independent Labor Vote, State Representative Candidates, 1882–1886

	Mean vote[1]	Percent	Number of fusion candidates elected
1882	2,124[2]	9.7 (est.)[3]	2
1884	2,020	7.3[4]	5
1886	3,606[5]	14.0[6]	3

Sources: Wayne County Election Records, 1884, 1886, Detroit Public Library; Detroit *Unionist*, November 20, 1882; Detroit *Evening News*, November 8, 1882.

1. Mean vote of candidates not endorsed by one of the major parties.
2. Based on four of five candidates. Returns for fifth candidate not available.
3. Estimated on the basis of incomplete returns.
4. Lower percentage in 1884 is the result of the larger turnout in a presidential year.
5. Revised vote total including estimated labor votes in precincts where labor votes were not recorded. See note 53 for further explanation.
6. Based on revised vote total.

to hold the machines together. The senatorial votes in the state legislature were often close in the 1880s. If a Republican endorsement might elect a labor leader in a normally Democratic district, the Democrats would be denied one vote toward the U.S. senator even if the successful labor candidate did not acknowledge any further obligation to the Republicans.[55]

Such cooperation involved moral and ideological contradictions for many labor leaders. How could a socialist in good conscience accept a nomination from Republican bondholders and monopolists? In 1880, for example, E. W. Simpson refused a Republican endorsement in his campaign for alderman. In 1886, Judson Grenell accepted Republican endorsements for state legislator and for deputy oil inspector, a patronage appointment, on the grounds that he could devote the resulting free time to the movement, but only after he had been assured that he could vote as he pleased in the state legislature. Charles Erb refused a similar offer from the Democrats in 1884.[56]

Ultimately the Independent Labor party devised a means of maintaining the semblance of independence and still using its balance-of-power position to advantage. It would nominate its slate prior to Republican and Democratic conventions. If either major party chose to endorse some of the labor candidates, fusion nominees could still be claimed as labor candidates first. This method resulted in victories for two of the party's seven state representative candidates in 1882, and five of seven in 1884. The swing character of the labor vote was particularly evident in the 1884 campaign. All seven of Detroit's state representatives were chosen on a citywide at-large basis. Each party could nominate seven candidates and each voter submitted a list of seven choices. The ILP nominated a full slate, including Grenell, Egan, Charles Erb, K. of L. district master workman J. D. Long, Lyman Brant (prominent in both the ITU and the Knights), and two other important Knights. Two of them were endorsed by the Republicans and three by the Democrats. All of the endorsed labor candidates were elected and all placed ahead of all other candidates. Thus, any labor nominee with a regular party endorsement beat any candidate of either party without the labor nomination. Five of Detroit's seven state representatives were labor organizers, and in the next two years, both major parties seemed to scramble frantically in pursuit of any labor leader who would talk to them.[57]

Sending a Knights of Labor leader or even a prominent socialist (Grenell) to the state legislature had tremendous symbolic impact and held out hope of immediate improvements in workers' situations through legislation sponsored by the ILP's representatives. The emergence of the Independent Labor party in a balance-of-power role confirmed activists' expectations of rising working-class power, and they believed that the ILP was on the verge of becoming the party of the majority of the city's workers. But this understandable pride and enthusiasm over their electoral victories often ignored the realities of their limited political base. A statistical analysis of the 1884 election results demonstrates, for example, that the party depended overwhelmingly on particular segments of the working class: in general, skilled workers; in particular, German skilled workers. Skilled workers provided an estimated 85 percent of all ILP votes, while about half of that 85 percent were from skilled Germans.[58] The party had virtually no support among non-German unskilled workers and only weak support among the unskilled Germans.[59]

The influence of the skilled Germans on the 1884 labor vote was so great that it might be argued that ethnicity was as important a determinant of labor-party voting as class. In only five precincts where Germans made up less than a quarter of the electorate did the ILP do significantly better than its citywide average.[60] Overall, the proportion of Germans among potential voters in a precinct was as good a predictor of the ILP vote in that precinct as the percent of potential voters who were working class.[61] In one sense the party's 1884 vote was still a class vote because the German labor vote was almost completely German working class.[62] Thus, nearly all labor voters *were* workers. But the party's inability to draw a significant proportion of votes from non-German workers, even when it was enjoying electoral victories, demonstrates how ethnic antagonisms continued to impede efforts to promote class consciousness beyond the neighborhood level. Until the 1886 campaign, labor-party voting correlated *negatively* or statistically insignificantly with every ethnic group except the Germans.[63]

Equally important for the movement, these election campaigns seriously aggravated debates over the objectives of labor politics. Most labor activists recognized that any far-reaching modifications in the industrial system necessarily involved legal and political changes which could not be won through negotiations with individual employers. Even unionists skeptical about long-range goals could be convinced that a variety of legislation had practical value: repeal of conspiracy laws against unions, safety legislation, maximum-hours laws, child labor legislation, incorporation procedures for unions. But while almost all labor leaders advocated some form of electoral activity, they were seriously divided over political goals and strategies. Labor politics, like almost all other aspects of Detroit's labor movement in the early 1880s, had dual effects. As a form of activity which both transcended the workplace and to some degree cut across craft and ethnic lines, it was a powerful practical and symbolic force toward class unity. Growing support for independent labor tickets between 1877 and 1886 reflected growing class consciousness, but the distribution of support also reflected continuing differences within the working class. Labor politics became an internal battleground of factional maneuvering, rival personal ambitions, and bitter emotional hostilities which eventually helped to destroy not only the Independent Labor party, but also the Knights of Labor and the spirit of class they represented.

The sources of these difficulties were both practical and conceptual. On a practical level all labor politics faced the same obstacles that had stymied the socialists in the late 1870s: established party loyalties among their potential electorate, weak or nonexistent precinct organizations, lack of funds, competition with established political machines able to offer patronage to their party workers, inexperience in the mechanics of electoral organization, hostility from electoral authorities, outright corruption and fraud. Although they did put together effective campaign committees in some neighborhoods, labor politicians never completely overcame these weaknesses. But they convinced themselves that the ultimate success of labor politics did not depend on beating machine politicians at their own game. Poorly financed amateur campaigners would always lose, they reasoned, unless they could mobilize voters on a different basis from the major party machines.[64]

Political activists believed that they could do so because, they argued, both major parties were virtually indistinguishable capitalist parties inherently incapable of responding to workers' real needs. While they understood that only a minority of workers agreed with them at present, the ranks of labor agitators were growing. The precedent of abolitionism in the previous generation lent credibility to a belief in the power of a dedicated minority. "Wage slavery," Labadie wrote in 1885, "may be wiped out as was chattel slavery. I am in hopes the influence of the earnest, intelligent minority will be strong enough to bring changed conditions through sheer moral force." But if not, change would come nonetheless as demonstrated by "the historical facts of previous social movements, including the anti-slavery movement and its ultimate success . . ." Politics as practiced by the major parties was "mere scheming for place," but the masses would recognize that "our industrial interests are the ones on which all others are based . . . Politics is our public business . . . to be attended to by ourselves, and no longer left to a few unscrupulous schemers."[65]

But any attempt to mobilize workers into an independent political movement faced serious conceptual difficulties. What should the ultimate objectives of such a party be? Was working-class political independence an end in itself, a means of developing class identity? Or should labor politicians seek alliances and compromises with the major parties in order to achieve immediate practical gains? Would incremental successes lead to a transformation of the industrial system or postpone more fundamental changes by blunting popular dissatisfaction without altering basic power relations? Could short-range and long-range goals be reconciled? Labor politicians faced a classic dilemma of leftwing politics: purity versus immediate results. The problem provoked bitter ideological debate, even though all factions recognized the need for internal unity.

Underlying divergent reactions to this dilemma were three separate justifications for labor politics: electoral activity as an alternative to strikes, confrontation, violence, or revolution; legislation as a means of correcting specific abuses; politics as a form of mass education toward fundamental social changes. The arguments were not necessarily mutually exclusive, and particular individuals might make various combinations of them, but the implications of the first two were far more reformist, and therefore compromise oriented, than the third.

The concept of politics as an alternative to revolutionary violence was particularly widespread. Labor leaders feared violence; the experiences of their entire generation from Tompkins Square to the Mollie Maguires to Haymarket suggested that violence might be more effectively turned against labor than used by it. The editors of the *Unionist* resolved the question "By Bullet or Ballot?" by arguing that the ballot was a more effective weapon. "A peaceful revolution at the ballot box will accomplish more for the elevation of the downtrodden than the bloody revolution of the sword." A Detroit correspondent to *John Swinton's Paper* agreed. "The ballot is the thing. A little piece of paper, with the proper principles will shoot further and with more force than a Redman's [illegible] gun."[66]

The ballots-not-bullets argument reflected widespread belief in American exceptionalism. Revolutionary violence might be justifiable, even admirable, in European societies where centuries-old tyranny left workers no other options, but America was different. Workers of many nationalities accepted this argument. A largely German working-class audience applauded the principal of the German seminary school when he contrasted American freedoms with the tyranny of Bismarck's Germany. Three thousand people had gathered to hear reports from German emigrees on the conditions of German workers under Bismarck's repressive antisocialist laws: "Our broad land, which has thrown off the shackles of a medieval civilization more effectively than any other . . . has been the star of hope of the oppressed of all climes . . . as an American citizen . . . deeply sensible of the responsibilities this privilege implies, I am here to listen to the grievances of a great nation . . . This is . . . a gathering . . . of American men and women who love their own freedom enough to sympathize . . . with the oppressed wherever despotism may raise his poisonous head."[67]

Not surprisingly, some radicals were skeptical of such faith in American political processes. Judson Grenell argued that "our so-called laws . . . are generally cunningly devised schemes to enable the few to rob the many."[68] And Labadie agreed that insistence on legality "is simply doing the work of capitalism . . . We will try all peaceable means [but] . . . our demands are just . . . if we can't succeed that way [then we must] . . . resort to revolutionary methods. The whining and making faces at the revolutionists is beneath the dignity of any one who is honestly and earnestly in this movement." Yet in a letter to Richard Ely written only a few months before this editorial, even Labadie confessed an abhorrence for violence. "The destruction of wealth in itself is an evil, and I am in hopes that a better social system will be established without the destruction of life and wealth."[69] For Labadie, then, politics might be a means of avoiding violence, but only if political action emphasized ideological education rather than short-range objectives. Judson Grenell agreed: "Amelioration is possible, but complete emancipation will come only when cooperation shall succeed competition . . . when landlordism and capitalism shall have been swept out of existence." Labadie was even more direct. "I notice that 'practical questions' almost always lead us to the support of some political mountebank who has no word of condemnation for the legalised methods of robbing the laborer of his earnings." Elections of such men were hollow victories. "Almost every time a 'labor' man gets a government position the labor movement loses an agitator . . . mere political action 'to get our man in'" was useless. "Our men are no better than anybody else's men when they are placed in trying circumstances. What is necessary is a change of system and not necessarily a change of men."[70]

Grenell and Labadie had no objection (as some of the more rigid SLP regulars did) to ameliorative measures. Agitators could not afford to isolate themselves in a mutual admiration society of fellow believers, but if they compromised their principles in order to make themselves more appealing to Republican or Democratic overtures, they destroyed the movement they were trying to build. "Workingmen of this country [cannot] . . . gain anything from either party by supporting or keeping in power either one or the other of the parties." Labadie argued that machine politicians who had scorned the movement a few years before were trying to seduce labor leaders because "the K. of L. is a power that must be either controlled or broken up if the political barnacles are to hang on to the 'ship of state.'"[71]

This suspicion of politicians and electoral politics in general was widespread. A correspondent to the *Unionist* advised workers to "stick to your unions and leave politics . . . alone. Somebody only wants to get a living off workingmen." The Knights' Shipcarpenters' and Caulkers' Local Assembly argued "that LA 2124 deems it unwise . . . to appoint as organizer in the K. of L. any person holding an office in the gift of any political party." The records of some of the labor politicians only aggravated these suspicions. In January 1885, Francis Egan, elected to the state legislature in 1884 as a labor candidate with

Republican endorsement, voted for the Republican candidate for house speaker rather than for the labor caucus' candidate, Lyman Brant. Hugh McClelland, another Labor-Republican, voted with Egan. The *Labor Leaf* denounced them as selfish and ambitious and declared that this announcement would constitute their political obituary, but Egan's political career was far from over. In August, he was appointed deputy labor commissioner and resigned his legislative seat. Labor commentators were convinced that the appointment to this lucrative post was his political payoff by the Republicans for his legislative vote.[72]

These experiences enhanced the position of those who sought to emphasize the Labor party's independence. Nevertheless, the attraction of coalition victories was nearly irresistible after the legislative wins of 1882 and 1884. Despite disappointments with men like Egan, labor legislators were instrumental in the passage of important legislation including the bill creating the State Bureau of Labor Statistics, a state ten-hour law, and important safety legislation.

But with each new campaign there were renewed proposals to forego coalitions or to find ways of guaranteeing the labor loyalties of fusion candidates. In December 1884, the ILP executive committee tried to prevent any disloyalty among labor representatives in the coming legislative session by forcing them to pledge not to participate in Democratic or Republican caucuses, but the futility of the action was revealed when Egan, who had voted against it, refused to comply. By November 1885, feelings on the issue were strong enough that a socialist correspondent to the *Labor Leaf* began campaigning for a fully independent labor ticket in 1886, a year in advance. When the ILP convention refused to support the demand for a completely independent ticket in September 1886, some thirty delegates (about one-fifth of the total) walked out.[73]

Yet despite all of these internal difficulties, the Labor party held together through the early 1880s and involved increasing numbers of union members in campaign activities and ideological debate. While these debates provoked discord, they also introduced participants to a theoretical dimension that was largely absent from day-to-day union affairs. For weeks before each election, hundreds of rank-and-file union members and Knights of Labor attended rallies, mass meetings, conventions, and demonstrations. This community character of the campaigns stimulated class feeling. A reporter from the *Evening News* who attended an 1882 election eve rally for "the workingmen" was impressed with the party's vitality and enthusiasm. Arbeiter Hall was packed as labor candidates addressed the audience in English and German, confidently predicting victory for the Labor ticket. By 1886, ILP activities were front page news. The final rally the night before the election had drawn 2,500 people. The following morning, 1,000 Knights of Labor poll workers, each wearing a red badge for identification, appeared at the polls to direct their supporters, supervise the activities of election officials, and try to prevent the ballot stuffing of previous campaigns.[74]

"So long as the idlers and rulers and robbers can keep the laborers contending with each other," Joseph Labadie had written in January 1886, "just so long will they feel safe with their privileges and plunder." By the summer and fall of that year, the growth of the Independent Labor party looked like just one more example of an emerging class consciousness that would threaten the "privileges and plunder" Labadie denounced.[75]

The Subculture of Opposition

The objectives of the unions, the Knights of Labor, and the Independent Labor party were outer-directed: to change the terms of employment, alter the relationships between employees and employers, produce political changes, reform society as a whole. But it was the inner life of the movement which made it into something more than a group of discrete organizations, a movement with a broad and distinctive cultural dimension. Psychologically this produced a millenarian quality like a religious crusade. "A mere trade union, with no other aim than to get a few cents a day more wages than the workers would get without organization, is a flabby institution that really is a hindrance to the best interests of the working people . . . ," Labadie declared in his "Cranky Notions" column. "Organization is only a means to an end, and if we have no higher aim in view than a puny two-by-four benefit we had better throw in the sponge."[76]

Labor activism was a cause and a way of life. Its roots were in the workplace and the neighborhood, the units of daily life. While union and Knights of Labor assembly meetings were usually monthy, biweekly, or at most weekly, the range of subsidiary institutions made it possible to integrate daily routines with the movement. Supporters were urged to do their regular shopping with a growing list of sympathetic tradesmen who advertised in the *Labor Leaf* and refused to sell scab (non-union-made) goods. "Help those who help you." Children were told to "boycott scab goods" and make sure there were union labels on the things their parents bought. Workers were encouraged to boycott saloons which sold nonunion cigars; four saloon keepers took the threat seriously enough to appeal to the Trades Council after their names were printed in the *Unionist* as offenders. A growing list of producers' cooperatives including a shoe factory, a cooperage, and an iron foundry appealed to workers to invest their savings and to buy cooperative goods. By 1886, the movement included a weekly labor press in both English and German, a workers' militia (The Detroit Rifles), regular debates in the Dialectical Union, a theater group, singing societies, and almost nightly social or educational events.[77]

Regular, almost daily, participation in these institutions was beginning to break down the barriers between workers of different nationalities and workers with varying economic experiences. Many of these subsidiary activities drew a wider range of participants than regular union business. Turnout at union-sponsored neighborhood picnics, dances, concerts, or dinners regularly numbered in the hundreds, and some of the most prominent labor lecturers filled large halls with overflow crowds of 3,000 or more. When the women of Florence Nightingale Assembly 3102 gave a strawberry and ice cream festival on a Wednesday evening in July 1885, people had to stand in long lines just to get in the door of the building, and so many people had to be turned away that the women apologetically assured readers of the *Labor Leaf* that another ice cream festival would be scheduled soon. Unions sponsoring group excursions hired entire trains or steamships for the purpose. The Detroit Sailors' Union chartered the steamship J. W. Steinhoff for its grand excursion to Toledo. The all-day affair cost fifty cents per person and promised that guests would be under the personal supervision of union president Andrew Forbes.[78]

More informal social life also centered around a number of saloons operated by prolabor saloon keepers. The larger saloons owned halls or meeting rooms above the main floor so that the establishment could double as meeting hall and social gathering spot. Sympathetic bar keepers allowed free use of meeting halls to labor organizations. On Christmas Eve 1884, five Knights of Labor assemblies expressed their gratitude to one "jolly saloonkeeper," Hiram Jackson, by presenting him and his wife "a handsome silver pitcher and goblets." The *Labor Leaf* explained that Mr. Jackson, who "has a very fine hall over the saloon which he gives rent free to labor societies," supported "the cause of labor, having been a union iron molder."[79]

The labor press provided a vital communication link which informed workers and their families of coming social events, advised them which products to boycott and which stores to patronize, and published full reports of major local events for those who had not been able to attend. The labor papers performed many other functions as well. Unions reported on current problems, informed members of special or emergency meetings, and explained reasons for organizing to unorganized readers they hoped to recruit. Craftsmen were advised on the state of their trades in other cities, whether work was available there or that workers should stay away. The prevailing wage rates in other cities were published so that workers could better understand the state of their industry and use that information in negotiations with employers. Complex concepts in political economy were explained in straightforward language, often through the medium of anecdotes or folk tales. Relatives of wandering workers sought lost sons. An announcement in October 1885 asked readers to be on the lookout for William Timms, a blacksmith, "Last heard of in Laporte, Ind. His parents are sick." Major radical thinkers such as Marx, Kropotkin, and Henry George were regularly featured with short biographies of their careers and expositions of their ideas. Feature pages included songs, poetry, recipes, jokes, local gossip, and short stories.[80] The offices of the paper functioned as an informal nerve center, discussion group, and flop house for itinerant workers. Out-of-town speakers and organizers would head for the *Leaf* office as they arrived, and the paper was able to present a running commentary on national events within the Knights of Labor from the information they provided.[81] As the labor press developed during the 1880s, the editing improved, the layout became more professional, the publication schedule became more regular, the size increased, and the circulation grew. In 1881, the *Times* reported a circulation of 1,500; by 1882, the *Unionist* claimed 30,000 in eleven issues, or over 2,700 per issue; and by 1885, the *Labor Leaf* set its goal at "10,000 subscribers by next year."[82]

The *Labor Leaf*, the Independent Labor party, the cooperatives, the various cultural events, the public demonstrations had grown together with the unions and the Knights of Labor to impressive dimensions by 1885 and 1886. Nevertheless, the subculture they served was a minority culture even among its own potential constituency, competing for support and allegiance with both the native middle-class culture and ethnic cultures. Indeed, even for many activists participation in movement activities was, at the same time, part of ethnic community

130

life. Few people had undivided loyalties. Even the most dedicated were still drawn by some of the values of the competing cultural systems. Many labor leaders pursued personal mobility and individual success along with group solidarity: Grenell for example, used his ties to the labor movement to launch a successful journalistic career with various daily newspapers.

Yet the subculture permanently affected the lives of its participants and the character of the entire city. The tone of the city's daily newspapers, the content of public political rhetoric, even the newspaper advertisements had all changed by the mid-1880s. The correspondence files that Joseph Labadie saved and later donated to the University of Michigan touchingly reveal the profound impact on Labadie and his friends. Letters from old comrades in their seventies and eighties, some still writing into the 1930s, continued to express the same values they had championed in the 1880s and pride and nostalgia for the experiences.[83]

The active participants of the subculture were a minority of the city's workers, but many more people must have participated occasionally in workers' institutions. The minority itself was both numerically impressive and psychologically important, including among its most active members an imposing array of working-class orators, political organizers, writers, and philosophers. How many people actually saw themselves as part of this cultural minority? We cannot say for sure, but recapitulation of the statistical evidence already presented suggests clear correlations between the rates of participation in each type of institution: union membership increased (including Knights of Labor) from 1,000 in 1880 to 5,000 in 1885; labor press circulation went from 1,500 in early 1881 to 2,700 in late 1882 and perhaps double that by 1886; the independent labor vote grew from 825 in 1877 to 2,106 in 1882 and 3,600 in 1886; labor parade marchers increased from 1,500 in 1880 to 3,000 in 1885. We cannot determine that these were the same people in each case, but the figures are certainly suggestive. At the leadership level, the same cadre of fifty to a hundred names shows up over and over again as union officers, stump speakers, parade marshals, political candidates, cooperative treasurers, newspaper correspondents, public spokespersons. Probably then, by 1885, there were some three to four thousand workers who participated in some ways in this subculture on a regular, almost daily basis. With their families, a conservative estimate of the total number of participants must be at least 10,000. As the incredible expansion of 1886 would indicate, a much larger number must have been involved or influenced on an occasional basis.[84]

The subculture defined itself by its opposition to employers, to great wealth, and to existing industrial conditions, not by a clear and consistent ideology. Participants had varying ideological assumptions and these differences stimulated internal debates which eventually became one of the contributing factors in the movement's partial dissolution, but internal ideological differences should not lead us to analyze the dynamics of the subculture purely in ideological categories. Many labor leaders really had no formal ideology in the sense of a carefully formulated philosophy that was internally consistent, and even those who did think in ideological terms displayed a high degree of eclecticism. In the early 1880s especially, the spirit of the movement was experimental; people considered a great variety of ideas and practical proposals to see which would work. "Any *ism* which conscientiously tries to improve the condition of the people," the *Labor Leaf* wrote in 1885, "should be considered fairly on its merits."[85] This exploratory and somewhat eclectic approach reflected the social realities of a city undergoing rapid industrial change. In 1880, the system of class relations in Detroit had not yet been fully worked out. Workers still debated the most fundamental definitions of their social perspectives, and several alternative strategies all seemed plausible to different groups of workers: individual mobility, craft elitism, antimonopoly political reform, ethnic solidarity, mass action, class solidarity, and socialism.

The language of organizers, the variations in the ways they used key terms, is one indication of this ideological fluidity. Detroit shoemakers, for example, in their 1880 declaration to fellow craftsmen, referred to a "wage class." The Knights of Labor used a similar concept, and their primary slogan was "Abolition of the Wage System." Yet the Knights were ambiguous, purposely at times, about what that meant, and they admitted a small number of non-wage earners to membership. Thus, consciousness of the primacy of the wage relationship did not necessarily imply a conception of workers as a class separate from small businessmen, professionals, and farmers.[86]

Even the definitions of *laborer* or *worker* were subject to disagreement. A correspondent to the Detroit *Times* in 1881, while discussing his views on political economy, made a special point of adding, "and I mean laborer to apply to the working man who directs large enterprises and employs labor as well as to the laborers employed . . ." The Detroit *National*, the local organ of the Greenback Labor party, had published a similar definition of workingmen three years earlier: "By 'work-ingmen' our organization means every man, who by his own legitimate and honest industry, provides for himself and his family. We care not in what field of labor he toils; whether his work be intellectual or physical; believing that there is no work worth the doing that does not, when completed bear the evidence that the head, the heart, and the hand have been united to produce it."[87]

The socialists ridiculed this all-inclusive definition. "Now why do the Nationals rave so about the 'bloated bondholders and bankers'? Do they not work? Are they not engaged in legal industry, and providing for their families by honest labor?" Although the socialists were willing to grant that work may "be mental, physical, or both combined . . . ," they denounced "all attempts to make the word 'workingman' include those who live by insidious scheming, and call it work." According to the socialists, "A workingman proper is a person whose means of exis-tence is his own labor."[88]

But while workers debated such conflicting definitions and con-sidered several strategies, all were influenced by a growing sense of class. The subculture of opposition was predicated on the assumption that there were differences between employers and employed. The gaps in wage levels and living patterns between workers and other classes substantiated this assumption. Labor agitators moved in a milieu in which the rhetoric of class was accepted and expected. Those labor leaders who sought to deny the existence of class conflict may have been expressing widely held beliefs in the dominant culture, but in 1885, they were going against the current of their own subculture. As craft unions began to switch affiliation to the Knights of Labor, as the Independent Labor party seemed on the verge of permanent acceptance by the city's political system, many labor leaders who had earlier op-posed the arguments of labor radicals submerged (if temporarily) their doubts.

There was a logical basis for cooperation among labor leaders of various ideological persuasions. Even when they argued about exactly who should be considered a worker, who was unproductive, and what was needed to rid society of the unproductive, men like Labadie, Greenbacker Henry Robinson, or ITU leader Lyman Brant could easily agree that something was drastically wrong with industrial society as they experienced it. All recognized that the natural law arguments of ideological conservatives justified social misery without offering any viable alternative. In a growing movement with an increasingly radical spirit, these philosophical differences might not involve serious tactical disagreements. If all could support demands for higher wages and better working conditions, if all campaigned for the same legislative reforms, if they trusted each other's sincerity and viewed each other's activities as part of the same whole, then the cultural unity of the movement would seem far more immediate than philosophical differences.[89]

In the period between 1880 and 1886, these preconditions were generally met; labor agitators of various philosophical persuasions usually combined forces. When even the most cautious and conciliatory labor unionists were attacked by antiunion employers and newspaper editors, there was strong pressure for labor unity. Nor was this simply a matter of convenience. The circle of labor activists developed a genuine spirit of community and comradeship. When Joseph Hockaday, a leader of the shipcarpenters, was unemployed in 1887, other labor leaders kept him going by hiring him to fix their homes. Joseph Labadie was one of those who hired him (to build a new house) although they were on opposite sides of the (by this time fairly bitter) factional division within the Knights. When the Detroit *Tribune* attacked John Devlin and J. D. Long in 1886, Labadie defended the integrity of "my friends and comrades" although he admitted he had serious philosophical differences with them. When a reader attacked the *Labor Leaf* for allowing a "rabid anarchist" (Labadie) in its columns, John Burton, the editor, (although he disagreed with many of Labadie's ideas) defended him with a vehemence that might have been reserved for some personal insult against himself.[90]

The growing radicalization of the labor movement in the early 1880s did not, at first, seem to interfere with such mutual regard. Representatives of all shades of opinion within it believed they were on the verge of a great breakthrough. The radicalization of the movement can be seen in many ways: the prominence of Labadie, Grenell, IWPA leader Henry Schulte, and many other socialists; the emergence of two IWPA sections in Detroit; the creation of a workers' militia (Detroit Rifles). Workers who wrote letters to the *Labor Leaf* applauded these trends. As one reader explained in August 1885:

> I saw in THE LABOR LEAF an advertisement for recruits for the Detroit Rifles. I would like to join . . . I think it is about time men woke up . . . The State, which ought to protect us, when we ask for good wages and treatment allows us to be shot, because the government of the State is in the hands of employers of labor, not the laborers . . .

This sort of thing has existed long enough, and only one way of preventing it seems possible. That is force. They force us by starvation and threats of violence to take their terms, but if we attempt violence, or even if we don't, the power of the State is used against us.

With union men well armed and accustomed to military tactics, we could keep Pinkerton's men at a distance . . . Employers would think twice, too, before they attempted to use troops against us. The men who fought for the union can fight just as well now, and will do it rather than be shot in detail.

Every union ought to have its company of sharp-shooters . . . learn to preserve your rights in the same way that your forefathers did. UNION.[91]

The *Labor Leaf* endorsed the idea of a workers' militia in its editorial column. "When there are robbers about it is a good thing to have a rifle handy. When you have a gun and know how to use it, and the robber knows you know how to use it, you are not so likely to have trouble . . . should trouble come, the capitalists will use the regular army and militia to shoot down those who are not satisfied. It won't be so if the people are equally ready, like their forefathers of 1776."[92]

In retrospect, there is an air of unreality about such revolutionary talk. Certainly not much came of it. Yet, in the pages of the *Labor Leaf* in the early months of 1886, it is striking how often writers resorted to the image of threatened revolution if all sorts of demands were not met. An ironmolder, using rhetoric typical that spring, declared in March 1886, "What the molders want is a pricelist and wages sufficient to save us from the poorhouse when old age comes. They ask for these peaceably; and they demand these in the name of justice. And if they are not shortly forthcoming, then let there be a revolution that will compel fair treatment . . ." Events seemed to substantiate the atmosphere of approaching social crisis. In March 1886, the *Labor Leaf* celebrated victories over Pingree and Smith and the Detroit *Free Press*, which had been the city's last major holdout as a nonunion printer. "A union shop after twenty years a rat office." Local brewers gained a reduction in their work day from fourteen to ten-and-one-half hours without any reduction in pay after a half-day strike. The following month the pace quickened even more. One Knights of Labor assembly initiated 135 new members in one night. The influx was just beginning.[93]

NOTES

1. Detroit Trades Council File, LC; Michigan *Truthteller*, April 2, 1880; *Labor Review*, March 1880.

2. Michigan *Truthteller*, May 21, 28, June 12, July 2, 1880; *Labor Review*, May, June 1880.

3. *Labor Review*, June 1880; Detroit *Post and Tribune*, October 17, 1880, clipping in Detroit Trades Council File, LC.

4. Detroit Trades Council File, LC; *Bulletin of the Social Labor Movement*, December 1880–January 1881; Detroit *Times*, April 10, 1880; Detroit *Free Press*, April 5, 1881. There are slight discrepancies among these sources about the numbers of affiliated unions.

5. Detroit Trades Council File, LC; *Labor Review*, October 9, September 11, 1880; Detroit *Times*, April 10, 1881.

6. *Labor Review*, October 23, 1880; unidentified clipping, Detroit Trades Council File, LC.

7. Detroit *Post and Tribune*, October 17, 1880; clipping, Detroit Trades Council File, LC.

8. Detroit Trades Council File, LC; *Labor Review*, October 2, 1880.

9. Detroit Trades Council File, LC; *Labor Review*, October 2, 23, 1880.

10. Detroit Trades Council File, LC.

11. Ibid.; Michigan *Truthteller*, April 2, May 21, May 28, June 12, July 2, 1880.

12. *Labor Leaf*, December 24, 1884.

13. *SBLS*, 1884, pp. 63–64.

14. *Labor Leaf*, November 1, 8, 1884.

15. *Labor Leaf*, January 14, April 22, 1885, June 23, July 21, 1886; Detroit *Evening Journal*, clipping, September 1, 1885, in Knights of Labor Scrapbook, LC.

16. *Labor Leaf*, January 14, April 22, 1885.

17. *Labor Leaf*, April 22, October 7, 1885.

18. *Labor Leaf*, October 7, 1885.

19. Detroit *Unionist*, April 30, 1883; *Labor Leaf*, April 8, March 11, 1885.

20. *Labor Leaf*, November 15, December 10, 17, 1884, April 1, 1885.

21. *Labor Leaf*, December 29, 1885. Grenell's estimate of 30,000 wage-workers is somewhat lower than calculations (38,000 in 1885) based on aggregate census figures, but in some occupations, these aggregates included supervisory personnel and the higher total includes occupations (such as domestic servants) which were not considered amenable to union organization.

22. *Labor Leaf*, December 29, 1885. Detroit *Evening News*, September 3, 1886. See chap. 5 for a more detailed discussion of this growth.

23. Detroit *Times*, April 10, 1881; Detroit *Free Press*, March 22, 29, April 3, 8, 9, 12, 13, 1881.

24. Contractors reportedly returned 600 axles to Baugh's because of poor workmanship, and at one point, the *Unionist* reported "over 50 percent of all the work done at this forge has to be thrown back in the furnace since the union left." Detroit *Times*, April 17, May 8, 1881; Detroit *Unionist*, September 4, October 30, 1882; *Labor Leaf*, January 6, 1886; *Labor Day Review*, 1892, p. 13. The National Stove Founders' Defense Association and the ironmolders' ongoing struggle with it are discussed in David Montgomery, "Workers Control of Machine Production in the Nineteenth Century," *Labor History*, 17 (Fall 1976): 503–4. Philip Van Patten argued that German-Irish rivalry within the union aggravated its other difficulties, Detroit *Free Press*, April 16, 1881.

25. *Labor Leaf*, December 24, 1884.

26. *Labor Leaf*, October 28, 1885; *Columbian Labor Day Review*, 1893, p. 26.

27. "Among the Molders," clipping, Detroit Labor Leaders File, LC; *Labor Day Review*, 1892, p. 13.

28. *SBLS*, 1884, pp. 73–74; "Among the Molders," clipping, LC; Trades Directory, Detroit *Times*, April 10, 1881; *KLDB*; *Labor Leaf*, November 26, 1884; *Labor Day Review*, 1892, p. 37, LC; *First Industrial History and Official Year Book of the Michigan Federation of Labor*, 1915, p. 29.

29. Minutes of the Washington Literary Society, LC; *KLDB*; *Proceedings of the Knights of Labor General Assembly*, 1882, p. 389. Between October 1879, and October 1880, LA 901 did not initiate a single new member (*Proceedings of the Knights of Labor General Assembly*, 1880, p. 213). No report was filed for 1881.

30. Minutes of the Washington Literary Society, LC; Knights of Labor— Michigan File, LC; Joseph Labadie to Powderly, December 7, 1879, TVP; Philip Van Patten to Powderly, August 13, 1880, TVP.

31. Labadie to Powderly, February 24, 1880, TVP; *Journal of United Labor*, p. 281; *Proceedings of the Knights of Labor General Assembly*, 1881, p. 266; The *Unionist*, August 7, 1882.

32. T. V. Powderly, *Thirty Years of Labor* (Columbus, Ohio, 1889), p. 631.

33. *KLDB*; *Proceedings of the Knights of Labor General Assembly*, 1882, p. 389; *Knights of Labor—Manual of Facts*, n.d., Burton Historical Collections, Detroit Public Library.

34. *Knights of Labor—Manual of Facts*, p. 7. Note the overwhelmingly craft character of the Knights in these years. This was true of the Detroit Knights throughout their existence. There is no evidence to substantiate the claims of Commons, Perlman, Grob, *et al.*, that the Knights were antitrade union, that mixed assemblies predominated, or that they recruited primarily among the unskilled.

35. *KLDB*; *Journal of United Labor*, p. 705; Detroit *Unionist*, July 24, 1882; Trevellick to Powderly, July 26, 1882, TVP.

36. *KLDB*; *Proceedings of the Knights of Labor General Assembly*, 1882,

p. 389; Labadie to Powderly, August 5, 1884, TVP; Detroit *Unionist*, December 4, 1882; *Journal of United Labor*, pp. 692, 969, 982; *John Swinton's Paper*, July 26, 1885; Richard Oestreicher, "Knights of Labor in Michigan: Sources of Growth and Decline" (M.A. thesis: Michigan State University, 1973), pp. 6, 15–16.

37. *Record of the Proceedings of the First Regular Session of the Michigan State Assembly of the Knights of Labor; Journal of United Labor*, pp. 705, 723–24; *KLDB;* membership in Detroit declined from 797 to 709 (*KLDB*) in 1884.

38. Detroit *Unionist*, October 23, 1882; *Spectator*, November 3, 1883; *Labor Leaf*, November 8, 1884. A seventh 1882 legislative candidate, SLP member Charles Erb, joined the Knights in 1879 but later withdrew to devote all his time to the SLP. The affiliations of the other two are unknown. Editors of the labor press included Labadie, Grenell, Charles Bell, J. R. Burton, Capt. J. M. McGregor, W. A. Taylor, T. M. Sheriff, and I. P. Granger, all Knights.

39. *Labor Leaf*, January 27, 1886; *Proceedings of the Knights of Labor General Assembly*, 1886, pp. 326–28; Detroit *Evening News*, September 7, 1886; *Reports* of the Officers of DA 50, January 10, 1888, p. 3.

40. For an example of a feminist perspective, see Rachel J. Davidson, M.D., gynaecologist, and president of Flint Equal Suffrage Association, to Powderly, February 26, 1884, TVP. Both Labadie and Grenell were strong advocates of women's rights and the *Labor Leaf* frequently reprinted articles from various feminist journals (although it also featured, on occasion, some decidedly nonfeminist humor). Grenell described his meeting with Susan B. Anthony at the 1880 Weaver convention as one of the high points of his career (Grenell, "Autobiography," p. 38).

41. An example is recorded in the *Minutes*, Cigarmakers' Union 130, Saginaw City, Archives of Labor and Urban Affairs, Wayne State University.

42. Detroit *Unionist*, April 16, 30, 1883.

43. *Labor Leaf*, May 6, 13, 1885.

44. *Labor Leaf*, June 10, July 8, 22, August 12, December 30, 1885, March 24, 1886; *Journal of United Labor*, p. 2041; *Proceedings of the Knights of Labor Michigan State Assembly*, 1885. David Boyd disputes this account of the Pingree and Smith strike, calling it "ill advised" and suggesting that the DA settled on unfavorable terms after the strike had collapsed. While some of the Knights' leaders were devious enough to call a capitulation a victory, Boyd's reminiscences were written over fifty years after the events; he worked for Pingree in the 1890s, and was personally close to him. David Boyd to A. Inglis, September 5 and September 25, 1938, LC. Boyd was a machinist and rank-and-file member of the Knights in the 1880s. He became prominent as a union organizer and Michigan Federation of Labor leader after 1900.

45. Norman Ware, *The Labor Movement in the United States* (New York, 1929), pp. 139–40; Donald L. Kemmerer and Edward D. Wickersham, "Rea-

sons for the Growth of the Knights of Labor in 1885–1886," *Industrial and Labor Relations Review*, 3 (January 1950): 213–20, dispute the influence of the Gould strikes; *Labor Leaf*, July 8, 1885.

46. For an example of suspension of ritual by leaders, see *Proceedings of the Knights of Labor Michigan State Assembly*, 1885, motion by Tom Barry to drop all "forms and ceremonies" for the duration of the convention, p. 6, which carried. E. J. Hobsbawm discusses the role and importance of ritual in *Primitive Rebels* (New York, 1965), chap. 9, "Ritual in Social Movements." Discussion of the Knights' paraphernalia is based on jobbers' advertisements in the labor press and a number of examples of these objects in the author's possession.

47. *KLDB;* Detroit City *Directory*, 1887. Not all of the LA's which I classify as having an occupational designation were craft unions. Wayne Assembly 7749 of car workers, for example, was officially designated a mixed assembly, indicating a multicraft character. Historians have generally misunderstood the nature of the mixed assembly. It was not necessarily anti–trade union. Some mixed assemblies were neighborhood social clubs (LA 2430). Some were essentially industrial unions or trade unions of several related crafts. LA 2697, Henry George Assembly, was essentially an ideological forum which took over some of the leadership cadre functions performed earlier by LA 901 as Labadie, Grenell, and several other prominent Knights transferred from 901. The nature and functions of mixed assemblies varied widely.

48. For a discussion of the constitutional structure of the Knights, see Ware, Appendix 2, pp. 381–89. Ware demonstrates that much of the constitutional theory was erratically enforced, and the constitution was often changed in order to ratify, ex post facto, actions already taken by powerful districts.

49. *KLDB;* "Among the Molders," LC. The membership of LA 8775 is an official figure from the 1889 State Assembly *Proceedings*. The membership of LA's 619 and 3954 are newspaper estimates, possibly unreliable. The *Advance and Labor Leaf* reported a membership of 249 for LA 619 (May 11, 1889), still a large figure but much less than 800.

50. Detroit *Unionist*, October 23, November 20, 1882; Detroit *Evening News*, November 1, 2, 3, 8, 1882.

51. Detroit *Evening News*, November 3, 1886; *Advance and Labor Leaf*, March 19, 1887; Wayne County Election Records, 1886, Burton Historical Collections, Detroit Public Library. Official 1886 returns gave four independent labor state legislative candidates an average of 3,169, but no labor votes were recorded in eight of the city's sixty-one precincts. The voting method makes it possible to estimate the labor vote in these precincts. Each voter cast seven state legislative votes for seven state representatives elected in a single citywide at-large district. In addition to the four fully independent labor candidates, three other labor candidates had been endorsed by the major parties and each of these ran ahead of the rest of the Democratic and Republican tick-

ets. In precincts where the labor vote *was* recorded, this plurality of Labor-Democrats and Labor-Republicans closely matches the vote received by the unendorsed labor candidates. Crediting labor candidates in the eight missing precincts with the fusion labor margin over regular party lines in those precincts would give the four unendorsed candidates an additional 437 votes. This may still underestimate the labor vote. Based on poll watchers' counts the *Advance and Labor Leaf* estimated the labor vote at 4,500.

52. *Unionist*, September 4, November 6, 1882.

53. Paul Kleppner, *The Cross of Culture* (New York, 1970) analyzes ethnocultural voting patterns in Detroit between 1888 and 1894, pp. 20–23, 204–14, and concludes that ethnocultural factors were more decisive determinants of voting behavior than class or economic factors. Kleppner's analysis is based on ward rather than precinct level returns, a poor unit of analysis given the heterogeneous character of Detroit's wards, but his conclusions are probably correct. For further analysis of voting patterns, see below.

54. These conclusions and the statistical analysis which follows in the text are based on Wayne County Election Records and a sample of potential voters drawn from the 1880 manuscript census and data provided by Olivier Zunz. For a discussion of the nature of these sources, see Note on Sources. The proportion of total labor votes coming from the German working class was estimated using a method similar to the one described by J. Morgan Kousser in "Ecological Regression and the Analysis of Past Politics," *Journal of Interdisciplinary History*, 4 (1973): 237–62. This yielded an estimate of 12.9 percent of German workers voting for ILP candidates, which would comprise 53 percent of total ILP votes. Given the quality of the original data and the limitations of this procedure, the results should be considered a rough indication of order of magnitude. The results from this method *are* consistent with a partial correlation analysis: Pearson's R for the correlation between labor vote and percent working class is .5569, but the partial correlation coefficient correcting for German working class is only .2987; i.e., percent German working class explains 72.3 percent of the effect of percent working class on variations in labor vote. (R^2_{wc}=.321; partial R^2_{wc} controlling for GWC=.089).

55. Melvin G. Holli, *Reform in Detroit, Hazen S. Pingree and Urban Politics* (New York, 1969), pp. 10–21; Judson Grenell, "Autobiography", p. 44.

56. Grenell, pp. 44–46; David Boyd to A. Inglis, November 29, 1938, LC.

57. *Unionist*, November 21, 1882; *Evening News*, November 6, 1884; *Labor Leaf*, November 8, 1884.

58. As noted in fn. 54, given the limitations of data and methodology, these results can only be taken as an indication of order of magnitude. See fn. 54 for the method of estimating these percentages. An alternative method, partial correlation analysis, suggests that the German preponderance among

skilled workers voting ILP was even greater. The percent *German* skilled workers explains 74.1 percent of the impact of percent skilled workers on variations in labor vote (i.e., $R^2_{SK}=.3221$; partial R^2_{SK} controlling for skilled German=.0799).

59. The partial correlation coefficient of labor vote with unskilled correcting for Germans is $-.082$.

60. Wayne County Election Records, 1884. Although percent Irish correlates $-.1940$ citywide, in four of these five precincts the percentage of Irish was well above the mean (mean percent Irish in the sample is 13.9 while the proportion of Irish in these precincts ranged from 21.0 to 52.6 percent).

61. With percent working class and percent German in the regression equation, the beta weights are .342 and .350 respectively. With Germans, skilled workers, and unskilled workers in the equation, beta weights are .388 for Germans, .296 for skilled workers, and statistically insignificant for unskilled workers.

62. Percent German working class explains 90.9 percent of the effect of percent German on variations in labor vote (i.e., $R^2_{Ger}=.3248$; partial R^2_{Ger} controlling for GWC=.0295); percent German skilled explains 92.7 percent of the effects of German working class on variations in labor vote (i.e., $R^2_{GWC}=.3113$; partial R^2_{GWC} controlling for skilled G=.0277).

63. Pearson's R:

	Native	*Canadian*	*British*	*Irish*	*German*	*Polish*
LV84	$-.6256$	$-.0211$	$-.1693$	$-.1940$	.5699	.0326

Other and unidentified
$-.1093$

In order to check that these correlations were not the result of variations in the class compositions of neighborhoods where different ethnic groups lived, I ran a series of partial correlations of each ethnic group with labor vote controlling for the percent *non*working class in the precinct with the following results:

	Native	*Canadian*	*British*	*Irish*	*German*	*Polish*
LV84	$-.2278$	$-.0851$	.1287	$-.1873$	.2996	$-.2643$

Note, however, that only the results for Germans and Poles pass a 95 percent significance test.

64. Even a cursory examination of election returns substantiates charges of false counts, although labor candidates were not the only victims. Candidates of all parties made such charges.

65. *Unionist*, October 30, November 6, 1882; *Labor Leaf*, October 21, 1885.

66. *Unionist*, October 2, 1882; *John Swinton's Paper*, April 20, 1884. The Tompkins Square demonstration against unemployment, held January 13, 1874, was attacked by police and several hundred were injured. The Mollie Maguires were a secret Irish organization (possibly part of the Ancient Order

of Hibernians) in the eastern Pennsylvania coal fields in the 1870s. Nineteen Irish coalminers were executed between 1877 and 1879 for alleged terrorist activities committed by the Molly Maguires. Supporters at the time and defenders since have been convinced the men were victimized for their labor activities. In 1887, four anarchists were executed for their alleged role in inspiring unnamed persons to throw a bomb at Chicago police during a demonstration in Haymarket Square the year before.

67. Detroit *Times*, April 10, 1881.

68. *Labor Leaf*, August 5, 1885.

69. *Labor Leaf*, December 30, 1885. Labadie to Richard T. Ely, July 4, 1885. Fine, "Ely-Labadie Letters."

70. *Labor Leaf*, February 10, 1886, January 6, 1886, November 4, 1885.

71. *Labor Leaf*, August 5, 1885, January 6, 1886.

72. Detroit *Unionist*, April 16, 1883; *Labor Leaf*, January 14, 28, August 5, November 18, 1885. The *Labor Leaf* was not alone in doubting Egan's motives. The Alpena *Labor Journal* charged he had "sold his position in the legislature to the Republicans for appointment as Deputy Commissioner of Labor," (July 2, 1886).

73. Detroit *Unionist*, November 20, 1882; *Spectator*, November 3, 1883; *Labor Leaf*, December 17, 1884, November 18, 1885; Detroit *Evening News*, September 3, 1886; *Labor Leaf*, September 29, 1886.

74. Detroit *Evening News*, November 2, 1882, November 2, 1886.

75. *Labor Leaf*, January 27, 1886.

76. Ibid., August 5, 1885.

77. Ibid., May 27, July 8, October 7, 1885; Detroit *Unionist*, December 4, 1882.

78. *Labor Leaf*, June 24, July 1, 8, 1885; Detroit *Unionist*, August 7, 1882.

79. *Labor Leaf*, December 31, 1884.

80. *Labor Leaf*, October 7, 1885.

81. David Boyd to A. Inglis, September 5, 1938, LC.

82. Grenell, p. 32; Detroit *Times*, April 24, 1881; Detroit *Unionist*, August 7, 1882; *Labor Leaf*, September 9, 1885; *Advance and Labor Leaf*, February 19, 1887; *Labor Leaf*, August 19, 1885. Copies of all these publications except the *Bulletin of Social Labor Movement* are available in the Labadie Collection, University of Michigan. The Detroit labor press has been the subject of an M.A. thesis: Siegfried B. Rolland, "The Detroit English Language Labor Press, 1839–1889" (Wayne State University, 1946).

83. Correspondence Files, LC.

84. See Oestreicher, Appendix 3, for background data on local labor leaders.

85. *Labor Leaf*, September 30, 1885.

86. Circular dated February 10, 1880, TVP. "Constitution of the Council of Trades and Labor Unions of Detroit, Michigan," Michigan *Truthteller*, April 2, 1880. The 1878 constitution of the Knights of Labor provided that up to one-quarter of an assembly's membership could be non-wage earners (usually farmers or artisans gone into business). Lawyers, bankers, liquor sellers, gamblers, and stock brokers were prohibited. Some scholars have exaggerated the proportion and significance of nonworkers in the Knights. In an 1888 survey of the Michigan SA, 4.4 percent of the respondents were farmers, and 4.3 percent were merchants and professionals (including small tradesmen), but this data was drawn from an overwhelmingly rural and small-town sample. There is no comparable data for Detroit. There were a few ex-wage earners turned politician or small businessman in the leadership in Detroit, but they were atypical. The Knights defended their choice of such men as public spokesmen on the grounds that their economic independence made them the only members not subject to employer reprisal. Only one of thirty-five early members of LA 901, for whom occupations are known, was not a worker. He was an ex-cigarmaker who operated a cigar and news stand.

87. Detroit *Times*, April 24, 1881; Detroit *National* cited in the *Socialist*, April 20, 1878.

88. The *Socialist*, April 20, 1878.

89. For example, see *Labor Leaf*, June 24, 1885, "Cranky Notes:" "They (The followers of various -isms) are fighting the same enemy, the same unyielding power that all labor reformers are fighting, and it is unreasonable to expect that all will use the same means of warfare."

90. Grenell, pp. 54–59; Detroit Labor Leaders File, LC; *Labor Leaf*, February 3, March 17, 1886.

91. *Labor Leaf*, August 5, 26, 1885.

92. *Labor Leaf*, February 17, 1886.

93. *Labor Leaf*, March 3, 10, 24, April 21, 1886.

5

A SUMMER OF POSSIBILITIES:
May Day to Labor Day, 1886

> The cry from every capitalistic quarter is now "Go slow!"
> But the cry comes too late.
>
> For years a few hated and despised agitators have warned
> people of breakers ahead, but they were looked upon with
> scorn and their warnings were unheeded.
>
> No power on earth can now avert a violent revolution
> . . . *the privileged classes* have invited a revolution and it
> will come down upon them with a relentless fury.
>
> The downfall of Capitalism is inevitable . . . When the
> revolution comes—and it isn't far off—he [a notoriously
> antiunion Wyandotte iron foundry owner] and the likes of
> him will pay the penalties of their brutal dominations, and I
> fear they may pay with their heads.
>
> Joseph Labadie, "Cranky Notions," March 24, 1886

One wonders what Mr. Muir (the foundry owner) and other Detroit manufacturers thought about Labadie's threat in the weeks that followed.[1] If any of them had a nervous disposition, the events of that spring must have been disconcerting. Since the summer of 1885 a series of dramatic strikes had been capturing national attention. The Saginaw Valley strike had shut down the state's most important lumber mills in July and August 1885. Two successful strikes conducted by the Knights of Labor against Jay Gould's Southwestern railroad system established the Knight's national reputation. That winter, as workers began to flock into the Knights of Labor in unprecedented numbers, local labor agitators launched a vigorous campaign to support a national general strike for the eight-hour day beginning May 1, 1886. As the deadline approached, the Detroit *Evening News* warned its readers that "the Greatest American Strikes [were] Impending." When a third great railroad strike broke out over the entire Gould system in March 1886, the *Labor*

Leaf's headlines expressed its belief that revolution was imminent. "THE REVOLUTION. Its Forerunner, the Great Railroad Strike."[2]

The 1886 eight-hour-day movement had been initiated by the nearly moribund national trade union federation, the Federation of Organized Trades and Labor Unions, at its 1884 convention. Although the federation was so weak that its own survival was in doubt, it had audaciously declared that "eight hours shall constitute a legal day's work from and after May 1, 1886." The federation had no funds, few followers, and had not specified how the eight-hour day was to be brought about, but scattered individuals and local unions seized on the idea as a way of mobilizing workers around a common demand. The Knights had nothing to do with starting the idea of an eight-hour deadline, but the notion fit perfectly into their vision of universal agitation and social reform. As the national strike fever spread through 1885, labor radicals, in particular, began to advocate a general strike for May 1, 1886.[3]

The eight-hour movement was first discussed in Detroit early in 1885. Charles Bell, a local leader of the IWPA, the Knights, and the typographical union, published "Pointers for Eight-Hour Agitation" in the *Labor Leaf* in February 1885. "The rate of wages does not depend upon the amount wage-earners produce," Bell argued, "but the amount they will consent to live upon and raise a family and perform labor." In a competitive economy, he reasoned, since the employer cannot fix prices, if workers demanded higher wages, employers would be forced to accept lower profits. Thus, although "the reduction of the hours would necessarily result in a reduction of the amount of wealth produced . . . this decrease in production would be a loss to employers . . . The hours of labor can be reduced until the production is just sufficient to replace the capital and sustain the wageworkers in their standard of living." If workers would simply refuse to work longer hours, the average standard of living would increase. In contrast, if workers accepted the advice of employers and moralists to live frugally, they were competing with each other and driving down the general living standard. The eight-hour movement would produce not only leisure and time for self-improvement, but a basic social advance. Higher wages would stimulate technological improvement and increase the general welfare. In the long run, reduction in hours would mean an increase in pay.[4]

The eight-hour day was not a new idea. Eight-hour leagues established by leaders of the National Labor Union had flourished in the 1860s,[5] but the notion that workers could alter the length of the working day by a single simultaneous mass act, rather than an incremental se-

145

ries of individual contracts or legislative initiatives, was new. The eight-hour deadline, in effect, amounted to an audacious assertion of workers' right and capacity to unilaterally redefine the social contract governing American class relations. The demand for immediate introduction had clear reformist implications beyond its immediate benefits. If workers could decree how long they would work, they could also dictate other terms of a renegotiated social contract. Radicals therefore viewed the eight-hour campaign as an open-ended reform, a first step toward a general transformation of the industrial system, not a cooptive amelioration designed to forestall more general change. It would be an impressive demonstration of labor's power. As workers recognized their power, organizers hoped, further demands would follow.[6]

Whether the workers who began to think about an eight-hour strike initially conceived of it in the same terms as its radical organizers is unclear. But as the idea caught on and gained a momentum that surprised even its organizers, it generated the excitement its instigators had imagined. For the first time in American history the possibility of a united and class-conscious working class seemed like more than the dream of radical theorists.[7]

Throughout 1885, plans for the eight-hour strike in Detroit slowly took on a definite form. In April 1885, the *Labor Leaf* announced the May 1, 1886, deadline for introduction of the "eight hour system." In July, the paper urged readers to begin to make plans for putting the system into effect on May 1, and in August, Labadie suggested a more specific mechanism—the formation of eight-hour leagues pledged to strike on May 1. Labadie and Henry Schulte kept up the demand for the May 1 strike into early 1886.[8] As the general tempo of labor agitation increased, the eight-hour idea began to catch on along with the Knights of Labor as a vehicle for its realization. Powderly opposed the idea of a general strike (as well as the rapid expansion of the order), but the Knights' most prominent leaders in Detroit were in the forefront of strike agitation.[9] Formal mass meetings publicizing the May 1 strike began in Detroit in early February under the auspices of a united front including the Trades Council, the SLP, the Knights, and the IWPA. The Detroit *Tribune* reported briefly on one of the first meetings in early February—a German eight-hour meeting of about 100 workers. By mid-February, meetings were being held nightly in different parts of the city. Labadie spoke three times in one week, twice for the Trades Council and once for the SLP. Other speakers that week included Charles Erb and Gustav Herzig of the SLP, Captain J. M. McGregor, Henry

Robinson, labor representatives Brant and Walthew, and August Spies, one of the Chicago leaders of the IWPA, as a guest speaker for the local IWPA.[10]

When, in the midst of this agitation, the Detroit Dry Dock Company decided to increase its shipcarpenters' hours from nine to ten, the shipcarpenters jumped the gun on the May 1 deadline by countering with a demand for eight hours. The company had paid its shipcarpenters $2.50 for ten hours the previous year. The mass enthusiasm for shorter hours had already been revealed when the men had agreed earlier in the year to accept a wage decrease to $2.00 in exchange for a reduction of the work day to nine hours. The Knights of Labor Shipcarpenters' Assembly 2124 held a meeting at Springwells (the suburban site of the dry dock) the first evening of the strike. Two hundred shipcarpenters attended, endorsing demands for the old rate of pay at twenty-five cents per hour, the eight-hour day (i.e., $2.00 for eight hours), double pay for overtime, weekly pay, no pay held back (the company, like many local companies, held back part of the pay for the entire season as a bond to prevent quitting), reinstatement for all strikers, and preference for Knights of Labor in new hires. Forty new members were signed up for the K. of L. assembly at the meeting.[11]

The same evening, 350 people met at Germania Hall to express their solidarity with the shipcarpenters and their support for the eight-hour day. Henry Schulte presided, as Charles Erb spoke, denouncing the company and arguing that workers were getting poorer. They had to "demand what their labor is worth." He suggested that local workers boycott all companies who used any of the Dry Dock Company's ships. Labadie and Herzig also spoke, proclaiming their support and announcing a Knights membership drive.[12]

By the next day, the newspapers reported that even the night watchmen and the errand boys had joined the strike in solidarity with the shipcarpenters. Workers had organized committees to patrol the docks for strikebreakers. If the employers tried to import Canadian strikebreakers as they had in the past, the workers would arrest the employer for violating the previously unenforced anti-alien contract labor law. The workers' committee appealed to the Knights DA to support their patrols and their agitation against imported strikebreakers, and to boycott all firms using non-union-made barges. A mass meeting sponsored by the DA three days later pledged the Knights' support for the duration of the strike. The Knights of Labor Shipcarpenters' Assembly had enrolled so many new members that the organization was difficult to manage, and they were considering dividing into two assemblies. Local shipyard workers who had never before considered joining a union were now solidly with the Knights of Labor for the eight-hour day. An old man spoke at the meeting with new-found fervor: "I have been told I am doing wrong in joining this strike. If I am, God forgive, but I don't know it. If any person will show me where it is wrong to ask pay for an extra hour's hard work I will go to the bosses, beg their forgiveness and begin work. But until this is explained to me I shall stand out, although I have a wife and seven children, to the bitter end." [13]

But the end was not bitter. After five weeks, the Dry Dock Company capitulated to all of the shipcarpenters' demands. Over 300 shipcarpenters had won the eight-hour day, and the Knights emerged not only as victors over the Dry Dock Company, but also as the symbol of imminent change. The May 1 strike took on even greater significance. On the day the shipcarpenters had settled with the Dry Dock Company, twenty-one brewery workers walked out of the Lion Brewing Company with demands similar to those of the dry dock workers. [14]

The shipcarpenters' strike demonstrated the underlying strength of the movement and the appeal of the eight-hour day. The Knights Shipcarpenters' Assembly 2124 had been agitating for years and could report only forty-five members by 1885, but it had led more than 300 men in the eight-hour struggle. The strike also revealed how the expectant atmosphere in 1886 gave what was initially a straightforward union struggle a transcendent quality. Workers had begun the strike only to resist an hour's increase, but they had quickly shifted to the demand for an hour's reduction and then to the whole list of additional grievances. As they began to patrol the docks with the assistance of the DA to enforce the anti-alien-contract labor law, the Knights were starting, in effect, to assume limited police functions. Objectively, all of the demands might still be classified as essentially bread-and-butter economic demands, but the movement behind them had assumed a millenarian quality. Perhaps for the first time workers believed they could change the industrial system. Solidarity meetings drew crowds much larger than the shipcarpenters' own meetings, and workers from other trades assisted in the boycott of firms using the company's barges. Grenell complained in early April that he and other organizers had spoken at so many meetings that all the movement's leaders were approaching total exhaustion, but the results were gratifying. Nightly mass meetings of several hundred were raising the specter of a class-conscious working class which gave all demands a symbolic significance far beyond the proposals themselves.[15]

The movement had generated the kind of enthusiasm which disrupted normal patterns of daily life and led people in directions that might have been unthinkable a few months before. In stable periods, workers' struggle for survival bred an inner caution and a defensive posture. Their problem was to accommodate to a hostile social environment without sacrificing too much of the cultural traditions which gave meaning to their lives and the strength they needed. For people who doubted the possibilities of drastically changing economic relationships, social relations appeared to be permanent and natural arrangements. From this perception, thoughts and actions which ran contrary to the existing structure of society seemed not only hopelessly utopian but personally dangerous; they threatened the individual's capacity to survive in apparently permanent institutions.

Once the existing social structure is thus reified, even minimal demands are difficult to justify rationally. Shorter hours might be a fine idea, but if it is necessary to strike to shorten the workday, the risks of losing a job which is the means of survival must outweigh the possible gains of an extra hour or two of leisure. The eight-hour movement could not justify itself by the normal calculus of risks and benefits. That large numbers of workers were willing to undertake dangerous actions (i.e., striking) in behalf of shorter hours implicitly indicated a consciousness of social alternatives beyond the demand itself, especially when the offensive nature of the eight-hour strike is compared to the overwhelmingly defensive character of major strikes in the previous decade.[16]

In the very process of taking normally unthinkable actions, even for limited demands, people's capacity to envision further alternatives expanded. When workers responded to Grenell's eight-hour speeches by telling him that they had asked their bosses for eight hours and employers had claimed they could not afford to operate on shorter hours, Grenell answered that they should "*demand an accounting*! Make every employer show his balance sheet! Let him not hide behind the phrase: *This is my business.*" Grenell was suggesting a rejection of property rights in a specific case, but he hoped that the example would lead people to more general conclusions about the whole concept of property rights. If the employer did not have uncontestable property rights over his business, then this implied a social definition of property; society could specify limits over how the property was to be used.

Once the justice of the shorter workday was assumed a priori, then alternative social arrangements necessary to make it possible followed. The normal order of priorities, of practicality over utopianism, was reversed. If examination of the employer's records revealed he could function under a shorter workday, then refusal to do so undermined his integrity and claims to social responsibility. He was either greedy or a liar. If he could not in fact survive, then that raised the possibility of systemic criticisms: what was wrong with a system which could not provide a minimal amount of leisure for its workers, and what changes were necessary to make that possible? Thus, once eight hours became a *nonnegotiable* demand, the door was opened for the most fundamental leap in mass consciousness: the concept of social alternatives.[17]

Some of the city's employers recognized their workers' mood. At the end of March, one of the cigar factories, Brown Brothers, suggested to its workers that they join the Knights of Labor. Pingree and Smith and the Detroit *Free Press*, both long-standing holdouts against the Knights of Labor and the typographical union, settled about the same time as the Dry Dock Company. Six small brewery owners accepted the eight-hour demand in April without a fight.[18]

By the last two weeks in April, new members were streaming into the Knights of Labor at the rate of several dozen per day. Seven hundred were initiated in two weeks—as many new members as the total membership of DA 50 only six months before. District Master Workman J. D. Long wrote in the *Journal of United Labor*: "The only trouble we have now is to keep men out of the Order."[19]

May 1 came on a Saturday. The banner headlines on the front page of the *Evening News* reminded readers that this was "THE FATEFUL DAY, Looked For With Anxiety by Employers and Employed," but judging from the accompanying story, local employers did not need to be reminded. Managers of the city's most important factories had shown "a keen appreciation of the signs of the times," according to the *News* reporter, and the stove companies had granted 10 percent wage increases in hopes of deflating the movement. The immediate impact of the general strike was difficult to gauge since Saturday was a short day for many firms anyway. The shipcarpenters and employees of six breweries had already been granted eight hours. The carpenters had reached a compromise with many of the city's building contractors—nine hours per day beginning one year from the present date. Strikes were expected in the rest of the city's breweries. Reports from other industries were very limited, but the situation was much quieter than many people had expected. Ministers devoted their Sunday sermons to the strikes. The Reverend H. C. Northrup of the Methodist Episcopal Church in a mildly pro-eight-hour speech claimed that May 1, 1886, "would ever be a memorable day in this country," but he was a bit vague on how it would be remembered.[20]

By Monday morning, it seemed that the whole affair might be anticlimactic. One more brewery owner had conceded, but the other brewery workers had struck. Sixty cracker bakers had struck for eight-and-one-half hours per day with five-and-one-half on Saturdays. The painters were demanding a nine-hour day instead of eight. Four hundred of them had agreed to go to work on Monday but to stop working after nine hours regardless of what employers said. Sixty lumberyard workers had struck in suburban Springwells. School janitors were scheduled to meet that night to discuss strike plans. But the strike was hardly a general strike. Editors of the *News* concluded that the lack of disturbance was "calculated to encourage the hope that the present difficulties may be adjusted, confidence restored and the wheels of industry started again, without that disastrous and widespread disturbance that a few days ago was predicted . . ."[21]

Their optimism was premature. The Michigan Car Works, which had laid off 125 men on Saturday, fired P. J. Clair Monday morning. Clair, a carpenter, had been the Knights of Labor organizer in the factory. The Knights had been organizing secretly in the car works for several weeks, but they had only a small nucleus and the organizers had considered a May 1 strike premature. Perhaps the company's management wanted to force the Knights' hand before the workers were ready. Certainly the mass layoffs on the first day of the projected eight-hour strike were provocative, and firing Clair left absolutely no doubt that company owners were ready to fight. The editors of the *News* contrasted the car works' managers' "lack of spirit and conciliation" with those of the stove companies, who had prepared for the strike by granting modest wage increases.[22]

On receiving word of his firing, Clair and a handful of friends went from department to department informing workers what had happened and urging them to strike. A growing crowd followed him as he forced his way into the plant manager's office. Clair's supporters demanded his reinstatement, a reduction in hours, and an increase in pay. With the expected refusal, the workers marched out of the factory shortly after noon. By one o'clock, as more workers left the factory, the crowd had swelled to an estimated 1,500. People milled around in front of the car works, filling the adjoining streets. The *Labor Leaf* conceded that the men had been "unorganized" and initially "the strike was little less than a mob." Various people shouted suggestions to march on other railroad car factories to shut them down. One group, allegedly armed with clubs, marched to the Spring Works, a nearby subsidiary of the car works. Others tried to shut down the Michigan Car Works foundry.[23]

The sheriff arrived with two deputies, but after surveying the situation, he just stood back and watched. His statements to the press suggested possible sympathies with the strikers. "I dread these strikes, but I will do all the law requires of me to protect property . . . What can I do against 2,000 men?" Forty city police arrived shortly thereafter with paddy wagons. Recognizing that their forces were still inadequate to control the crowd, they stationed themselves between the car works and the Spring Works to break the workers' line of march, but the 300 employees of the Spring Works had apparently seen the crowd coming before the police arrived, and the Spring Works was already shut down before the police set up their lines.[24]

The crowd began to march systematically from one factory to the next, calling on other workers to join them. The car workers' step-by-step movements suggest advanced planning. At the very least, the possibility of joining the May 1 strikes must have been widely discussed before the car works firing triggered the Monday afternoon walkouts. As the crowd went from factory to factory, the plants emptied almost spontaneously, sometimes in advance of the arrival of the marchers. Little explanation was necessary, so that if there had not actually been some advance planning, there had at least been enough prior discussion to make many workers in other factories psychologically ready to join a strike as soon as it presented itself. Newspaper reports asserted that workers in many factories had been driven out against their will, but the newspapers' own accounts of the successive shutdowns, as well as the willingness of workers in all of these factories to remain on strike on following days after the crowd was gone, imply exactly the opposite conclusion.[25] By late afternoon, the number of strikers had swelled to 3,000, and a committee had been set up to establish demands.

The symbolic emotional character of the strike is perhaps best revealed by this tendency to formulate strike goals only after decisive action had been taken. The workers had shut down one factory after another as a display of power, a gesture of defiance. Where plant managers were willing to defer to this spirit, people remained at work and those who had struck seemed to feel that to do so was no breach of solidarity. The stove works, whose managers had made a gesture to the workers' power in the prestrike wage increase, continued to run throughout the strikes at other factories. At the Griffin Car Wheel Works the plant superintendent agreed to meet with the marching strikers when they arrived and offered his employees a reduction from ten hours to nine and a fifteen-cents-per-day wage increase. Both the car wheel employees and the strikers seemed satisfied as the factory resumed work.[26] It was as if the city's workers had collectively decided to establish the principle of negotiation; any concession was sufficient because it established the workers' right to set terms and therefore opened the door to future gains. Perhaps for this reason the Griffin Car Wheel settlement was almost immediately seized upon by the car workers' committee. By Monday evening their demands were reinstatement of Clair and nine hours with a fifteen-cent-per-day wage increase for all car workers.

The car workers' action had provided the catalyst that had been missing over the weekend; the display of mass marchers shutting down a succession of factories stimulated further militance in other trades which had hesitated to take action. By that evening the number of painters pledged to nine hours had tripled to 1,200. Brewery workers, who had already shut down all of the breweries that had not accepted eight hours, escalated with actions against saloon owners who were selling beer made by the struck companies. Already the previous weekend the *News* had noted the sudden emergence of "union beer only on tap" signs all over the city. On Monday evening, workers began systematically entering saloons selling nonunion beer, ordering "drinks for the house," and then refusing to drink it and walking out without paying. By Tuesday, most of the brewery owners had capitulated. Hostile actions by some employers further swelled the ranks of strikers. The Diamond Match Company, for example, locked out 235 workers.[27]

The tone of Tuesday's newspapers, which included reports of "A RIOT IN CHICAGO" and "Serious Trouble Anticipated in Milwaukee" as well as "General Discontent . . . In All Quarters" of Detroit, reflected the suddenly changed situation. Editorials in the Detroit *News* had been sympathetic to the eight-hour movement all spring despite some apprehension about the strike, but the paper's editorial position shifted dramatically after Monday's events. As the strike continued to escalate each day, the editorials criticized and ridiculed the workers. At the same time, they tried to calm middle- and upper-class readers. "KEEP COOL," the newspaper pleaded on Wednesday as the editor warned, "The average conservative citizen—that is the citizen who has accumulated property and is tolerably satisfied with his prospects—will read his paper with mingled feelings of fear and indignation." The workers for whom the editors had expressed sympathy a few days before were now in their eyes nothing more than "mobs of foreigners," but that in itself was comforting because "mobs cannot live without food, and food can be had only by work." "There isn't an average of two day's supplies in the houses of any of these disorderly foreigners who are now inebriating themselves with cheap beer and the cheaper socialist fustian of their orators . . . the humility and weakness begotten of hunger and necessity will succeed the flamboyancy engendered by beer. The desire to overturn and regenerate society will give way to the urgent necessity of satisfying the demand of that most potent of tyrants, the human stomach."[28] Stories were also designed to dampen the enthusiasm of strikers. A recapitulation of strike events in Tuesday's *News* led off with headlines suggesting that prominent local leaders, including Joseph Labadie, were critical of the strikes. Yet the accompanying story revealed that it was a minor disturbance at Springwells that a few labor leaders had questioned, not the strikes at the car works and other major factories. Stories repeatedly implied that the strike wave was collapsing, that strikers were returning to work, "The End Approaching," only to report two or three days later that the strike continued unabated. It is not clear whether major employers were pressuring the newspapers or editors were acting on their own conceptions of civic duty. Perhaps in a conflict atmosphere, class loyalties were strengthened on both sides.[29]

The polarization of the community was also manifested in the way local authorities mobilized against the strike. All policemen had been ordered to serve double duty Monday night, and the city's superintendent of police had issued orders to precinct captains to ignore routine business. Except for extreme emergencies, police were to remain in station houses for massing at strategic points. The police superintendent claimed the city's entire police force could be concentrated at any point in the city within twenty-five minutes. Some business owners threatened to take action on their own. Harry Newberry, secretary and treasurer of the Steel and Spring Works, was quoted by one reporter as he confronted some of the workers who had just shut down his factory: "I've got a right to defend my property from any mob, and tomorrow I'll be on hand prepared to shoot the first man who tries to stop the engine."[30]

Strike leaders, in comparison, exercised restraint. When 2,000 men, including several hundred sympathizers, arrived at the Michigan

Car Works by 6:30 Tuesday morning to prevent any strikebreakers from entering the factory, P. J. Clair urged them to remain peaceful. The strike was spreading on its own accord, and the men had to organize themselves and avoid provocative actions. The men remained in the streets in front of the factory discussing the strike. Speeches were given in English, German, and Polish. By evening, workers had created an effective strike committee. To demonstrate their discipline and organization, as they left the men formed into military ranks and marched in formation down Russell Avenue to Gratiot and up Michigan Avenue before breaking ranks to return home.[31]

They returned Tuesday evening to "one of the largest gatherings of workingmen ever held in this city," a solidarity meeting which overflowed into the streets because it was too large for any hall in the city. Three thousand people heard speeches by Frank Reichlin (a leader of the shipcarpenters' LA and a DA 50 executive board member), A. M. Dewey (of the typographical union and the DA), Clair, George Vornberger (chairman of the German Central Labor Union), and Charles Erb, recently elected Trades Council president. Erb contrasted the "McMillan's palaces" with the workers' homes. "Machinery was introduced for the welfare of humanity and not to oppress labor and benefit a class." As he compared the car shops to prisons, declaring "the men want one hour less imprisonment," the audience broke into cheers. "Stand firm," Erb advised them.[32]

On Wednesday, the number of shorter-hours strikers topped 5,000. The Peninsular Car Company's employees remained at work Monday and Tuesday because the company's pay day was on Wednesday. The workers had decided to continue work until they had been paid since most had no savings or other resources to carry them through even a short strike. They would join the strike around noon Wednesday.[33] Strike leaders carefully planned a dramatic series of marches to emphasize this addition to the strikers' ranks, enlist community support, and demonstrate the movement's growing power. Workers were to gather at the Michigan Car Company Wednesday morning. They would march across town through various working-class neighborhoods and arrive at the Peninsular Car Company as the Peninsular's workers left the plant. A second march that evening was to return to the large square in front of the Michigan Car Works where workers from both car companies would be joined by striking workers from other industries in a massive rally.[34]

A *Tribune* reporter received permission from strike leader Clair to march at his side and witness the day's events. The reporter's descriptions of both the marching strikers and enthusiastic observers revealed a mixture of fear and grudging admiration for the workers' discipline and determination. Two thousand marchers arrived at the Michigan works, according to the reporter's estimate. If his guess is accurate, the march included a substantial proportion of sympathizers: the number of Michigan Car Company strikers had been estimated at only 1,200 the day before. Clair and a group of strike marshals organized the marchers into military formation, dividing them into "troops by trade" or squads of forty. The quickness with which this was accomplished and the orderliness of the march impressed the reporter, who had probably expected the mobs of unruly foreigners his editors had been describing. The march proceeded quietly until it entered residential neighborhoods described by the reporter as "working class districts." There the car workers seemed to be a symbol for the entire community's grievances, acting not just for themselves but for the working class as a whole. The reporter stuck close to Clair at the head of the march, apparently convinced that Clair's presence was necessary for his safety. People shouted from windows and rooftops, waved, and gestured their approval. "Good Luck!" "Give it to 'em." "That's the stuff for the laboring man." As they arrived at the Peninsular works, they were joined by the Peninsular workers, and the combined crowd heard speeches by strike leaders in English, German, and Polish.[35]

That evening the workers marched a second time down two of the city's main thoroughfares, Gratiot and Michigan avenues. As the estimated 2,500 marchers arrived in the large square in front of the Michigan Car Works, they merged with a crowd of more than 1,000 already there. The police maintained a low profile: a corporal's guard of only twenty men watched from across the street. Speakers pursued the same theme of class division that Erb had emphasized the night before. Vornberger, speaking in German, argued that workers built Pullman's cars but could not afford to ride in them. A. M. Dewey followed him in English with a similar argument. The strike was part of the larger struggle of contemporary society. Workers deserved a share of the profits of industry. Strike leaders warned the workers about police infiltrators in the Knights of Labor and business threats of vigilante violence. Henry Robinson described conversations with business leaders the past two days. "I don't fancy this strike business at all," one employer had told Robinson. "We will organize an armed league and shoot those fellows all down if this thing keeps on." Robinson ridiculed such threats of violence, but a speech by an old Irish worker employed at the Peninsular Car Works implied that workers were ready to meet force with force. James Barney said "he had been an old soldier and had enlisted for another war."[36]

The system of daily marches and mass meetings developed during the first few days continued throughout the strikes. The meetings and marches fulfilled several practical and psychological functions. Workers kept busy and remained directly and immediately involved in the movement. In some ways, the lack of formal organization helped to maintain this involvement. There was no official bureaucracy to organize picket lines, establish demands, arrange publicity, and maintain communication; the workers had to do these things themselves. While a small group of informal leaders assumed decision-making roles, these decisions had to be validated daily by the strike meetings. There were no means of applying sanctions on individuals who failed to meet the obligations of solidarity except through informal group pressure. Mass picketing at plant gates bolstered spirits as well as intimidating those who might have otherwise considered returning to work. Continual reaffirmation of solidarity was essential. If the strike started to break and any sizable number of strikers returned to work, the position of the remainder would be untenable. The car workers had no union or contractual protection, no seniority rights. The companies could rehire anyone they wished. Those who remained on strike once the companies began hiring again could easily be refused employment. The strike meetings were thus a ritual of reaffirmation; each striker publicly presented himself daily and reasserted solidarity with the group.

The meetings were also the primary means of communication, essential because of both the hostility and inaccuracy of newspaper coverage and the multilingual character of the strikers. At strike meetings, strikers could be informed in their own languages of the progress of negotiations and assured that newspaper reports of back-to-work movements were false. Newspaper descriptions of nearly all major strike meetings noted the presence of speakers in three languages: English, German, and Polish. Meetings also provided an opportunity to arrange emergency assistance for families who needed it. On Friday, May 7, for example, thirty-five loaves of bread and fourteen pounds of cheese were distributed to needy workers during a meeting of 500 Peninsular Car Company employees.[37]

The marches served many of the same functions as strike meetings and mass picketing, but they also established solidarity beyond the plant level and visibly demonstrated the overall strength of the shorter-hours movement. Except for a few of the largest and most important meetings, meetings were for the workers of a particular plant. Michigan Car Company workers congregated at the Michigan works, Pullman Company workers at the Pullman factory, Peninsular workers at the Peninsular works; painters held painters' meetings, brewery workers held brewers' meetings. Mass marches were designed to bring everyone together from all of the striking factories. They were a gesture of class power and as such also served a crucial purpose in the negotiating process. The *Tribune*'s editors expressed middle- and upper-class reaction to the marches in an editorial on Thursday, May 6. "Bloodshed in other cities and the unsettled state of labor in Detroit contributed to the feeling of uneasiness among the citizens generally yesterday . . . The sight of hundreds of men marching through the streets to the music of their heel taps was not an inspiring sight."[38]

A surprising number of companies began to offer concessions to the strikers almost immediately after the marches began. The master painters refused the striking painters' demand of nine hours but offered a half day on Saturday or a fifty-five-hour week. Most of the brewery companies accepted the eight-hour day by Wednesday. One brewery owner who hired scabs and held out until Saturday finally settled and agreed to pay the union a $780 indemnity for his intransigence: $50 for each day he had refused to settle, $35 for each union member he had fired, and $50 to cover the union's expense of printing boycott circulars against him. The Globe Tobacco Company offered its workers a choice between eight hours six days per week, or longer hours Monday through Friday with only half days on Saturdays (the workers chose the latter). The stove companies, who had already granted a 10 percent wage increase on May 1, offered two hours off every Saturday if their men would stay at work. Even the Michigan Car Company agreed to negotiate and offered to accept the reduction from ten to nine hours per day if the men would accept a corresponding wage decrease instead of an increase.[39]

These concessions must be viewed as a direct response to the spectacle of mass marches. The strikes had not been underway long enough to represent any serious economic pressure on firms. Some employers may have offered concessions because they had sympathy with the movement, but even if that was the case, the marches and the strikes had been essential prods. The eight-hour system had been actively discussed for months before the strikes began, but few employers had been willing to make any concessions at all until the eve of the strikes, and the extent of such concessions expanded tremendously as the mass marches dramatized the strike.

The strike wave reached its peak by the weekend of May 8 and 9. On Saturday, May 8, the *Tribune* estimated the number on strike at 5,146. The strikers represented a cross section of Detroit's industries. In addition to 3,400 employees of four railroad car manufacturers, there were painters, cracker bakers, lumber mill workers, sewer construction laborers, chair and match factory employees, steam forge workers, foundry workers, tannery workers, sailors, lumberyard workers, coopers, and a variety of other metal trades. Yet even this list greatly underestimates both the number and range of participants in the shorter-hour movement. Close to a thousand strikers had already returned to work under successful settlements, while thousands more who had threatened to strike had negotiated some reduction in their workday before the strike deadline. The total number of workers who had struck for shorter hours since March or had arranged shorter hours through negotiations was probably nearly double the *Tribune*'s estimates.[40]

But the significance of the shorter-hours movement lay not only in its numbers. For the first time the labor movement superceded the multiplicity of fragmentary forces to tap a broad constituency of workers outside its ranks. The shorter-hours campaign cut across the competing loyalties of ethnicity, craft, neighborhood, and status. Polish-, German-, and English-speaking workers pledged their solidarity to each other. Skilled workers who had reached satisfactory agreements with their own employers engaged in widespread sympathetic boycott actions for workers still on strike. Bricklayers, masons, and carpenters refused to work on buildings employing painters while the contractors and master painters had not settled with the painters.[41]

More than half of the shorter-hours movement's participants had not belonged to any labor organization prior to the strikes. Thousands of them now joined the Knights of Labor and various trade unions. When Wendell Phillips Local Assembly 4293, P. J. Clair's assembly, met during the first week of the strike, the hall was filled to capacity with members standing in the street outside. Clair went inside with a long list of names to be considered for membership, and a mass initiation quickly followed.[42] The painters' local assembly (1820) claimed 400 members by the second week of the strike and had made plans for a cooperative paint company. The coopers' union enrolled its entire membership in the Knights and became a new local assembly. The tailors' union followed suit.[43]

Even employers who steadfastly refused to accept the workers' strike demands tried to appear conciliatory. When the Michigan Car Company workers refused the company's offer of nine hours with nine hours' pay, the company's manager offered to allow representatives of the workers to examine the company's books in order to convince them that a wage increase or even the old rate of pay for nine hours (i.e., ten hours' pay for nine hours) was impossible.[44]

Daily strike marches continued into the second week, but by the third week, some strikers began to weaken. The car workers had begun to organize a car workers' union: 464 workers had paid one dollar each as an initiation fee, and nearly twice that number had been at the union's first meeting. The car companies were adamant, however. The superintendent of the Michigan Car Company, apparently retracting earlier offers of conciliation, vowed to keep the factory closed all summer if necessary. Final pay checks had kept the workers going up to this point, but many families were beginning to face real distress.[45]

On Tuesday, May 18, the Pullman workers, upon receiving word of the collapse of the strike at the main Pullman factory in Pullman, Illinois, voted to return to work, but the Michigan and Peninsular car workers decided to continue the strike and to prevent scabs from entering the factories by force, if necessary. On Monday, they had ringed the Michigan Car Company with a mass picket line. When a supervisor, Engineer Metzenfeldt, pulled his revolver on the pickets, he was stoned. The company had recruited scabs from out of town, but apparently the car workers had received information about this and had prepared themselves. A group of strikers had hidden behind coal cars in a railroad siding near the factory entrance. When the police began to escort the strikebreakers into the factory, at a prearranged signal the hidden strikers climbed on top of the railroad cars and began pelting the scabs. The factory remained closed for the day. But the following day the police were better prepared. Seventy police ringed the Michigan works early Tuesday morning to prevent strikers from getting close to the factory. The "Cleveland scabs" arrived heavily armed and entered the factory at gunpoint. While some strikers had reportedly also been seen with revolvers, they were not ready to undertake a gun battle in order to keep the strikebreakers out.[46]

By the end of the third week of the strike, the car workers' position was growing desperate. A benefit ball held in midweek raised $900 for their support, but that would not go far for some 2,000 car workers and their families. On Wednesday, May 19, shots were reportedly fired at strikebreakers at the Michigan Works, and a group of Polish strikers told strikebreakers, "You are going to be killed," but the strikebreakers avoided confrontation on Thursday by arriving at the factory at 2:00 A.M. On Thursday, Clair went to visit James McMillan, owner of the Michigan works, to convince him to change his position. McMillan refused, and although the car works strikers were still solid, the end was clear.[47]

By Saturday, May 22, most of the factories in the city, other than the car works, had resumed operations. The car workers were becoming increasingly isolated. As reports began to circulate that the car companies were advertising widely in Cleveland and other cities for new workers, a trickle of car workers began to reapply for work. Many applications were refused while other workers were told to come back next week. The car works strike was becoming a lockout. Clair was not to be rehired under any circumstances. The Polish laborers at the Michigan Car Company pledged to stick with Clair. "One go, all go" a group had reportedly declared in pidgin English at a weekend strike meeting, but by the middle of the next week, it was clear that this was a futile gesture. Clair formally absolved them of any obligations to him. Some workers stayed out with him, nonetheless, while the company refused to rehire about half of those who applied. When the Michigan Car Company officially resumed operations on Wednesday, May 26, there were still about 1,000 workers on strike in the city according to the *Tribune*, but by June 1, the only group of workers still reported out on strike were 150 painters.[48]

Yet the car workers' defeat and the collapse of the eight-hour strike did not have the discouraging consequences that might have been expected. Evaluated from the immediate point of view of the eight-hour demand, the movement had been at best a mixed success. It had not produced a general strike: at its peak less than a fifth of the city's industrial workers were on strike, and the total number of participants including those who arranged compromise settlements without striking was only one-third.[49] For the more than 3,000 car workers, the strike resulted in no tangible improvements. But most of the other strikers had received some concessions. At the end of May Grenell estimated that 5,000 workers had gained some reduction in hours since May 1, with an average decrease of eight hours per week. Twenty-four hundred stove company employees had received a 10 percent wage increase. These results were impressive. The city's labor movement had had no more than 5,000 members at the end of 1885. "In spite of what the capitalistic press say, the short hour movement has been more successful than its most optimistic friends dared to anticipate."[50] But the movement's greatest importance was not the immediate gains. The eight-hour movement had brought thousands of workers who had never before participated in labor organizations into a bitter conflict which revealed to them, and to their employers, their potential power. Dozens of employers who had never previously recognized labor organizations or the concept of collective bargaining had been forced to negotiate with their employees. Skilled and unskilled, natives, Germans, Poles, and Irish had come together in the crisis atmosphere of a protracted strike and for the first time learned to act together. While they had been beaten this time, the experience convinced them that there could be a next time, that they could change the industrial system. Class relations had been changed in Detroit in a way no amount of writing, speech making, or exhortation could ever have accomplished.

Union and Knights of Labor membership, which had increased rapidly in the weeks before the strike, now shot up even faster. At the first meeting of the carworkers' union held after the end of the strike, P. J. Clair submitted a list of nearly 2,000 names of workers who wished to join the union. The Knights especially, with their image as a universal class organization, expanded at a staggering rate. Detroit Knights of Labor membership had probably been under 1,000 as late as December 1885. Several hundred joined in the early months of 1886; 700 in the last two weeks of April 1886 and at least another 500 in the first two weeks of May. But over 2,000 more joined between the end of the strike and the first of July and an additional 3,000 between July 1 and September 1. Membership was increasing so rapidly that official totals were already out of date by the time they were reported to national headquarters. By the end of the summer, the *Evening News* estimated Knights of Labor membership in the Detroit area at 8,000, nearly twice that reported to the general secretary treasurer on July 1, and total union and Knights of Labor membership at over 13,000, compared to only 5,000 just eight months before.[51]

Even more important than this quantitative leap was the qualitative leap that went with it. Thousands of new members fresh with the enthusiasm of direct action entered into the daily activities of the oppositional subculture that activists had so laboriously nurtured for the previous decade. If these people could be permanently incorporated

162

into the reinforcing world of a counterculture, the spring and summer surge of labor activity could lead to a fundamental realignment of the balance between the competing cultural systems that had divided the city's workers. The mood in Detroit during the summer of 1886 reflected widespread belief in history in the making—a belief that such a realignment was taking place. The newspapers for the first time treated normal business of labor organizations as major news. Biographical studies of local labor leaders became regular fare in the feature pages.

Actions by employers also suggested a belief in the rapidly growing power of labor. Some employers displayed an almost hysterical belligerence—firing anyone even associating with the Knights of Labor and locking out their employees at the first sign of any demands. Others were conciliatory, almost obsequious, fawning over the Knights' DA executive board, and offering all manner of free gifts to be given away at the scheduled Labor Day celebration. Both reactions suggest uncertainty, a sense that employers also believed that power relations were changing, and they would either have to fight or accommodate themselves to a new power.[52]

The invigorated labor organizations prepared to utilize their gains. The Independent Labor party, confident that fall elections would validate the belief in the movement's new strength, began organizing for the fall campaign in early summer. A massive convention was planned for the first week in September with more than 150 delegates elected from all of the city's labor organizations.[53] The Knights opened a new Labor Headquarters in May with meeting rooms for unions, Knights of Labor assemblies, and other workers' organizations. Free reading rooms stocked a full selection of labor papers and gave workers a place to relax.[54] Educational programs flourished, reflecting the desire of the large numbers of new members to learn more about the movement's philosophy as well as the fundamentals of political economy. LA 901 reported in late June that it had distributed 10,000 eight-hour tracts since the beginning of the eight-hour campaign and sold 300 copies of Grenell's booklet, "Robbers of the Nineteenth Century." LA 2348 ordered 100 subscriptions to the *Labor Leaf* for use by its members, and the Machinists and Blacksmiths' LA (7750) ordered another fifty. In August, a labor play, produced by the Knights, played to packed houses at the Detroit Opera House, one of the city's largest theaters.[55]

The culmination of the summer and the high point in popular participation was the Labor Day Parade held on September 6. The previous fall's march had been held at night, like most movement activities, so as not to conflict with work schedules. Perhaps the best indication that workers believed in August 1886 that they could make history, that they had seized at least some power over their own destinies, was the decision to hold the march and celebration on a Monday at midday. Labor Day was not a legal holiday. Unlike all other holidays, the idea did not come from a legislature, or city council or mayor, or corporate executive, but from the workers' own organizations. The first Monday in September would be a workers' holiday not because some outside authority gave them permission, but because enough workers decided it would be a holiday by going to the march instead of going to work. Employers would be forced to recognize the workers' decision because too few people came to work to run the factories. Thus, although those who promoted the idea scrupulously avoided the use of the term, in effect the first Monday in September was to be made a general holiday through a general strike.[56]

The evening demonstration the year before had drawn 3,000 marchers. Some workers had been scared away from that march by rumors that employers had hired Pinkerton agents as spotters to record names of participants for reports to employers. Subsequent firings had confirmed the rumors. Firings for union and Knights of Labor membership had not ceased in the year following the October 1885 march. The planned September 6 public holiday was an audacious undertaking. Despite all the events of the spring and summer, and especially after the failure of many of the May strikes, workers were still aware of the potential danger of publicly identifying themselves with the labor movement. Predemonstration publicity treated the day as a light-hearted affair—a parade followed by a massive family picnic—but if only 3,000 workers had shown up, the consequences might not have been so light hearted. Typographical union parade chairman Robert Ogg alluded to this in an understated personal appeal to all printers in the last issue of the *Labor Leaf* published before the demonstration: "It behooves us at this particular time to show our strength."[57]

They did. Workers began arriving at Grand Circus Park, the staging area, more than two hours before the scheduled starting time. Marchers had been assigned to eleven divisions according to trade, industry, and organizational affiliation. Each division had a marshal who organized the marchers into ranks. Although "the sidewalks and every available space was occupied by sight-seers," many trades had been drilling in anticipation of the march, and they sorted themselves out with a minimum of confusion. When Chief Marshal Judson Grenell gave the order to march, there were, according to the *Labor Leaf*, "Ten Thousand Men in Line." Marching four abreast with banners, floats, and carriages for speakers and the members of Florence Nightingale Assembly, the procession was three miles long, "the first division entering the gardens [Miller's Gardens, the destination] about the time the last division started from Grand Circus Park."[58]

It was a workers' march and a workers' holiday. Although thousands of friends, family, and curiosity seekers lined the parade route or waited at the gardens, except for a few small visiting delegations from other cities, the marchers were all affiliated with various Detroit labor organizations. The class character of the holiday was clear in the responses of home owners along the parade route. While many homes were decorated with banners, and residents along the way greeted thirsty marchers with ice water, the *Labor Leaf* noted that "the only private residence on Jefferson Avenue [a well-to-do neighborhood] which was decorated was that of Moses W. Field [a local Greenback-Labor politician], who himself stood in front and received a tribute of cheers to signify his courtesy was understood."[59]

Floats and banners depicted the activities of the various trades. The printers' float included a working press printing facsimile copies of the *Labor Leaf*. The cigarmakers' float represented "a scab cigar factory decorated with a 'golden pheasant'" [an allusion to a brand name of one of the local nonunion shops] and with union leader Sam Goldwater, as a tyrannical owner, threatening "the scabs" with his whip. The car workers' union turned out 1,500 men behind a miniature freight car. Slogans included the usual range of reform proposals, but some reflected the tone of new militancy. "One significant motto," the *Labor Leaf* noted, "read 'Divided we can beg; united we can demand,' and thousands of the spectators appreciated its meaning."[60]

At the gardens, speech makers kept things short, but Henry Robinson's closing speech evoked a great response. Robinson spoke with his small daughter at his side.

> I do not represent any large interests. I certainly do not represent bags of dollars nor piles of bricks nor any of those things wrung from the workingman. I have with me today my daughter. She is a bigger interest than all the millions of dollars represented in the big interests. Gentlemen, I wish to bring about such a condition as will give my daughter and your daughters and your sons a chance to get a fair shake in life after we have gone . . . history shows that the aristocracy

had not been satisfied with robbing the workers of their earnings, but they have also striven to despoil them of their virtue. We all know that our aristocracy is the same as that
which history has painted for us. It is my object to change the
system which permits such things.[61]

As the finale of the greatest "uprising of labor" in Detroit's history,
Robinson's speech was optimistic. But on reflection, the *Labor Leaf* observed two days later, "That the masses of the people are awakening
was shown by the bodies of organized wage workers who paraded . . . ,"
but that was just a beginning. "It requires brains to map out a plan of
action . . . and difficulties . . . are sure to crop up."[62]

The events of the spring and summer had shaken many people
loose from their traditional loyalties and normal patterns of daily life,
but if the heightening of class consciousness which had resulted was to
continue, the movement had to be able to provide both practical and
psychic substitutes for the older loyalties and ways of living that workers were abandoning. The structure of industry, the social and cultural
divisions of the city were as yet unaltered. The movement had to be
able to fulfill some of the hopes it had aroused and to create stable ways
of maintaining and reinforcing a sustained emotional hold over supporters while the struggle continued. The pattern of rapid growth and
the millenarian expectations which had accompanied it are characteris-
tic of oppositional social movements. But the rapid collapse of movements which fail to find ways of stabilizing their support is also char-
acteristic.[63]

Periods of intense pursuit of social change are historically quite
atypical. Normally for most people not only is the world of public policy
and social decisions quite divorced from their daily experiences, but
attempts to influence power and decisions, to "make history," are
fraught with danger—threatening their capacity to survive, to protect
their families, to sustain their values and beliefs. Most people learn to
avoid activities that may get them into trouble, disrupt the stability of
daily life, or threaten family integrity, especially when their experiences teach them that prospects for changing history, i.e., altering the
basic demands of daily life, are quite limited. People internalize part of
what they have been forced to accept. Especially in stable periods
when most of people's expectations for everyday life are met, they will
express satisfaction with things as they are, even hostility against those
who seek to change them. Those who question the quality of daily life

are questioning something most people have been forced to accept, but would like to believe they had chosen freely. Yet on a deeper level, perhaps partially unconscious, there are still resentments about power-lessness, about the nature of everyday life. Sometimes people are pre-sented with opportunities to express those resentments; more often ex-ternal circumstances disrupt the stability of daily life, and when the people affected by these disruptions can identify the source of their difficulties and find a means of expressing their anger, cumulative re-sentments have explosive potential.[64]

For many working people in the 1880s, industrialization was just such a disruption. In the previous decade, the labor movement had usually not been strong enough to provide much protection. On the contrary, simple membership in the Knights of Labor, or even buying a labor paper (as many of the incidents already described demonstrate), could lead to dismissal, and others more cowed by hunger were waiting to take any available place; risks seemed to outweigh possible benefits. Workers might have adjusted to the disruptions of their lives if the em-ploying class had been willing or able to bargain with skilled workers and to give all workers a minimum level of security, dignity, and per-sonal freedom in their private lives—that is, to provide what Ameri-cans conceived of as the rights of an American citizen. But the employ-ers did not. Nearly every dramatic national episode of apparently spontaneous activity from the bottom, from the 1877 Railroad Strike to the Gould Southwest strikes, Homestead, and Pullman in 1894, began as a resistance movement to actions initiated by employers: wage cuts, firing union organizers, union busting, speedups, and changes in work rules. The extent of the eight-hour strikes in Detroit in 1886 was the result of the Michigan Car Company's decision to lay off workers on May 1 and fire Clair on May 3. Workers who faced the disruptions of the 1870s and 1880s lived in close proximity and shared a common threat. The eight-hour movement and the rise of the Knights of Labor provided a way to express their feelings. The explosion of 1886 was the result.

But people could not sustain intense opposition or maintain new loyalties unless their attempts to make history could be reconciled with the demands of everyday life. Amidst the glowing reports of the sum-mer of 1886 there were glimmerings of this problem—increased evi-dence of internal dissensions within the movement, conflicts between unions and the Knights of Labor assemblies, between skilled and un-skilled workers, between radicals and conservatives within the move-ment. Detroit workers were still divided. But now the stakes were quite different. The movement appeared to be on the verge of real power. How was that power to be used and for what ends? Around what goals? What symbols could sustain the loyalties of new and enthusiastic converts? In a summer of limitless possibilities the general belief that they were making history seemed a sufficient basis for unity. It would not be for long. Within weeks the atmosphere of solidarity was shattered, and with its loss went much of the potential power the movement seemed to have created.

NOTES

1. *Labor Leaf*, March 24, 1886.

2. Norman J. Ware, *The Labor Movement in the United States, 1860– 1895* (New York, 1929), pp. 139–50; Detroit *Evening News*, March 7, 1886; *Labor Leaf*, March 31, 1886.

3. Ware, pp. 252–53; Philip S. Foner, *History of the Labor Movement in the United States* (New York, 1955), 2: 98–103.

4. *Labor Leaf*, February 4, 1885. Bell's arguments closely resemble those of Ira Steward discussed in David Montgomery, *Beyond Equality* (New York: 1972), pp. 249–60.

5. Montgomery, pp. 136–37, 234, 302–11.

6. *Labor Leaf*, February 4, 1885, March 24, 1886.

7. A variety of recent case studies also characterize the eight-hour movement and the 1886 labor unrest in this way. See Paul Buhle, "The Knights of Labor in Rhode Island," *Radical History Review*, 17 (Spring 1978): 39–73; Steven Ross, "Strikes, Knights, and Political Fights: The May Day Strikes, the Knights of Labor, and the Rise of the United Labor Party in Nineteenth-Century Cincinnati," unpublished paper, Knights of Labor Conference, 1979; and Jama Lazerow, "'The Workingman's Hour': The 1886 Labor Uprising in Boston," *Labor History*, 21 (Spring 1980): 200–220. Leon Fink analyzes the rise of independent labor politics in 1886 from the same perspective (*Workingmen's Democracy: The Knights of Labor in Local Politics, 1886– 1896* [Urbana, 1983]). This approach sharply contradicts a number of earlier studies of the eight-hour movement which saw it as an indicator of rank-and-file interest in bread-and-butter, pure-and-simple unionism *as opposed to* utopian and millenarian visions. See, for example, Marion Cotter Cahill, *Shorter Hours: A Study of the Movement Since the Civil War* (New York, 1932).

8. *Labor Leaf*, April 22, July 8, August 26, 1885, January 27, 1886.

9. Ware, p. 152.

10. Detroit *Tribune*, February 12, 1886; *Labor Leaf*, February 17, 1886.

11. *Labor Leaf*, February 17, 1886; Detroit *Tribune*, February 15, 16, 1886; *Journal of United Labor*, p. 2041.

12. Detroit *Tribune*, February 15, 1886.

13. Detroit *Tribune*, February 16, 19, 1886.

14. *Journal of United Labor*, p. 2041; *Labor Leaf*, March 17, 1886; Detroit *Tribune*, March 17, 1886.

15. *KLDB; Labor Leaf*, April 7, 1886.

16. Bruce Brown, *Marx, Freud, and the Critique of Everyday Life* (New York, 1973), pp. 12–13.

17. *Labor Leaf*, March 31, 1886.

18. Detroit *Evening News*, March 8, 28, 1886; May 1, 1886; *Journal of United Labor*, p. 2041; *Labor Leaf*, March 24, May 5, 1886; Detroit *Tribune*, March 15, 1886. The cigarmakers' union later claimed that Brown Brothers sought Knights of Labor membership to get the Knights' label after being denied the union's label, and accused the Knights leaders of collusion with the manufacturer. The DA withdrew the KL label shortly after the cigarmakers complained. In any event, the company's desire to get a union label indicates its judgment of the labor movement's influence on buying habits.

19. *Labor Leaf*, April 21, 1886; *Journal of United Labor*, p. 2041; Detroit *Evening News*, June 3, 1886.

20. Detroit *Evening News*, May 1, 2, 1886.

21. Detroit *Evening News*, May 3, 1886.

22. Ibid.; Detroit *Tribune*, May 4, 1886.

23. Detroit *Evening News*, May 3, 4, 1886; Detroit *Tribune*, May 4, 1886; *Labor Leaf*, May 5, 1886.

24. Detroit *Tribune*, May 4, 1886; Detroit *Evening News*, May 4, 1886.

25. Ibid.

26. Ibid.

27. Ibid.; *Labor Leaf*, May 5, 1886.

28. Detroit *Evening News*, May 4, 5, 1886; Detroit *Tribune*, May 4, 1886.

29. Detroit *Evening News*, May 4, 8, 11, 1886.

30. Detroit *Evening News*, May 4, 1886; Detroit *Tribune*, May 4, 1886.

31. Detroit *Evening News*, May 4, 5, 1886; Detroit *Tribune*, May 5, 1886.

32. Ibid.

33. Detroit *Evening News*, May 5, 1886; Detroit *Tribune*, May 6, 1886.

34. Ibid; *Labor Leaf*, May 5, 1886.

35. Detroit *Tribune*, May 6, 1886.

36. Detroit *Tribune*, May 6, 1886; Detroit *Evening News*, May 6, 1886.

37. Detroit *Tribune*, May 7, 1886.

38. Detroit *Tribune*, May 6, 1886.

39. Detroit *Tribune*, May 6, 7, 1886; Detroit *Evening News*, May 4, 7, 8, 9, 1886.

40. Detroit *Tribune*, May 6, 7, 8, 1886; Detroit *Evening News*, May 4, 8, 1886; *Labor Leaf*, May 5, 12, 1886.

41. Detroit *Evening News*, May 7, 1886; Detroit *Tribune*, May 8, 1886.

42. Detroit *Tribune*, May 7, 1886.

43. Detroit *News*, May 9, 10, 11, 13, 1886.

44. Detroit *Evening News*, May 9, 1886.

45. Detroit *Evening News*, May 11, 13, 14, 1886; Detroit *Tribune*, May 13, 14, 1886.

46. Detroit *Evening News*, May 17, 18, 1886; Detroit *Tribune*, May 18, 19, 1886.

47. Detroit *Tribune*, May 19, 21, 1886; Detroit *Evening News*, May 20, 1886.

48. Detroit *Evening News*, May 22, 24, 26, June 1, 1886; Detroit *Tribune*, May 26, 27, 1886.

49. Based on all newspaper reports and estimates, the total number of strikers in Detroit in May 1886 was about 5,600 to 5,800 (U.S. Commissioner of Labor 1887 *Report* lists 4,483.) The total number of industrial workers in Detroit in January 1886, according to statistics in the *Tribune*, January 10, 1886, was 32,217. Perhaps 3,000 more had negotiated compromises or struck before May 1, and 2,400 stove company employees had received wage increases. Even including the stove workers and the compromise settlers, the total number of participants in the shorter-hours movement had been under 35 percent of the industrial work force.

50. Detroit *Labor Leaf*, May 26, 1886.

51. Detroit *Evening News*, June 3, 4, 1886; *Labor Leaf*, December 29, 1885; *Proceedings of the Knights of Labor General Assembly*, 1886, pp. 326–28. The only membership figure verified by per capita tax records is the Knights DA 50 official total of 4,679 reported on July 1, 1886. Detroit *Evening News*, March 7, May 6, 12, June 18, 1886; *Labor Leaf*, May 19, June 9, 1886.

52. *Labor Leaf*, June 23, 30, August 4, September 1, 1886.

53. *Labor Leaf*, July 7, 28, September 1, 1886; Detroit *Evening News*, September 3, 1886.

54. *Labor Leaf*, June 9, 1886.

55. *Labor Leaf*, June 23, September 1, 15, August 4, 18, 1886. The play seems to have been modeled on Martin Foran's novel *The Other Side*, which is analyzed in Montgomery's *Beyond Equality*, pp. 220–21. Its vague antimonopolism was too conservative for the editors of the *Labor Leaf*, who wrote a critical review (August 18, 1886).

56. The idea of a September Labor Day had been started by the New York City Central Labor Union in 1882.

57. *Labor Leaf*, October 7, 28, September 1, 1886. Ogg's statement may also reflect the emerging rivalry between the trade unions and the Knights of Labor and a desire to prove the strength of the unions relative to the Knights. The Pinkerton incident in the 1885 demonstration is described in the 1893 *Columbian Labor Day Review*, LC.

58. *Labor Leaf*, September 1, 8, 1886; Detroit *Sunday News*, September 5, 1886. The *Labor Leaf*'s estimate of the number of marchers was corroborated by the daily newspapers. The *News* estimated 9,000 and the *Tribune* 8,000 to 12,000.

59. *Labor Leaf*, September 8, 1886. Field, a prominent businessman, was chairman of the Greenback-Labor state central committee.

60. Ibid.; Detroit *Evening News*, September 7, 1886.

61. *Labor Leaf*, September 8, 1886.

62. *Labor Leaf*, September 1, 8, 1886.

63. Paul Kleppner, *The Third Electoral System 1853–1892* (Chapel Hill, 1979), argues that the 1886 surge in labor voting did not lead to any realignment of voting patterns because of the failure to stabilize the movement's support (pp. 365–66).

64. Richard Flacks, "Making History *vs.* Making Life," *Working Papers* 2 (Summer 1974): 56–71.

6

THE DECLINE OF THE SUBCULTURE
OF OPPOSITION

The events of the spring and summer of 1886 had not changed the basic
ethnic and sectoral divisions within the city's working class, but had
temporarily offered means for superceding them and an atmosphere in
which the arguments for class unity seemed more compelling than they
had before. But the sudden expansion of working-class activity also ex-
acerbated increased tensions within the labor movement and the subculture of opposition.

Before 1886, labor activists with differing ideological worldviews,
ethnic perspectives, and immediate economic interests had exercised
restraint whenever conflicts emerged. They were convinced that they
needed each other and therefore were willing to view working-class opponents as misguided comrades, but comrades nonetheless. This practical and ideological commitment to unity was reinforced by a set of
common experiences. The same core of activists had been working together since the late 1870s. While they originally came from different
cultural traditions, they had forged close personal relationships during
these years. Most were in their thirties and forties, all were skilled
craftsmen, many from the same trades.[1]

Factional Divisions within the Labor Movement

The influx of the mid-1880s raised dramatic possibilities, but in two
ways it also undermined the conditions that had insured previous unity
and stability. First, the movement's vastly expanded base brought in
thousands of new people who did not have the same experience of political cooperation. While the backgrounds of these people varied
widely, most had high expectations, the enthusiasm of new converts to
a religious crusade, but little practical organizational knowledge about
how their expectations might be fulfilled. Second, this new situation

172

forced leaders to make explicit strategic decisions on divisive issues that they had previously been able to avoid.

The events of 1886 magnified the labor movement's size and significance, catapulted the labor question into central prominence, and polarized Detroit. Vast additions of members, strike victories over long-standing opponents, and mass demonstrations convinced labor leaders that they were on the verge of real power. If they responded correctly to this crisis, they might realize the dreams they had fought for. People were watching them to see if they would make the right decisions. The wrong choice might alienate this new audience. In the summer of 1886 activists became more harshly critical of factional opponents whom they believed were advocating exactly the wrong things, exactly what would alienate this potential constituency.

At times these debates seemed to suggest a left-right ideological split within the movement. At other times factional struggle seemed to be centered around organizational rivalry between the Knights of Labor and the trade unions. But a closer examination of factional alignments on the three key issues—politics, trade unionism, and the Haymarket defendants—reveals that cleavages were not consistently along either ideological or organizational lines. Instead we find shifting alliances among four factions: craft conservatives, German socialists, independent radicals, and artisan reformers.

On almost every major issue on which serious differences of opinion emerged, these complex factional alignments also developed. Strict political independence, fusion politics, or no politics at all had advocates in both the Knights district assembly and the Trades Council. When the ILP opted for fusion politics in 1886, the campaign committee included both district assembly and Trades Council representatives, and the opposing faction likewise included both union and Knights of Labor members. When the issue of clemency for the Haymarket defendants arose in 1887, the district assembly and the Trades Council each split right down the middle. Even on matters of trade union policy such as the question of craft autonomy, there was no neat division between the district assembly and the Trades Council; the district assembly had its trade faction while the Trades Council included numerous spokesmen who agreed with Knights of Labor that narrow craft unionism was obsolete.

Any attempt to understand what happened in Detroit, the parallel national decline of the Knights of Labor and the rise of the American Federation of Labor, and the accompanying changes in working-class consciousness must go beyond the simple dichotomies of either organizations or philosophy (reformism versus business unionism, for example) on which scholars have often depended. Each of the major labor organizations, both locally and nationally, had internal divisions just as serious as those between organizations. To characterize the struggles of the late 1880s as the Knights versus the unions, as most scholars have done, misses the significance of internal conflicts, the cooperation of groups in both the Knights of Labor and the Trades Council with each other against factional opponents in their own organizations, and the ways in which factional disputes among labor leaders reflected underlying cleavages within the working class. The roots of each faction can be traced both to the differing economic circumstances of different types of workers and to the differing political cultures of the competing ethnic cultural systems. While the correlations are not completely consistent, the mass support for each faction came more from particular economic sectors and particular nationalities than from others.[2]

Craft Conservatives

Craft conservatism was based on the higher wages, greater status, and better bargaining position of secure craftsmen, especially those in crafts that had not yet undergone fundamental changes in the organization of work. Craft conservatives were unionists because they recognized the potential leverage of their bargaining position and wanted to protect it. Where manufacturers could not threaten them with imminent technological obsolescence, they often saw no real need for alliances with other crafts or other groups of workers. Their power was based on their ability to maintain a craft monopoly, and in that endeavor, actions of other groups of workers, even in their own locale, had far less direct impact than those of fellow craftsmen in other cities—hence their preoccupation with their craft.

Their unions remained relatively aloof from all supra-union bodies, whether the Trades Council, the district assembly, the Independent Labor party, or any of the other cultural and cooperative bodies established during the 1880s. Extreme examples like the local lodges of the railroad brotherhoods avoided all contact with other labor organizations. Others, like the printers and the building trades, participated actively in the council but refused all commitments which might limit craft autonomy. While they might be interested in politics in order to secure specific legislation correcting health and safety abuses, they were generally not interested in long-range proposals for social change.

174

This conservative political orientation was consistent with cultural traditions. Drawn from trades which were disproportionately native or Irish, they reflected the conservative majorities within those communities. Few craft conservative leaders had backgrounds either in radical republicanism or radical Irish nationalism.

They usually worked with fellow craftsmen in small shops, for small contractors, or in small self-directed work crews within large factories, so that they had relatively few immediate work experiences with other workers who had a different perspective. When they seemed to depart from the principle of craft autonomy, for example when the ironmolders allied with the Knights, they did so more to get added muscle against better organized and more powerful employers than to pursue the Knights' reformist objectives. Craft conservatives were often militant; they adhered rigidly to their own codes of solidarity and often contributed generously to other striking unions. But such mutual self-help was a practical as much as an idealistic doctrine.

Many craft conservatives had been swept up in the elan of the early 1880s, but by 1886 or 1887 they were beginning to have second thoughts. Universal organization emphasizing class rather than craft loyalties, and the militant posture that went with it, seemed to threaten their interests. It raised the possibility of subordination of craft interests to a higher authority. Equally important, intense class polarization might actually weaken their bargaining position by stiffening the resistance of employers to all labor organizations.

German Socialists

Yet, as the radicalization of the Trades Council in the early 1880s demonstrated, the craft conservative faction did not command the loyalties of all craftsmen. The labor movement's left, as well as its right, was primarily craft based. Some, like the cigarmakers or shoemakers, found themselves in trades with prospects very different from those of more secure crafts. German craftsmen identified with a radical ethnic heritage. Still others, like Labadie and Grenell, drew their intellectual inspiration from the more radical interpretation of native republicanism. But this left was itself divided.

One group was what Grenell called the straight-backed socialists— at the leadership level primarily SLP and IWPA members and at both leadership and rank-and-file levels overwhelmingly Germans. Although the SLP had dwindled in numbers and significance since the late 1870s, its most prominent members had considerable organizational

175

skill. More importantly, their stature did not depend on the fortunes of the party. They ran the German unions and played key roles in such ethnic institutions as free thought societies, the Turnerverein, and anti-prohibition leagues. Given the relative insularity of Detroit's Deutschtum, the rest of the labor movement depended on them to insure the continuing support of German workers.

In both philosophy and practice, they anticipated the conceptions of elite organization and theoretical purity developed by Daniel De Leon in the 1890s and by Leninists in the twentieth century. Their reactions to developments in the 1880s were dictated by their desire to win support for socialism. Initially, the Knights seemed promising to them because of the order's emphasis on trade amalgamation and class organization, but the SLP turned against the Knights when it became clear that the order was moving in a reformist, rather than a revolutionary, direction. While a sizable number of German workers joined the Knights by the mid-1880s, most of the German radical leadership viewed the organization with skepticism at best, and the SLP directed its energies to the Trades Council and the German Central Labor Union. They failed to commit the Trades Council to socialist policies, but they did elect many of their members to council office and exercised considerable influence in council proceedings. They supported the Independent Labor party as a possible transition to a genuine socialist party, but they were more interested in the party's potential to bring workers closer to socialism than in its capacity to win elections or secure legislation; therefore, strict independence, even if that meant sure defeat, was to be preferred to coalition victories.

Independent Radicals

In response to the German socialists a left independent of the SLP emerged. Men like Labadie, Grenell, Dolan, and Simpson were all SLP alumni. They had tangled with the German stalwarts since the 1870s, and while they became convinced that the socialist critique of capitalism was valid, they considered the Germans aggravating and ineffective. They moved from the party into the Knights. Almost exclusively American, Canadian, or British, ethnicity as well as ideology separated them from the Germans. They were radicals, but their radicalism owed more to native republicanism (or in a few cases English Chartism) than to socialist theory. While they accepted a vague conception of socialism, they were more concerned than the Germans with immediate results, and also in contrast to the Germans, they welcomed ideological eclecticism, reacting positively to the other reformist notions of the 1880s: the Single Tax, cooperation, reform politics, and philosophical anarchism. Intensely democratic, militant unionists, capable labor veterans, their long term strategy depended on the capacity of the Knights of Labor to combine a radical class perspective with practical results. They had played key roles in the initial organization of the Knights and most of the oppositional cultural institutions in the early 1880s. Personally they were more widely known than the leaders of any of the other factions, but in the factional infighting of the late 1880s, their backgrounds were a source of weakness as well as strength. Their interpretation of republicanism was a distinctly minority current within their own cultural communities, so that they were less able than the leaders of other factions to draw on the resonance of their ideas with a mass cultural base.

Artisan Reformers

While independent leftists like Labadie remained prominent throughout the 1880s, the district assembly began to slip from their control just as the Knights were beginning to realize their expectations. A new group of leaders, representative of the marginal trades who flocked to the Knights in the mid-1880s, took increasing control of district assembly affairs. A few had been among the founders of the Knights in Detroit, but most had entered the movement's leadership only in the mid-1880s. Several had first attracted attention as local assembly strike leaders in 1886. Most of the others had become known through their activities in the Knight's cultural and political efforts, especially as candidates of the Independent Labor party. A distinct group, separate from the radicals who had established the Knights in Detroit, they swept the elections for district assembly offices in January 1887. None of the leaders of the left who had played such an important role in the rise of the Knights in Detroit remained on the district assembly executive board.[3]

This new group of leaders were reformist, but not radical. While the group included several Irish Catholics, their rhetoric and style had strong pietist overtones. Many were active in fraternal and prohibitionist organizations. Most were skilled workers, artisans, but artisans with a very different background and social perspective than the other three groups. Only six of the seventeen district assembly board members elected in 1887 had been prominent in the local labor movement before 1884. Eight of the seventeen were not industrial workers during the time they served on the board. Six, including all five of the district officers, held appointive political office (five Democrats, one Greenback-Republican), one was a clerk in a hardware store, and the eighth, Captain McGregor, was a ship's captain and *Advance and Labor Leaf* editor.[4] More importantly, only two of the entire group had worked in a trade in which there was a strong craft union (one cigarmaker who was expelled during the year for crossing a picket line and one ironmolder).[5] Thus, in contrast to nearly all of the labor leaders in the other three factions, these reformers did not rise to leadership via prior activity in a trade union; only three had held major union offices outside of the Knights of Labor.[6]

Some scholars have suggested that such men were not really workers, but were middle-class reformers, political hacks, or quacks, but only one of these seventeen men (Robinson) comes close to fitting that description. While half of them were not working at their trades during their tenure in office, all came from working-class backgrounds, and several resumed work after short periods in leadership positions. They tended, however, to be particular kinds of workers: artisans from marginal crafts in which craft dilution had already destroyed much of their artisan status—three shoemakers, a hatter, a woodworking-machine hand, a cracker baker (the most industrialized sector in the baking industry), a railroad-car painter, two semiskilled stoveworkers. The shoemakers had witnessed the destruction of the Crispins, and the three metal workers (a molder, a pattern maker, and a polisher) had seen repeated victories of the stove companies over the molders' union.[7] Thus, as a group, they either had little experience with unionism or experiences which would lead them to doubt the effectiveness of trade unionism. In contrast, their political efforts had been moderately successful. Their political orientation, their belief that the district assembly should avoid alienating voters, made sense based on this personal background.

They were workers, and they were sincere reformers. There is no evidence that they were personally or politically corrupt, that they used their offices to line their own pockets. District Master Workman Long found himself unemployed and nearly unemployable after retiring from district assembly office. His successor had similar problems. John Devlin, who appeared to be the most opportunist of the group in the mid-1880s, abandoned a successful career as a Democratic politician to join the pitifully weak Populist party in Michigan. When radicals accused them of selling out for the spoils of office, they reacted indignantly. And if they could hear the modern scholarly descriptions of themselves as middle-class hacks, they would be equally shocked.[8]

Their desire for respectability, for a sense of dignity, came as much from their background as skilled workers as did their reformism. They were reformers who identified with an earlier age in which a deserving artisan could expect that hard work and self-denial would eventually lead to the status and security of an independent master craftsman with his own shop. Several had failed in attempts to achieve this goal, and they saw the emerging corporate system destroying the rights and status of the artisan-citizen. That such men had mass appeal is a reflection of the widespread nature of their fears about the implications of industrialism. Descendants of a long republican tradition, they opposed a concentration of employers' power and a competitive individualism which degraded the artisan, but as they were quick to point out, they had nothing against honorable employers who respected artisan rights.

Each of these four groups represented a major constituency. The leaders of each were genuinely popular with their following. The factional struggle certainly included elements of personal rivalry and petty ambition, but ultimately the existence of such factions was based on the heterogeneity of Detroit's workers—the variations in their backgrounds and experiences. All four of the factions existed throughout the 1880s, but their alliances shifted. These shifts were the decisive factor in the changing fortunes of the Knights and the unions.

Factional struggle thus grew directly out of the varied experiences and backgrounds of Detroit's working class. Internecine conflict had, however, another unanticipated consequence. Bitter factional battles disrupted and consumed the organizational infrastructure of an expanding subculture of opposition. Thousands of workers were beginning to look at their own experiences and formulate a critique of the industrial system, but people who came from diverse cultural backgrounds and varying economic circumstances could not act together without formal vehicles for discussion, cooperation, and mobilization. Factional battles destroyed those vehicles. Without a broad array of formal institutions, the labor movement had no way to integrate the thousands of new recruits into a stable alternative (or complement) to the ethnic cultures to which they still belonged. The surge of the mid-1880s could not lead to a permanent realignment of working-class loyalties without that integration.

Politics: The Collapse of the Independent Labor Party

The opening round of the factional battles was the ILP nominating convention held on September 2, 1886. The events of the spring and summer had raised hopes that the ILP could finally aspire to major party status and real political power in the city. That possibility, however, forced the competing factions' contradictory conceptions of politics into the open. For the German socialists, anything other than an unambiguously proletarian and anticapitalist party was now retrogressive at best, traitorous at worst. To craft conservatives and artisanal reformers, such a posture appeared inflammatory and reckless. Craft conservatives, if they were interested in politics at all, hoped for cross-class political alliances that could lead successfully to ameliorative legislation, while artisan reformers viewed politics as the means of rescuing the republic from the threat of class polarization and degradation imposed on them by unscrupulous monopolists. Artisan-citizens hoped to prevent the development of class boundaries, not to sharpen them. The independent radicals found themselves caught between these increasingly divergent paths. While they shared the militant and anticapitalist stance of the German socialists, their own native republican origins made them less eager to ground their radicalism in purely class terms. Equally important, they had separated themselves from the German socialists most sharply by their rejection of ideological purity and belief in the necessity for appealing to as broad a political base as possible, hoping to bring what they viewed as a politically immature but potentially sympathetic mass audience along slowly. More than anything else, they hoped to preserve the fragile unity of the movement.

Activists had been gearing up for the battle all summer. The German socialists hoped to use renewed criticisms of the alleged corruption of labor politicians who had been elected on fusion tickets in 1884 as an ideological wedge by committing all future ILP candidates to "strict independence." Spearheaded by SLP leaders, a number of radicals began organizing within their unions and Knights of Labor assemblies to elect convention delegates pledged to a full third-party ticket with no endorsements from "the old corrupt political parties." The ILP campaign committee was to be empowered to remove any candidate accepting such an endorsement and substitute someone else. At the same time, their factional opponents argued more vociferously than before for just the opposite course: now was the time to seize opportunities for new alliances.[9]

The convention opened with a symbolic fight over election of the meeting's chairman, normally a pro forma decision. The socialists nominated Sam Goldwater, a cigarmaker and spokesman for the "strictly independents," against artisan reformer Andrew Forbes, District Assembly 50's recording secretary and president of the seamen's union. Goldwater received only thirty votes from the more than 150 delegates, but Forbes was a highly respected veteran organizer, and Goldwater a newcomer to Detroit. On a series of credential fights for various delegations, the vote was much closer. The socialists challenged the Greenback delegates, who counter-challenged the SLP. The convention compromised by seating both. The most controversial delegate was Francis Egan, former Trades Council president, ILP legislator, and deputy state commissioner of labor. Critics charged that Egan had sold out to the Republicans in order to receive his political appointment. By a vote of only seventy-five to sixty-eight, with about a dozen delegates abstaining, Egan remained.[10]

Nine delegations, mostly Germans, including representatives of the cigarmakers' union and the Carl [sic] Marx and LaSalle Knights of Labor assemblies, had been elected with orders to withdraw from the convention if it turned down the antifusion resolution. The debate grew bitter. James Murtagh of the typographical union denounced the sponsors of the resolution as socialists and disrupters. Charles Erb, bordering on hysteria according to one newspaper account, had to be physically restrained. As the final vote revealed a three-to-one margin against strict independence, Gustav Herzig called on "all truly independent labor delegates" to leave the hall. The nine pledged delegations and a few other individuals, about thirty delegates in all, followed him from the hall.[11]

With the withdrawal of the radical strict independence faction, the balance of power within the convention shifted to the right. Delegates who sought a close working relationship with politicians in the major parties now dominated the proceedings. The list of candidates reflected their control. Although some prominent labor politicians most objectionable to the anticollaborationists were not chosen, notably Egan, the slate demonstrated exactly the kind of ticket-balancing philosophy which the bolters opposed. Most of the candidates had important connections in the Democratic or Republican parties, several were chosen primarily to represent ethnic constituencies, and a number of them had only a tenuous relationship to the labor movement. Bernard

O'Reilly, for instance, was a shipcarpenter and secretary of the ship-carpenters' assembly of the Knights of Labor, but more importantly, he was an incumbent Democratic alderman and part of the inner circle of local Irish Democrats. Thomas O'Donnell, an iron worker, was report-edly nominated for state representative because he claimed support among both iron workers and Irish Americans. He had never been mentioned before in the labor press. After receiving a Democratic en-dorsement in October, he denounced all of the non-Democratic Labor nominees and publicly pledged his support to the straight Democratic ticket. He was removed from the Labor ticket a week before the elec-tion. Other state representative nominees included George Walthew, a lawyer and incumbent Labor-Democrat; Conrad Bettinger, a German Republican elected to the legislature in 1882 and narrowly defeated for reelection in 1884; and John Rairden, who ran a night school which catered to a working-class clientele. Only two of the twelve nominees could have been considered left of center within the labor movement: Judson Grenell and August Wettlaufer (owner of a small cigar factory), both moderate socialists.[12]

Delegates tried to patch things up by electing a campaign commit-tee including representatives from all factions. The party's nominees provoked bitter criticism, however, not only from the seceding faction of radicals who made plans for another convention to nominate a fully independent workingmen's ticket, but from other sources as well. John Burton, editor of the *Labor Leaf*, had consistently tried to steer a middle course in his editorial policies, criticizing narrow craft union-ists for failing to understand the need for systemic reforms at the same time that he opposed extreme polarization and class conflict. But the Labor ticket deeply troubled Burton. The choice of candidates smacked of rank opportunism.

As he surveyed the list of candidates, Burton tried to be diplo-matic. In a number of cases he simply omitted the customary ecstatic praise. One candidate was described as "safe," another "well known," and a third "a fluent speaker." But in at least two cases, Burton could not restrain himself. O'Donnell's nomination, according to Burton, was entirely inconsistent with the movement's principles. O'Donnell had no record of labor activism and there was not even any solid evidence that he really had the backing he claimed. O'Reilly's nomination raised even more serious issues. As alderman, O'Reilly had been implicated in a number of bribery and graft schemes. A year before, Burton had denounced him as a disgrace to the labor movement, and now he re-

printed his earlier article describing O'Reilly's alleged role in municipal corruption.[13] O'Reilly, O'Donnell, and some of the other nominees
reacted angrily to Burton's articles. The ILP campaign committee organized a boycott of the *Labor Leaf*, but Burton pledged that he would
stick to his guns.

Even within the paper's normally congenial staff, emotions flared.
Labadie, who had decided to oppose both fusionists and strict indepen-
dence-ites, argued that political action would only disrupt the economic struggle. Grenell, representative of the dilemma of the independent radicals, found himself caught in the middle between Burton's
suggestions of corruption, Labadie's denunciation of politics in general,
and other close associates within the seceding group who supported
politics but opposed collaboration with the "old parties." As a candidate and a leading advocate of the ILP's fusion policy, he felt compelled
to defend the party. Burton, Labadie, and the Goldwater group all
struck Grenell as unrealistic, utopian, and impractical. To publicly denounce the Independent Labor party in mid-campaign could only diminish the movement's effectiveness without accomplishing anything
positive. Grenell's initial replies to the ILP's critics were phrased in the
tone of a disappointed friend, but as criticism grew more vitriolic, particularly with the radical left's charges of selling out to capitalist parties, his articles and speeches displayed obvious tension. Perhaps he
felt particularly vulnerable to the sellout charge because he had accepted a post as deputy oil inspector from the Republicans in 1885, a
position which carried a salary of $1,200 (double a printer's normal an-
nual income) with few duties. By mid-October, Grenell repudiated his
former SLP associates in the "Goldwater gang" and denounced them all
as liars.[14]

The "Goldwater Gang" proceeded with its plans for a rival ticket
convinced that they were the true voice of the city's organized workers.
A manifesto, signed by Goldwater and six prominent SLP members,
announcing their convention, stated that the previous convention had
been "manipulated by office holders of the old parties against the interests of the working people . . . it is a demonstrated fact that the Democratic and Republican parties are the common enemy of the working
people, and in the interests of monopolies . . ." workers could do
better. "The ten thousand men in line in the demonstration of Monday,
September 6, proved that they are enough to act independently."[15]

But when the workingmen's convention finally met, the factional
alignment of delegates remained essentially the same as it had been at

the earlier ILP convention. The majority once again repudiated the strictly independent position and then quickly voted to adjourn. The dissenters, who remained behind, agreed they could not field a ticket of their own, but vowed to work for the defeat of candidates they considered to be in collusion with capitalist politicians. Labadie attended the convention as an observer and was horrified at the "bitter feeling" on both sides. Men who had worked closely together for years were denouncing each other in the harshest possible terms. Such bitterness could set back the movement for years. The experience strengthened his conviction that labor organizations should avoid politics.[16]

Labor candidates, who had confidently expected to carry Detroit only a few weeks before, found themselves on the defensive, attacked by major party conservatives as advocates of class war and by dissenters within the labor movement as corrupt manipulators. Many of their campaign speeches were devoted to justifying their actions, hoping especially to neutralize the criticism coming from their own ranks. Testimonial letters to the *Labor Leaf* from friends and neighbors defended their honesty and integrity. Yet despite campaign rallies of over 2,000 people, a small army of campaign workers, and much hoopla, on the verge of the election, the ILP looked like a sinking ship. When O'Donnell abandoned the labor ticket less than two weeks before the election, Grenell pleaded with labor voters: do not abandon the whole ticket because of the deficiencies of a few of the candidates.[17]

The results were not as disheartening as they might have been. Three of the seven state representative candidates, all endorsed by the Republicans, and two of the state senatorial candidates (one endorsed by the Republicans, the other, O'Reilly, by the Democrats) were elected, and the unendorsed candidates unofficially averaged about 1,600 votes more than in 1884. With the slightly smaller turnout in an off-year election, that meant the ILP had doubled its percentage of the vote (from 7.3 percent in 1884 to 14.0 in 1886).

Perhaps potentially more important, the party had substantially broadened its electoral base. The increased ILP vote was primarily the result of a massive influx of unskilled workers, an influx which was especially strong among unskilled Germans and Poles, but which cut across ethnic lines including unskilled workers of all nationalities and producing high ILP totals in several ethnically heterogeneous but heavily working-class precincts. Several examples illustrate these trends. The third precinct of the Thirteenth Ward, with a voting population half unskilled German, increased its ILP percentage from 8 percent in 1884

184

to 22 percent in 1886. The Polish majority fourth precinct of the Ninth Ward jumped from 4 percent ILP in 1884 to 30 percent in 1886. In the newly created second precinct of the Fifteenth Ward, 90 percent working class, but ethnically divided (one-third native, no other nationality over 22 percent), the ILP received 36 percent in 1886.[18]

While German workers were still the strongest source of ILP support, for the first time they provided less than half the ILP votes.[19] Unskilled ILP voters outnumbered skilled workers. Thus while the ILP still captured less than a quarter of the working-class vote, the vote was decidedly more proletarian and more representative than ever before. Not surprisingly, these tendencies were particularly evident in the precincts surrounding the largest factories where strikes had taken place that spring. The events of the previous year had started to break down the divisions within the working class.

But party organizers had entered the campaign expecting far more than a few victories for fusion candidates and a moderate expansion of their electoral base. Compared to the 13,000 members claimed by the unions and the Knights of Labor, or the more than 10,000 workers who had marched on September 6, 3,600 labor votes were a crushing disappointment. Without major party alliances, the ILP would still not be a serious contender for local offices; no unendorsed labor candidate was even close to being elected.

And the campaign had seriously aggravated bitter debates about the direction of the labor movement which threatened to destroy the movement's solidarity just at the time it was trying to cement the loyalties of the thousands of new members who had joined that spring and summer. The Goldwater Gang had followed through on its threats to disrupt the campaigns of ILP candidates who had been endorsed by "capitalist parties". Their opposition may have cost Labor-Republican Henry Robinson a congressional seat. Robinson lost by 1,500 votes out of 34,000.[20] ILP spokesmen blamed the defeat on the combined opposition of upper-class Republicans and ultra-left labor activists. While Robinson ran exceptionally well in such normally Democratic areas as the Polish section of the Ninth Ward, he ran far behind other Republicans in the well-to-do parts of the Second Ward, and especially poorly in a number of East Side German working-class precincts that were usually the ILP's stronghold.[21] A statistical analysis of these precincts confirms the influence of the Goldwater Gang. While the ILP vote soared in nearly all German precincts, it declined in several near East Side precincts, a neighborhood with a preponderance of skilled

Germans, the center of German working-class radicalism for the previous decade, and the precincts which had been the strongest ILP supporters in previous campaigns. In four of these precincts, the Goldwater Gang's opposition probably cost the ILP at least 400 votes.[22]

The spectacle of some of the city's most committed labor activists sabotaging a Labor party campaign was the final blow for those who were beginning to doubt the wisdom of political activity altogether. To Joseph Labadie, the campaign proved that politics only disrupted the labor movement, creating "bitter feeling . . . Let us close up the breach once more and turn our faces toward the common enemy—capitalism."[23] Yet the close of the campaign did not end the furor over political strategies as Labadie hoped. Underlying the debate over politics were basic issues: Should the labor movement attempt to be a class movement representing the interests of workers as a class, a political reform movement seeking allies from all classes, or simply a loose confederation of occupational groups? Should the movement pursue a strategy of confrontation or conciliation? Was its image to be radical or respectable? Should labor leaders seek influence in the established institutions of society or continue to develop independent counter-institutions?

With the close of the campaign, conflict emerged on an even wider scale. Radicals and artisan reformers within the Knights of Labor split bitterly over the issue of the clemency campaign for the Haymarket defendants; pro–trade union elements in the unions and within the Knights began to clash with the Knights' leadership over the issues of trade and craft rights; and key decisions by national and local Knights of Labor leaders raised serious debates over internal democracy within the Knights.

Meanwhile, the conduct of important Knights of Labor leaders in the following months seemed to vindicate the criticisms of people like Labadie and Goldwater. In early 1887, key Irish Democrats in the pro-Powderly artisan reformer faction in District Assembly 50 abandoned the ILP for the local Democratic machine. District Master Workman J. D. Long had already advocated such a course at the end of the 1886 campaign. He was appointed city assessor. John Haire of the district assembly executive board became sidewalk inspector and then assistant assessor. John Devlin, a district assembly executive board member and former Democratic state representative, had been appointed U.S. consul at Windsor in charge of customs at the end of 1885. By 1887, he had filled the customs house with Knights of Labor appointees, twenty-three in all, including even the renegade labor candidate

Thomas O'Donnell. By the fall of 1887, the *Evening News* was accusing the Democrats of trying to bribe labor leaders for influence in language that might have come from the Goldwater Gang.[24]

In September 1887, the ILP decided to run the strict independence campaign demanded by the German left the previous year, but acceptance of the noncollaboration policy was a hollow victory. Leading labor politicians ignored the order and campaigned openly for the major parties. At the Democratic county convention Knights of Labor leaders Long, Haire, and Brant publicly proclaimed that they were Democrats, not Labor party men, and several Labor party poll workers distributed Democratic rather than Labor party tickets on election day.[25]

Many activists became convinced that labor politics was a fruitless endeavor inevitably dominated by self-seeking and corrupt individuals. By election time, most former ILP members had apparently reached Labadie's conclusion: the whole mess should be avoided. When Labor party supporters tried to introduce a Labor party resolution at the Trades Council the week before the election, Trades Council President Fildew ruled the question out of order, and his ruling was sustained by a nearly three-to-one majority.[26]

Not surprisingly, the 1887 campaign was a disaster. Henry Robinson, the mayoral candidate, polled only 1,653 votes while most of the rest of the ticket ran far behind him. By 1888, the Labor party had given up. Labor leaders who wanted to enter politics sought major party nominations. The Trades Council expressed opposition to a few major party candidates who were particularly objectionable, but otherwise refrained from political activity. District Assembly 50's position was similar. It circulated a political catechism, or list of questions for candidates, and the *Advance* published the candidates' answers. A handful of labor leaders were elected as major party candidates, but independent labor politics was dead. The subculture of opposition ceased to have an independent political voice.[27]

Widening the Breach: The Knights, the Cigarmakers, and the Trade Unions

Throughout the spring and summer of 1886, readers of the *Labor Leaf* received periodic reports of growing disputes between the national leaders of the Knights of Labor. A key group of trade union leaders also complained that the Knights had violated fundamental union precepts:

187

Knights of Labor assemblies had initiated scabs, individuals who had been expelled from unions for misconduct, or workers who were violating union work rules; the Knights had collaborated with employers against unions, offering Knights of Labor labels to companies that had been denied union labels, signing contracts at below union rates, even taking the jobs of striking union members; Knights of Labor officials in various localities had pressured union locals to dissolve and enter the Knights of Labor. But before the end of 1886, these disputes had few local counterparts.[28]

Relations between the Trades Council and District Assembly 50 were quite amicable. They collaborated in the political campaigns of the ILP from 1882 through 1886, combined efforts for the marches of 1880, 1885, and 1886, worked together in the eight-hour campaign, and both supported subsidiary labor institutions such as the labor press, clubs, cooperatives, and club rooms.

Given the history of the Knights in Detroit from 1878 to 1885, this close working relationship was quite natural. The first Knights of Labor assemblies in Detroit had been created by socialist and other reform-minded unionists who hoped to broaden the scope of union policies and activities, but they remained active in their unions and continued to support trade unionism. The Knights of Labor in Detroit was primarily trade-based throughout its history. Of seventy local assemblies known to have existed in Wayne County between 1878 and 1892, only nineteen were true mixed assemblies and seven of those were in small out-county towns. In the early 1880s, the Trades Council and the district assembly shared officers so that the distinction between them broke down at the leadership level. There was little competition between them for members before 1886. The Knights organized trade bodies in crafts with weak or nonexistent national unions. Although the district assembly absorbed a few locals from the Trades Council before 1885, none of these were in the industries which formed the mainstays of the council. Not until late 1885 did District Assembly 50 charter any assembly which was in direct competition with a member of the Trades Council.[29] Thus, while there were occasional local disagreements between unions and the Knights of Labor, they were nothing beyond the normal course of minor interorganizational disputes, no more serious than similar occasional squabbles between various trade unions. The most important cleavages within the local labor movement were ideological and ethnic, not organizational. Roughly the same debates took place within both the district assembly and the Trades Council and both were divided along right-left lines.

During the summer and fall of 1886, however, this local harmony broke down. The initial trigger was sharply divided local reaction to the national dispute between the International Cigarmakers Union and the national leaders of the Knights of Labor. The number of local workers directly affected by the dispute was quite small—only a few dozen—but the issue became a symbol for more fundamental conflicts between craft conservatives, radicals, and artisan reformers over the proper objectives and methods of organization.

The cigarmakers' dispute had been simmering since the early 1880s. Initially a split in the large New York City local of the International had led to the formation of a rival national union, the German socialist Progressive Cigarmakers. By the mid-1880s, both unions and a large number of Knights of Labor cigarmakers' assemblies were involved in a national jurisdictional battle within the cigarmaking industry. When the Progressives temporarily joined the Knights to combine forces against the International in 1886, the International began rallying discontented craft unions in other trades for open warfare against the Knights. Some half-hearted attempts at conciliation by both sides fell through, and in December 1886 the discontented craft unionists led by the International Cigarmakers held a convention in Columbus, Ohio, to form the American Federation of Labor to direct their war against the Knights. Powderly countered in February by ordering immediate enforcement of a resolution, passed at the Knights general assembly the previous fall, outlawing dual membership in the Knights of Labor and the International Cigarmakers. All Knights of Labor cigar workers had to leave the International or leave the order. In effect, all union cigarmakers were summarily expelled from the Knights of Labor.[30]

Throughout 1886, local union and Knights of Labor leaders had tried to keep Detroit's cigarmakers out of the national battle. Despite some verbal sparring, the three factions of local cigarmakers agreed to accept a local peace pact which included local withdrawal of the Knights of Labor cigar label, maintenance of the International Union's wage scale, and mutual recognition of each other's union cards. When Gompers gave a speech in Detroit in May 1886, entitled "Scabs, Knights of Labor, and Unions," in which he argued that all tobacco workers except International members were scabs, local International supporters were not yet willing to accept his position. Occasional incidents in the local tobacco industry and a number of other industries did suggest a reservoir of minor dissatisfactions, but until the end of 1886, a semblance of unity was maintained.[31]

The February 1887 expulsion order produced the crisis Detroit activists had tried to avoid. Although there were only twelve or thirteen dual members in Detroit facing expulsion, the order necessitated an immediate and unequivocal decision on an issue with overwhelming symbolic importance. Was Powderly's decision legally binding on the district assembly? Could Powderly summarily expel members without proper cause? If so, what did that say about democracy in the Knights of Labor? Would the district assembly honor the order or fight it? Did this signal a declaration of war on the unions?[32]

Those facing expulsion included pioneer Detroit Knights Hugh McClelland and Thomas Dolan, both charter members of LA 901. "I am a Knight of Labor," Dolan explained, "was a charter member of 901, and have never done anything to offend the order, but will be compelled to go with my trade union. My living is there . . ." McClelland, also a cigarmaker and a former Labor legislator, agreed. An impressive array of local labor leaders expressed their horror at the expulsion order, and the issue dominated the pages of the *Advance and Labor Leaf* for the entire month of February. Even Andrew Forbes, hitherto closely identified with what was rapidly emerging as the "administration" faction in the district assembly, came out for the opposition. "I should stand by my union in preference to the Knights of Labor if such an order was issued to my trade."[33]

But the new district assembly leadership elected in January was dominated by the artisan reformer faction sympathetic to Powderly and hostile to trade union grievances. Probably at their instigation, Burton was removed from editorship of the *Labor Leaf*. Captain McGregor, his successor, took a strict administration line. The International Cigarmakers had ordered a boycott of the Knights of Labor cigar label, McGregor claimed, arrogantly demanding the Knights surrender their label when the Knights actually represented more cigarmakers than the International. The Knights could not stand idly by and see their rights infringed upon. In Detroit, so far, the district assembly had taken no action to defend itself, and, as a result, the International's label had almost totally replaced the Knights' label. The expulsion order was an act of self-defense totally justified by the events of the past year.[34]

At Judson Grenell's suggestion, the district assembly tried to patch things up locally by proclaiming formal acceptance but ignoring the expulsion order in practice. Dolan, McClelland, and other local cigarmakers affected by the order remained within the Knights, but the compromise did not really satisfy partisans on either side.[35]

A vigorous and increasingly bitter debate over the relations between the Knights of Labor and the unions filled the columns of the *Advance and Labor Leaf.* Organizers who had been comrades for nearly a decade denounced each other viciously. Even more disastrous, the invective spilled over into public forums and mass meetings called for very different purposes: to discuss trade union policies, for example, or to inform prospective members of the advantages of organization. It became literally impossible to hold any labor gathering in Detroit without engaging in factional debate. At a meeting of brewery workers in March 1887, pioneer Knight and independent radical Thomas Dolan spoke at length on the superiority of the unions. In April, rivalries between the ironmolders' union and the rapidly growing Knights of Labor molders broke out into the open. The union refused to honor Knights of Labor cards in shops where it predominated, and the Knights retaliated by threatening to cross union picket lines in the event of a strike. Knights of Labor sailors complained about a similar situation on Great Lakes ships docking in Detroit. They could not find work because of union opposition to their Knights of Labor membership.[36]

In the tobacco industry, the International quickly established its supremacy. The Knights tobacco workers' assembly lost all of its members (several hundred the year before) except the hundred or so at the Globe Tobacco Company. And Globe employees remained with the Knights only because the firm had a union shop contract with the district assembly. To the reformers in the district assembly the Globe agreement was their model of the virtues of arbitration. Company royalties to the district assembly for the use of the KL label were described by the district assembly's officers as an example of "profit-sharing" and an exercise in labor-management cooperation. "Such training removes the antagonistic spirit too common between employer and employed." But disgruntled company employees disputed these grandiose claims and argued that the company paid lower than average wages. The so-called shared profits were a ruse which did not even make up the wage differential between Globe and other companies.[37]

While the rivalries in Detroit's tobacco industry were settled with the virtual disappearance of the Knights except at Globe, the union and the Knights were more closely balanced in the iron foundries. By 1887, the union had bounced back from its near destruction by the stove companies in the early 1880s. A majority of the workers in several small shops had rejoined the union, and important nuclei of union members in the large stove companies were advocating representation by the ironmolders' union. Yet the Knights, whose membership policies were less restrictive than the union's, were also growing rapidly, in direct competition with the union. Devlin Assembly 3954 had branched out from the carshops to the Peninsular Stove Works, and a second molders' assembly, Garland Assembly 619, would organize several hundred more at the Michigan Stove Company in 1888.[38] At the same time, local metal manufacturers had escalated their attack on established pay scales and work rules. In early 1887, the three major stove companies— Detroit, Michigan, and Peninsular—all joined a national stove manufacturers' alliance designed to break the resistance of the ironmolders' union to the Berkshire or "bucks" system. Union spokesmen argued that the real purpose of the employers' pact was to destroy unionism in the metal trades. Employers consciously exploited the rivalry between the Knights of Labor assemblies led by artisan reformers and the unions led by craft conservatives but endorsed by the radicals increasingly alienated from the reformist leadership of the Knights' district executive board.[39]

Some leaders on both sides recognized the costs of interunion rivalry and attempted to combine efforts. Among working ironmolders, there seemed to be a basis for cooperation. The union had encountered rough going in Detroit throughout the 1880s. For this reason union molders had established Knights of Labor assemblies in order to draw support from the larger organization. Union leaders admitted in public debate in June 1887 that "the Knights of Labor have done for labor in Detroit what the union never could have done . . ." But involvement of the District Assembly 50's executive board in the negotiating process had disastrous consequences.[40]

Under the Knights of Labor rules, the district board had great power over the negotiations of local assemblies. Locals needed district assembly approval to engage in strikes or boycotts. Equally important, except for very large locals, local assemblies were almost totally dependent on the district for organizing the community support and assistance that was essential to strike victory. Leaders of many assemblies were also recent converts, inexperienced in the mechanics of negotiations. For all of these reasons, the district executive board was able to exert great leverage over locals to name it as the negotiating agent. Locals often did so with some reluctance. The *Advance* admitted, for example, that strikers at the Wilson Brothers Carriage Works in March 1887 had "at first refused to submit their affairs to the executive board of District Assembly 50" and had finally done so under duress. District assembly officers reported the negotiations with Wilson Brothers had produced a satisfactory settlement, but apparently the workers did not agree. In August, the Carriage Workers' Assembly (LA 6182) threatened to withdraw from the Knights of Labor if the proposed Carriage Makers' National Trade District, which would have taken them out of District Assembly 50's control, was not approved.[41]

Negotiating efforts by the District Assembly 50 executive board with the Hart Manufacturing Company in February and the stove companies in May and June of 1887 produced similarly unsatisfactory results. At Hart Manufacturing Company, ironworkers had been locked out following a series of disputes over work methods and piece rates. The company had introduced a new device for making hinges, claiming the old machine was less efficient. They cut the piece rate on the hinges accordingly. The employees argued that all pay cuts were totally unjustified. They denied the company claims of the greater efficiency of the new hinge-making machinery. Moreover, no improvements had been made in the manufacturing of other products, but piece rates had been cut there too.[42]

Iron Molders' Local No. 31 and Knights of Labor LA 3954 had been competing to organize the shop for some time, but when the new disputes arose they joined forces to fight the changes. The union wanted to turn the lockout into a strike and boycott the company's products, but the Knights, upon the suggestion of the district leadership, proposed binding arbitration instead. The union, with some hesitation, agreed. The district assembly approached the Hart management with the idea and agreed that the company would name one representative, the district assembly another, and then these two would agree on a neutral third representative. The district assembly's representative was *Advance* editor Captain McGregor.[43]

To McGregor, the importance of the case had been the willingness of the company to accept a negotiated settlement. Arbitration, he hoped, would set a precedent for other industrial disputes. His reaction reveals why the assumptions of the district assembly's artisan reformers made them poor negotiators. Although McGregor had been appointed as the labor representative to the arbitration committee, he apparently conceived of his role not as the representative of the iron workers, but as a spokesman for the philosophy of arbitration and class harmony advocated by his fellow reformers on the district executive board. They hoped to portray the Knights as a respectable body which accepted its responsibilities to public welfare. Honorable employers, they believed, would respond to this spirit of harmony. This goal carried at least as much weight in McGregor's thinking as the grievances of the locked-out workers. He was an outsider to the industry but apparently took no steps to provide himself with documentation independent of the company statistics. When the workers failed to provide hard data for their side, a job which might reasonably have been considered McGregor's as their negotiator, he essentially capitulated to the company position. The district assembly claimed a victory for arbitration, but from the workers' point of view, the "victory" amounted to district assembly approval for the company-sponsored cuts.[44]

The district assembly executive board played a similar role in the final showdown with the stove companies. In April 1887, Henry Cribben, president of the Stove Manufacturers' Defense Association, arrived in Detroit to confer with local employers. Union leaders were aware that the employers' association had recently sponsored lockouts in St. Louis in opposition to wage demands and to enforce the bucks system. As part of the Manufacturers' Association agreement, member firms agreed to accept patterns from other association firms engaged in labor disputes. Cribben had brought St. Louis patterns to Chicago, and molders there struck in solidarity with fellow iron workers in St. Louis. He brought the same patterns to Detroit hoping to force the Detroit firms to take up the slack from the struck firms in St. Louis and Chicago. The union wanted to strike, but Knights of Labor leaders once again urged caution and negotiation. A strike would throw more than 3,000 stove employees out of work, causing distress to their families and threatening to depress the entire city's economy. It was in the public interest to avoid a strike by submitting disputes to arbitration.[45]

The stove companies did not agree; they locked out their employees in mid-May, declaring they would not reopen until the workers accepted the bucks system and the disputed patterns. Molders opposed the bucks system on both moral and practical grounds. The whole idea of putting skilled craftsmen "in the position of subcontractors . . . [who] enrich themselves at the expense of the men who do their work . . . [was] repugnant to our ideas," one molder explained to a Detroit *News* reporter. Equally important, the practice could be used to bypass the trade's apprenticeship rules. Bucks could be trained to do a single task. While they would not have the skills of a real molder, they could learn their one job adequately in far less time than it took to become a molder. Such semiskilled workers could then be substituted at much lower wages for more highly paid union molders. The semiskilled workers would undercut the position of the union molders but would have no bargaining power of their own, since their training had been confined to a single task and they could not switch to another employer who used slightly different methods.[46]

Spokesmen for the manufacturers claimed that they had the molders' best interests at heart. Some old men could not get along without assistance. If the Knights and the union had their way, such experienced employees would have to be fired. What the labor organizations demanded was "tyranny," a denial of the individual molder's right to choose. The leaders of District Assembly 50, according to Peninsular Stove Company President Moran, were "juveniles . . . sucking at the pap of public office . . . stirring up discontent and trouble among the workingmen simply to prolong their power."[47]

Moran's remarks hit too close to home for comfort. Knights of Labor leaders pointed out that Moran himself was city controller and had placed his own relatives on the city payroll. Certainly for him to criticize the district assembly's leaders for their political appointments was a case of the pot calling the kettle black. Yet Moran's remarks, as he must have known, merely echoed the growing criticism Knights of Labor leaders were receiving from their own ranks. Moreover, public sentiment seemed to be turning against the strike. Although the editors of the *News* recognized that the shutdown of the stove companies was a result of the manufacturers' desire to "test" the Knights, they blamed the Knights for the continuation of the strike. If the dispute was really between molders who wanted to use bucks and those who opposed the use of bucks, a strike against the company was "ill conceived," according to the editors. This strike was an example of the problem with the Knights—too many strikes.[48]

Two days after Moran's outburst, the district assembly leadership settled with the stove companies. A "treaty" was signed which seemed to grant victory to both sides. Old men who needed assistance would be allowed to hire bucks, but the bucks system would be officially done away with. The bucks system was thus outlawed but kept intact at the same time. The arrangement would be carried out according to rules worked out by employees and employers in each shop. Once again public image was apparently the primary concern of district assembly negotiators. Blamed by the newspapers for prolonging the strike in disregard of public welfare, the district assembly leadership quickly retreated. Despite Moran's obviously self-interested motivations, perhaps his charges of political opportunism were justified. Maybe they did fear that unpopular strikes could lose votes. After a rather lame denial of the charges, in which district assembly spokesmen admitted that five of twelve board members held appointive political office, district assembly officials were strangely silent.[49]

Dissatisfied molders, however, did not keep quiet. In the days and weeks following the signing of the agreement, it replaced the cigarmakers' issue as the focus of factional controversy within the local labor movement. Predictably, the vagueness of the agreement allowed countless opportunities for abuse. Union molders complained about a month later that union militants were being systematically discriminated against by the stove companies. Molders were paid on a piece rate basis with deductions for imperfections in workmanship. The companies, critics insisted, victimized union supporters, while appearing to stay within the agreement, by discounting or refusing perfectly acceptable work. As expected, the district assembly's investigating committee denied the charges, claiming that the inspectors who had rejected the work included Knights of Labor members, and the kickers were IMU members who were just trying to stir up trouble in order to break up the Knights. But molders disputed the district assembly's findings. The *Advance* reported that "several molders have already left the assembly and joined Union 31, because, they say, the Knights of Labor do not take enough interest in technical trade matters, and this puts them at a very great disadvantage. They also object that men who are not practical molders cannot know all the schemes to which the bosses resort to beat the men, and therefore cannot guard against these abuses by contract."[50]

A molders' public meeting during the closing days of the lockout demonstrated how the struggle had stimulated factionalism rather than drawing the molders closer together. More than 400 molders gathered for speeches by leaders of both IMU No. 31 and the Knights molders' assemblies, as well as a variety of leaders from both the district assembly and the Trades Council. Sam Goldwater, representing the Trades Council, obliquely attacked the Knights when he suggested that iron-molders could avoid future difficulties by organizing. John Bauer, master workman of LA 3954, leapt to his feet to point out that the molders were already organized in the Knights of Labor. Gustav Herzig continued the attack more directly when he pointed out that the Knights' national leader was paid $5,000 per year. Bauer was once again on his feet to repond to this "gratuitous insult," (although the remark was true). IMU local organizers criticized the Knights' negotiating tactics in the stove-works disputes, although their tone was less vitriolic than Goldwater's and Herzig's. Only the IMU International representative, astonished at what he heard, was detached enough to redirect the other speakers to their conflict with the companies instead of each other; in a couple of hours of speech making, he pointed out, nothing specific had been said about the current difficulties.[51] However, speakers ignored the IMU representative. Preoccupied with hardening factional lines, they were more interested in attacking each other than settling the practical problems at hand.

While the debate looked organizational, the Knights versus the unions, the alliances between leaders with quite different aims and ideological assumptions suggests that factionalism was based on something more complex than organizational rivalry. The Knights' position in these disputes was attacked by both conservative craft unionists in the leadership of IMU No. 31, socialist trade unionists like Goldwater and Herzig, and independent radicals in the Knights like Labadie, Grenell, and Dolan. They were defended by spokesmen representing the dominant artisan reformer faction in the district assembly leadership. Thus what appeared to be a struggle between two organizations, the Knights of Labor and the Trades Council, actually involved all four factions in the leadership of the Detroit labor movement. Some contemporary observers, as well as later scholars, ignored these subtleties and the deeper divisions that were behind the immediate questions of factional dispute.

The four groups had been present all along, but they had maintained peace until 1886 through the unifying role of the Knights of Labor. The Knights had been able to play this role because activists from both factions of the left as well as the artisan-reformers saw it as the most promising vehicle for changing the industrial system. Some craft conservatives had been disinterested or even hostile to the idea, but they found themselves isolated by the concurrence of the other factions and the excitement generated by the Knights' apparent success. When the Knights became a major force in the city, even craft conservatives may have started to rethink their assumptions. If they could use the Knights' power against employers without sacrificing craft autonomy, perhaps the organization would be valuable. But as the district assembly demonstrated its unwillingness to respect that autonomy, craft conservatives renewed their attack on the Knights in the series of disputes we have just examined. However, although their opposition had been long standing, it was not decisive.

The decisive change was the shift of the two left factions to the craft camp. The resulting realignment of forces escalated the factional struggle which ultimately destroyed the Knights in Detroit. The sequence of events was crucial. While craft unionists had expressed grievances against the district assembly leadership for some time, it was only at the end of 1886 and the beginning of 1887, that is after the left began to challenge the new district assembly leadership, that the issue of craft rights began to be seriously argued in the *Labor Leaf* and that radicals came out on the side of craft autonomy and craft rights. The timing suggests that the left took up the cause of craft rights not so much out of a deep-seated concern with craft grievances but as a weapon against the reformers in the district assembly, whom they were opposing for other reasons.

Politics and the public posture of the Knights were their real concern. The German socialists who walked out of the ILP convention over the issue of collaborationist politics, the Goldwater Gang, suddenly recognized the miseries of the International Cigarmakers or the ironmolders after the election. Leftists who had denounced craft narrowmindedness for years suddenly became the champions of craft rights. Of course, the German socialist left had been less than enthusiastic about the Knights for some time. They had opposed reformism all along. The more critical and dramatic shift was the new hostility of the independent left to the leadership of the Knights. They had been the order's founders in Detroit and its early leaders. Now they saw the organization moving away from the path they had charted for it. Labadie lamented early in 1886, well before the most bitter factionalism, that the influx of new members did not understand the order's true purposes, its real principles.[52]

The independent left joined the attack on the district assembly leadership because the problems of the craft unions, in their opinion, were symptomatic of more fundamental problems with the organization's direction. The working-class army was courting respectability more than social change. Powderly was hobnobbing with corporation executives and sabotaging the struggles of his own members. He was cavalierly violating the organization's constitution with increasing frequency, making a mockery of internal democracy. Most importantly, he had joined the "cowardly attack" on the men unjustly accused of the bombing at Haymarket Square in Chicago in 1886.[53]

Powderly, Haymarket, and the Destruction of the Knights of Labor

> There has been much dissatisfaction expressed with the results of the last year . . . and much of it has been with Mr. Powderly . . .
>
> *Labor Leaf*, December 29, 1886

Local reaction to Powderly followed the same factional lines and same sequence as the response to the District Assembly 50 leadership. Artisanal reformers enthusiastically supported Powderly, while both radical factions grew increasingly critical. To critics, the leadership of the district assembly and the national leadership were the same types of people making the same mistakes with similarly disastrous consequences. District assembly leaders sprang to Powderly's defense. As a result, by mid-1887 internal debate within the Detroit Knights of Labor had polarized into self-consciously pro- and anti-Powderly factions. There had been indications of local dissatisfaction with Powderly as early as the beginning of 1886, but the eventual leaders of Detroit's anti-Powderly faction were slower to attack Powderly directly than to attack his local counterparts. While opponents later admitted that they had had fundamental doubts about Powderly for quite some time, they were reluctant to express these feelings openly. The Knights were under attack in the press, from corporations, from some of the unions. Powderly was a public symbol of the Knights. To attack him might give comfort to the enemy, might hurt the organization. Men like Labadie, Grenell, and Dolan, the independent radicals in the Knights, did not want to bring about the downfall of the organization they had worked so hard to build. Their criticisms both of Powderly and of the District Assembly 50 leadership were based on exactly that fear—that inept leadership was destroying the order, but kicking, unnecessary or unjustified complaining or nonconstructive criticism of leaders, was among the harshest epithets of the labor culture.

As he began to change his mind about Powderly, Labadie moved cautiously. He suggested obliquely that Powderly could be removed from office without harming the labor movement. "The existence of the [labor] organizations does not depend upon the few men who have been honored by their fellows with prominent positions . . . ," he wrote in December 1886. "When the men who are now prominent in the movement fail to carry out the objects of the organizations they will be cast aside and others will take their places." Even Labadie's angry diatribes against the cigarmakers' expulsion order stopped short of any personal

denunciation of Powderly. The critical issue which finally turned Labadie and the other radicals in Detroit implacably against Powderly was
Haymarket.[54]

Labadie had not hesitated to defend the anarchists accused of
throwing the bomb, and he had been joined in this position by Burton,
Grenell, and the rest of the *Labor Leaf* staff. Only a day after the bombing, the *Labor Leaf* blamed the incident on the Chicago police who
"didn't mind their own business" and attacked a peaceful demonstration of workingmen.[55] Labadie was shocked, as he read various labor
papers they received regularly at the *Labor Leaf* offices, to discover that
most other labor papers had reacted quite differently. "I do wish the
labor papers would stop distributing the nasty puke the capitalist papers have seen fit to cover their dirty sheets with about the Chicago and
Milwaukee troubles. Don't be fools because your enemies want you to
be." "The Beastly police," Labadie argued, got what they deserved.
They had come to crack heads but "instead of cracking heads they got
cracked." Sentiment for the dead policemen was "a good deal of mush."
If a "body of men goes to break up any kind of meeting they should go
at the peril of their lives. If it is necessary to use dynamite to protect
the rights of free meeting, free press and free speech, then the sooner
we learn its manufacture and use and power the better it will be for the
toilers of the world. Anything is better than beastly submission to
wrong and injustice."[56]

Labadie's defense of the Haymarket defendants earned him a
warm letter of thanks from August Spies written from Cook County jail
shortly after the trial:

> Friend Labadie,
>
> If you would send us one or two copies of "Labor Leaf"
> regularly, we should consider it quite a favor . . . It is most
> gratifying to us to see that in the general stampede of cow-
> ardly retreat there are at least some voices who boldly and
> fearlessly proclaim the Truth.[57]

Some of Labadie's associates were not so sure. In particular, they
objected to his support of the use of dynamite, even in self-defense.
Henry Robinson challenged Labadie to a debate at the Dialectical
Union on the question of justifications for throwing the bomb. The public vote at this meeting was divided exactly equally, twenty-three to
twenty-three, but more important than the vote was the hysteria the debate provoked. Many of those present had refused to vote for fear of

being identified with the issue, and one who did was hounded out of town. John Goldring, a free-lance house painter, had declared publicly that he would have thrown a bomb, too, under similar circumstances, and his business partners and neighbors were so outraged that he decided to leave Detroit.[58]

But as news of the trial of the Haymarket defendants began to circulate, the balance of working-class opinion shifted more in Labadie's direction. Regardless of the question of armed self-defense, the men were not getting a fair trial. The prosecution had presented no evidence tying any of the defendants directly to either the planning or the execution of the act. Instead, they were being tried for their ideas, the prosecution asserting that their violent ideas provoked whoever had actually thrown the bomb. When news of the guilty verdict reached Detroit, the *Labor Leaf* labelled the decision a "legal outrage" and began to solicit funds for an appeal. Henry George Assembly 2697 explained why it had decided to contribute to the defense: "While this assembly does not believe that violent or revolutionary methods, in the sense of killing people and destroying property, are the true way to bring about social-economic changes, yet we do believe that even revolutionists have rights that should be respected, and we are willing to aid them in maintaining those rights."[59]

When Lucy Parsons arrived in Detroit in January 1887 to speak in her husband's behalf, the city's police superintendent tried to pressure hall owners to refuse to rent to her and absolutely forbade a political meeting on Sunday. But Mrs. Parsons spoke to a packed house at Germania Hall on Saturday night, explaining the details of the case, and the audience responded warmly. She remained in Detroit for nearly a week, speaking at other public meetings and at Knights of Labor assemblies. For Burton, Labadie, Sam Goldwater, and the others who had supported the defendants from the beginning, it was an intensely emotional experience. Parsons, a brother Knight, was being railroaded, they believed, by Chicago millionaires as revenge for the eight-hour movement. A red scare atmosphere had been created. *Labor Leaf* correspondents noted that newspapers all across the country, including movement papers, were refusing letters and articles sympathetic to the condemned men. If Parsons could be convicted on such flimsy evidence, who might be next?[60]

Yet Powderly was responding to this red scare with red-baiting of his own. In April 1887, according to Labadie, during a speech at Harrisburg, Pennsylvania, he had dramatically pulled an American flag out of his pocket and waved it while he denounced all those who supported the red flag.[61] At the Richmond, Virginia, general assembly in October 1886, he had opposed a clemency resolution, arguing that "under no circumstances should we do anything that can, even by implication, be interpreted as identification with the Anarchist element. Their blind, unlawful act has cast a stain upon the name of labor which will take years to wipe out." Powderly not only refused to question the guilt of the Haymarket defendants, but he also blamed them for all of the order's problems. "Instead of owing them sympathy we owe them a debt of hatred for their unwarrantable interference at a time when labor had all it could do to weather the storm." While he finally voted for a compromise resolution which asked for mercy but emphasized the Knights' disapproval of "infractions of the law," his confession of hatred probably came closer to his real feelings. Although he had voted for the resolution, he used his influence against all actions by the Knights in favor of the clemency campaign.[62] His supporters at the state and local level emulated him, trying to brand administration critics as anarchists and revolutionaries. In August, the Michigan State Assembly passed an anti-anarchy and revolution resolution after intense debate, but refused resolutions censuring adminstration conduct.[63]

Both in Michigan and nationally, anti-administration leaders began to line up support for their side as well. At the national level the general executive board was split. Tom Barry, a local hero to many Michigan Knights, had been drifting further and further from Powderly almost from the day of his reelection to the board in the fall of 1885. By June 1886, he was publicly at odds with Powderly at the Cleveland GA. In November, when Barry was sent to direct the Chicago packing-house workers' strike, Powderly betrayed him by calling off the strike in the midst of the negotiations. Barry insisted that they had been on the verge of victory. The break with Powderly was complete; Barry toured the country denouncing him. Barry was joined in oppositon by W. H. Bailey, a leader of the Knights' Coalminers' National Trade Assembly 135. Powerful districts in New York and Chicago, antagonized by Powderly's position on the Haymarket case, sympathized with Barry. Both sides began looking toward the upcoming Minneapolis GA for a showdown, not only on the Haymarket issue, but on Powderly's conduct as master workman. Barry, who was in close contact with many of Powderly's opponents, kept Labadie informed of developments in the internal struggle. "Kicking in Labor circles seems to be the order of the day all over the country," Barry wrote him in June 1887, " . . . if we would kick against Capitalistic oppression we would have kicking enough." In July, he wrote Labadie to ask "how Detroit is fighting."[64]

They were fighting, indeed. In July a Cooperative Publishing Company took over ownership of the *Advance* and appointed Labadie editor in chief. With McGregor demoted to business manager, the tone of the paper shifted once again. Criticisms of both local and national leadership received greater prominence, while union activities were treated more favorably. After a few weeks, McGregor gave up journalism and returned to his position as ship captain. In August, Labadie decided to run for GA representative in open opposition to Powderly's policies. GA candidates were being clearly identified as pro- or anti-Powderly, both by the press and by their supporters, as battle lines were drawn. The state assembly had elected a pro-Powderly slate, so that the Detroit election had even greater significance. Despite the dominance of pro-Powderly elements on the district assembly executive board, the influence of Labadie, Grenell, Burton, Dolan, and others had made District Assembly 50 a maverick district for some time. They had refused to enforce the cigarmakers' expulsion order, decreed their unwillingness to accept all constitutional changes made since 1885 because they had not been properly ratified, and even sponsored a movement for a new constitution designed to decentralize authority in the organization. Labadie was a pioneer Knight, founder of the order in Michigan, and a consistent advocate of radical views—symbolically, perhaps the most *anti* anti-Powderly candidate possible. His election as GA delegate would express the strongest possible condemnation of the existing leadership and would have widespread repercussions outside Detroit.[65]

Labadie campaigned unequivocally against Powderly. Summarizing Powderly's deficiencies in an *Advance* editorial, he argued that Powderly was "not a bad man," but he had demonstrated he was a "poor leader." He had condemned the eight-hour movement only weeks before the May 1, 1886, deadline, thereby weakening the campaign. His cigarmakers' expulsion order was arbitrary and unconstitutional. His leadership of the Southwestern strike had been "half-hearted" and had interfered with the workers' efforts. Instead of opposing the attack on the Chicago anarchists as an attack on the whole labor movement, he had joined in the criticism of them. His acceptance of re-election for a two-year term (with a salary increase) at Richmond instead of the customary one-year term was a move away from democracy within the order. His advocacy of temperance demonstrated his lack of socioeconomic analysis; intemperance was a product of poverty and to treat it as a separate moral issue diverted the movement from real reforms. And most importantly, power had gone to his head; he had become susceptible to "capitalist flattery" and the desire for public approval from those who should be his enemies. Obviously, Labadie had much of the local leadership of the district assembly in mind when he made these criticisms as well, for he concluded that "new blood infused into the general offices, from the highest to the lowest, would be a benefit to the order."[66]

Labadie's election, by a two-thirds majority, indicated deep disaffection with the current leadership. As critics had hoped, the local newspapers took his victory as evidence that District Assembly 50 "sets itself squarely against the present administration." A proposal by the pro-Powderly faction to limit Labadie's prerogatives by specifying how the district wanted him to vote on key issues also lost overwhelmingly, reinforcing this impression.[67]

The GA opened in Minneapolis on October 4, 1887, amid a series of credential fights in which the Powderly forces attempted to prevent seating radical delegates on various technicalities. The real fight, as everyone knew, would be over the clemency campaign for the condemned Haymarket men. With the execution only a month away, emotions on both sides of the issue had almost reached hysteria. Supporters of clemency were convinced that an unequivocal resolution by the country's most powerful labor organization would influence political leaders who would make the final decision on the appeals for commutation. The convention's decision might make the difference between life and death. Powderly was equally resolute in his determination to dissociate the order completely, not only from anarchism, but even from any clemency campaign.[68]

The climax came on October 10 on a resolution by James Quinn of New York District Assembly 49. Avoiding any reference to ideology or the nature of the trial, Quinn tried to commit the GA to commutation on the basis of opposition to capital punishment. Despite the moderate tone of the proposal, pro-Powderly delegates tried to shout him down, and Powderly tried to dispose of the matter by ruling the motion out of order. After some parliamentary wrangling, an anti-Powderly delegate appealed the ruling of the chair. Defeated 121–53, the anti-Powderly forces moved to reconsider, forcing the debate that Powderly obviously wanted to avoid.[69]

Powderly monopolized the floor and pulled out all the stops. He invented anarchists' attempts to assassinate him, alluded to sinister plots by the International (anarchist) to dominate the Knights for evil purposes, and threatened the delegates with responsibility for destroying the order if they allowed it to become associated with anarchy. It was an "illogical, cowardly, brutal, and violent" performance, Labadie charged later, but the majority of the delegates were cowed.[70]

The opposition was furious, and the convention degenerated into a shouting free-for-all of charges and countercharges. Powderly, now sure of his ability to control the majority, tried to have his opponents on the GEB, Barry and Bailey, removed by calling for new elections of officers and board members. Elections were not scheduled for another year, but Powderly and his associates engineered a scheme whereby they would all submit their resignations, call for new elections, and all would be reelected except Barry and Bailey. But the plot was too transparent, and Barry and Bailey refused to resign. Barry responded with a tirade including a veritable inventory of administrative abuses, and Labadie presented evidence of Powderly's own socialist past in order to show the hypocrisy of the master workman's pious antiradicalism.[71]

Finally, a group of opposition delegates, nearly a third of the entire convention, including Labadie and a large group of Chicago delegates, walked out of the assembly and met in another hall to discuss strategy. They decided to hold a rump convention in Chicago on the way home from the GA. Thirty-five delegates attended, forming a tentative organization under the name of the Provisional Committee, designed to either take over the Knights or establish a rival group. The committee issued a manifesto outlining the long series of abuses committed by Powderly and urging locals and districts to pledge their support to the Provisional Committee.[72]

A veritable war within the Knights of Labor ensued. Powderly returned home and immediately began drafting letters to anyone and everyone on the anarchist plot to take over the Knights of Labor. "I have a favor to ask," began the standardized attack: "Traitors to the cause of Labor have gained entrance to our Order and would tear down the edifice which it has taken years to build . . . I have for eight years as GMW striven . . . to build an organization . . . but profane hands have been laid upon it and the men who gathered in Chicago and gave out that hostile declaration to the world, did so, only because Anarchy could not rule our Order."[73]

As one of Labadie's associates on the Provisional Committee, John Ehmann, noted, Powderly's strategy was "simply dub the kickers who protested against the manner in which things were conducted in Minneapolis as Anarchists, and under the prejudice which that word excites, prevent any further discussion of the question."[74] The Provisionals were actively organizing, nonetheless, in New York and Chicago. They had organized a district assembly of their own in Chicago, another district assembly in Brooklyn was ready to join, and so were several Philadelphia locals.[75] Litchman admitted to Powderly that the outcome of the power struggle was impossible to predict. "Since the Order started no crisis so grave has been upon it." At Minneapolis the officers had admitted a drop in membership of more than 200,000 since July 1886, but Litchman confessed three weeks after the GA that the decline was really much more serious than that. "The per capita tax for October 1, 1887, has been paid on but little over 350,000 members . . . a falling off of 150,000 since July 1, 1887 (the basis for the officers' claim of 485,000 at Minneapolis). It will be impossible to keep this fact secret." Their apparent victory at Minneapolis, Litchman thought, should not blind Powderly to the weakness of their position: "It would need but little to turn against us many who were on our side at Minneapolis . . . many who voted with us were only lukewarm in their fidelity."[76]

In the weeks immediately following the GA, Litchman's fears that the administration's position was weak were substantiated in Detroit. Labadie returned determined to arouse the Detroit Knights against Powderly and to drive the Powderly forces from local office in the district assembly. In an informal report to the *Advance* on the GA and the rump convention in Chicago, Labadie predicted that the Provisional Committee would draw at least 100,000 members away from the order. On the advice of Charles Seib, the Chicago leader of the Provisional Committee, Labadie decided to try and recapture the district assembly rather than join the secessionist movement immediately, but he did formally announce that "I have declared open warfare upon those who use this order or the labor movement for immediate gain at the expension of its future development. The present general officers of the Knights of Labor must go before the Order can proceed on its rightful mission towards a just settlement of social and industrial evils. Large salaries and large powers have unfitted them to lead a labor movement successfully."[77]

Powderly and his Detroit supporters were afraid that Labadie might carry out his goal. Powderly wrote A. M. Dewey, a Detroit associate, just after the GA asking him to rouse opposition against Labadie. "Labadie," Powderly declared, was "a man who is known to oppose the true principles of Knighthood . . . I have been told that Labadie did not represent the true sentiments of District Assembly 50, if that is true I want those who do not approve of Labadie's actions to demonstrate their power during the coming year." But while Powderly assured Dewey that "there are good men in the Order in Detroit . . . ," he admitted that "I am acquainted with no one there in whom I have confidence outside of Devlin and yourself." [78]

Dewey and Devlin did what they could. Dewey denounced Labadie's *Advance* article on the Provisional Committee and tried to refute Labadie's charges at the district assembly meetings, but although he claimed that "hundreds of people, in the order and out of it, have congratulated me . . . ," he did not seem to be having much success. He complained to Powderly that "my defence of the officers of the Order from attacks of that element within our own ranks which would wreck the movement upon the shoals of anarchy, has made it necessary for me to seek employment elsewhere . . . The Labadie gang in Detroit have determined to make it 'hot' for me here, and I don't propose to give them the chance any longer." Dewey had left Detroit and begged Powderly to hire him as editor for a proposed expanded version of the Knights' national *Journal*. [79]

Devlin did not panic as easily as Dewey, but he also doubted that he could hold District Assembly 50 for the administration. Labadie's charges were "most unfair and unjust," but Devlin admitted that the executive board had made serious "errors . . . in its disposition of the funds and sometimes in its action upon matters reffered [*sic*] to it." Labadie was "devious" and "we had quite a time in the D. A. last Evening." The situation had gone too far for the district assembly officers to handle themselves. "Something must be done and that Soon to counteract the influence of Bro Labadie and those who are as I believe trying to ruin the Order in this District. I believe and Bro Long DMW & others who do not take stock in anarchy, that it is absolutely necessary that you should come to Detroit and set yourself and the GA right before our Brothers." [80]

Labadie had hoped to be elected as district master workman. But the tension of the unsuccessful last-minute struggle to save the Haymarket defendants seemed to sap his energy. He had been scheduled to present his formal report on the Minneapolis convention, which the district assembly intended to print and circulate to other districts, early in

November, but at the last minute he was ill and could not attend the meeting. He resigned as editor of the *Advance and Labor Leaf*, and he was not featured among the keynote speakers at a final local sympathy rally of 2,000 supporters a week before the November 11 execution. He finally presented his report three days after the execution. Powderly, he charged, was "as much responsible for the murder committed in Chicago last Friday as anyone connected with that most unfortunate affair."[81]

Labadie vowed to continue his war against Powderly, but in the weeks that followed he appeared to retire from labor affairs. He took a new job with the Detroit *Sun* as Grenell took over the editorship of the *Advance*. No private correspondence from him in the months after the execution has been preserved, but his actions suggest a deep depression over the outcome of events. He was sick much of the time, his "Cranky Notes" column appeared irregularly, there were fewer reports of public speeches than in previous years, he decided not to run for district assembly office, and he threatened to quit the organization to which he had devoted nine years of his life.[82]

With Labadie's decision not to run for district master workman, the opposition fixed its hopes on Thomas Dolan. Dolan was a popular candidate. He had been a labor activist in Detroit since the early 1860s, a pioneer Knight, and a prominent union cigarmaker, but by the time of the election in January 1888, the balance was shifting once again away from the opposition.[83]

The Powderly faction brought in a new face to replace DMW Long. A. W. Vicars had been on the district assembly executive board in 1887, but he was far less well known than men like Long, Devlin, or Dewey. Devlin nominated Vicars; Labadie nominated Dolan. No one could be confused about the meaning of the election. On the first ballot the vote stood Vicars: forty; Dolan: forty-one; three scattered, with several not voting. Dolan led by one, but on the second ballot, the undecided votes swung to Vicars. He was elected by a margin of forty-five to forty-three. From then on, the administration faction swept all offices. "Labadie and Company were completely routed," Devlin gloated. As a token peace gesture, Labadie was appointed district statistician, but as the *Advance* admitted, it had been a "complete victory for the administrationists."[84]

But it was a Pyrrhic victory. At the installation of new officers on January 24, Vicars and Worthy Foreman Joseph Hockaday tried to smooth the ruffled feathers of the opposition—Vicars with a collection of platitudes that combined generous doses of Labor Day rhetoric with a bit of radical jargon, Hockaday with a speech reminiscent of Jefferson's inaugural address ("I know no administrationists or anti-administrationists. I know them only as Knights of Labor"). But the image of the Knights had been permanently tarnished, and most of those who had grown dissatisfied were now convinced that the organization was beyond repair.[85]

Spurred on especially by Sam Goldwater, radicals in both the Trades Council and the Knights of Labor tried to swing local sentiment behind the AFL. Goldwater had been the Trades Council delegate to the AFL convention at the end of 1887, and he was impressed with Gompers and the AFL. The Knights had always accused the trade unions of being too conservative, but Goldwater pointed out that Gompers and the AFL had appealed for clemency for the Chicago anarchists while the Knights had not. The Knights were not a "legitimate labor organization" at all, he decided, and he began making public speeches to that effect. Apparently other trade unionists began to agree with him. In late July, they elected him Trades Council president, and six weeks later a number of unions refused to march with the Knights on Labor Day. By October, he and Labadie had begun to make plans for a Michigan Federation of Labor as a statewide AFL affiliate. When the MFL finally met in February 1889, Labadie was elected its first president.[86]

But the Trades Council and the MFL were no more congenial to disgruntled radicals than the Knights had been, and in the intensely factional atmosphere, opponents in the council made few efforts to placate them or even maintain a superficial appearance of unity. In February 1888, the Trades Council voted down a proposal for strictly independent political action by a two-to-one margin, and in August, it again defeated a similar motion. A motion to prohibit any Trades Council officer or delegate from holding appointive political office was also defeated, as was a Central Labor Union proposal in October to sponsor a mass meeting in commemoration of the Chicago martyrs.[87] Votes on all of these issues revealed a hardening of earlier factional lines. Craft conservatives on the council, emboldened by the disarray of the Knights and the apparent vindication of their earlier skepticism about far-reaching schemes for social change, now carried the council on all of these issues. They consistently outvoted the coalition of German socialists and independent radicals who were trying to push the council into replacing the faltering Knights as the voice of class militance.

The Knights of Labor did not fade away immediately, but rapidly falling membership figures decisively undercut their capacity to present themselves as the voice of universal organization and reform. By the

209

beginning of 1888, Knights of Labor membership in Detroit had fallen by nearly two-thirds from the 1886 peak.[88] District Assembly 50 lost members steadily during 1888, dropping from 2,620 just before the October 1887 GA to 1,277 by August 1888.[89] Some of the drop could be accounted for by the transfer of several large assemblies out of District Assembly 50 and into national trade districts. Many trades within the Detroit Knights were dissatisfied with the District Assembly 50 leadership, but they were quite reluctant to leave the order entirely. By 1889, only about half the LA's in the city belonged to the district assembly. Even after such assemblies as the barbers (7,439), longshoremen (10,413), and Florence Nightingale Assembly (3,102) joined the Trades Council, they maintained dual membership in the Knights of Labor.[90]

As late as 1890, there were still thirty-six Knights of Labor assemblies in Detroit, but by the end of the year, key assemblies were rapidly transferring to the Trades Council. Five shoeworkers' assemblies switched late in the year; the large streetcar workers' assembly lapsed, and a street railway union was formed; the Brass Finishers National Trade District, which had its headquarters in Detroit, was reorganizing as a national union; and the carworkers' assemblies were folding. By 1891, there were only eleven assemblies. The following year, as Globe Tobacco Company cancelled its long-standing agreement with the district assembly, and Florence Nightingale Association (new name) dropped its KL affiliation, the district assembly ceased to exist.[91]

There is no record of any Knights of Labor assembly in Detroit after 1892, although the Knights may have maintained a vestigial existence. A Knights of Labor Hall was still listed in the 1894 City *Directory*, and a handful of railroad workers questioned by State Bureau of Labor Statistics investigators still claimed Knights of Labor membership in that year. As a meaningful organization, however, the Knights did not function in Detroit after 1891.[92]

By 1892, local labor leaders were already writing *post mortems* on the Knights. Captain McGregor, even though he had been identified with the pro-administration faction, attributed the death of the Knights to corruption and inefficiency in its leaders. Labadie, writing many years later, still saw the Knights' destruction in more personal terms. The "crushing blow" had been Powderly's refusal to allow passage of the clemency resolution at the 1887 Minneapolis GA.[93]

In retrospect, much of the factional bickering of the late 1880s appears quite predictable. The positions that leaders of each faction took in these disputes seem consistent with the logic of the political cultures out of which they came. Conservative craft unionists may only have been acting out the values of their native and Irish compatriots. The class-harmony arguments of the district assembly's artisan reformers could have come straight out of any republican reformer's speech from twenty years before. The intransigence of the German socialists had been evident for more than a decade. And perhaps the attempts of native radicals like Labadie and Grenell to push republican values in a radical direction had been based on a misperception of republican assumptions all along. It is tempting to view the outcome as inevitable. Yet for a decade they had cooperated to create institutions that helped to bridge the differences between cultures, bridges that had made a movement possible.

The destruction of the Knights of Labor had serious repercussions for the subculture of opposition. The Knights had provided its organizational cohesion. Not only was their demise intensely discouraging for all who had placed such high hopes on the order's success, but their failure also removed the broad base of support for the subculture's other formal institutions. Few of these institutions could survive without it. Thousands of workers who had enthusiastically rushed into the movement in 1886 found themselves confronted with a bitterly squabbling leadership throughout the late 1880s. Without a rich internal life to hold the workers, most simply drifted off, wondering whether any plans to remake society were, after all, hopelessly utopian.

"Will the butter come?"

The trouble with the whole army of the discontented is that they are tired of churning so long and seeing no signs of butter. Agitation, education, organization, is all very fine at the first go off, but what is the prospect? When will these dreams of ours materialize? It matters but little whether the "administration" be justified or not. The point of contest is will the butter come? Can it be we are churning skim milk? Is the virtue gone out of our membership? Has personal ambition and jealousy come in to frustrate our purposes?

Advance and Labor Leaf, December 8, 1888.

The discouragement of activists like Labadie was not confined to the leadership of the movement. Mid-1886 was one of those brief rare moments when people believed almost anything was possible. Joining the

Knights of Labor, striking for eight hours in May, marching as a public declaration of commitment on Labor Day had all involved serious risks of reprisal. Yet thousands had done so defiant of those risks. They were making history, and in the new cooperative commonwealth, workers would no longer be subject to arbitrary firing.

But the demands of everyday life have a way of intruding upon those who are making history. People cannot suspend consideration of immediate needs and risks without seeing some results for their efforts. How long could they expect to churn and "see no signs of butter?" Workers were regularly being fired for union and Knights of Labor membership: more than a dozen cases were described in the *Labor Leaf* in only eight months between September 1886 and April 1887. "An injury to one is the concern of all" had little meaning if the Knights could not, or—as in the case of the Chicago anarchists—would not, defend those who had joined the cause.[94]

When workers demanded action in response to employer reprisals, their feuding district assembly leaders urged patience and caution. Perhaps that was wise counsel. The long-term strike record of most labor organizations had not been encouraging, and even the most radical labor veterans urged emotional restraint and careful planning before calling a strike. But the district assembly's leaders' pompous way of combining advice with preaching was extraordinarily objectionable to many workers. Maybe when an employer fired a worker for Knights of Labor membership, the district assembly could not get the job back, but it was insulting when District Master Workman Vicars announced that "the ordinary wage slave cannot grasp the money, land, and other vexatious questions . . . in his present mentally crippled condition." And if that "mentally crippled" wage slave had the audacity to suggest a strike or boycott as a remedy, Vicars argued that such "intimidation and coercion only result in pitting class against class."[95]

Such rhetoric conformed to the republican vision of artisan reformers, but in reality class was already pitted against class. Turn the other cheek was not a popular message. The moralizing tone that went with it was equally divisive. Many of the district assembly's officers were active prohibitionists. Their pietistic sermons were standard fare to native republicans, but temperance speeches outraged other workers. When John Devlin blamed the KL-AFL strife on the drunkenness of the AFL leaders, not only was he making an absurd claim, but he was also echoing the arguments of employers who blamed workers for drinking themselves into poverty. J. F. Bray reacted indignantly to

Devlin's temperance speeches. These prohibitionists "belong to the 'goody-goody' class and have no affinity for the wage workers. They are the same breed of fanatics that have persecuted reformers in all ages for the assumed good of their souls." A great many workers agreed with him, and when the new Knights of Labor constitution in 1887 had a temperance clause, several local assemblies withdrew en masse. The Germans, in particular, were incensed at the temperance campaign, and by the spring of 1888, there was only one German local assembly left in Detroit.[96]

If they could not drink, could not strike, and could not boycott, what could they do when employers fired them for joining the labor movement? "Education the Pre-eminent Principle of the Knights of Labor," Master Workman Vicars declared in his inaugural address. "Would you answer an old K. of L. a question or two?" wrote one veteran to the *Advance* in 1888. "Education is the cry of our general officers. How long are we to be before we get graduated in this labor movement?"[97]

There is no way to sample the opinions of a representative group of Detroit workers to see what they felt about the pious pronouncements of Vicars and Devlin or how many identified with the criticisms of the opposition. However, the membership trends of Detroit's labor movement, as well as the fortunes of the subsidiary labor organizations, suggest that a substantial proportion, perhaps a majority of those who had participated in the upheaval of 1886, were not only disappointed with the Knights but disillusioned about the possibility of any kind of successful action. The labor movement claimed 13,000 members in Detroit in 1886: 8,000 Knights and 5,000 trade unionists. Even if that figure exaggerated the number of dues-paying members, nearly that many actually participated in strikes or demonstrations in mid-1886. Within a year, the combined total membership of the Knights of Labor and the trade unions was no more than 8,000: about 3,000 in the Knights and 5,000 in the unions. Total estimated union membership in 1892 was 7,100. Most of the 2,000 or so workers that remained with the Knights in 1889 had shifted to the Trades Council by 1891.[98] But what of the thousands of others who had participated in the mid-1880s? Despite the intervening population growth and industrialization of more than a decade, Detroit union membership still hovered at a little under 8,000 in 1901. Thousands of Knights of Labor had permanently left the movement.[99]

Even more important, however, is what else went with the disillusioned Knights. The Labor party had collapsed by 1888. The Co-operative Boot and Shoe Company announced its closing in April 1888. Most of the other cooperatives followed in the next year or two. The Detroit Rifles were never mentioned after 1887. The *Advance and Labor Leaf*, after more than five years of uninterrupted weekly publishing, closed in late 1889, no longer able to meet its costs. When John Burton's monthly *Onward* ceased operations the following year, Detroit was without a regular English-language labor press for the first time in more than a decade. One by one, the organizations that had made up the infrastructure of an active subculture had gone. The cooperative work traditions, the spirit of mutuality that lay at the heart of the subculture of opposition continued. But lacking formal organizational vehicles they lost much of their oppositional character. Equally important, without a formal mechanism like the Knights for linking this spirit with a larger vision that went beyond the neighborhood and workshop level, it lost much of its sense of immediacy. The labor movement survived, but with far weaker connections to the majority of workers outside its ranks.[100]

The movement that remained in the 1890s was quite different from that of the 1880s. It did a fair job of protecting its members' wage rates: wage levels for unionized trades generally went up in the early 1890s. But it was a movement which ceased to speak for workers as a whole, which no longer addressed itself to the continuing patterns of rapid change in the city, a movement which no longer made serious efforts to expand, a movement without a vision.

NOTES

1. DLL.

2. Most of the standard labor histories of this period are organized around organizational conflict between the Knights and the AFL, especially those following in the Commons-Perlman tradition. Perhaps the most influential recent example is Gerald Grob's *Workers and Utopia* (Chicago, 1969), which emphasizes ideological differences between the supposed reform unionism of the Knights and the business unionism of the AFL. Grob's arguments are a reformulation of Selig Perlman's treatment of the Knights and the AFL in *A Theory of the Labor Movement* (New York, 1928). Jama Lazerow, "'The Workingman's Hour': The 1886 Labor Uprising in Boston," *Labor History*, 21 (Spring 1980): 200–220, is a case study critical of the Grob-Perlman thesis.

3. DLL; *Labor Leaf*, January 5, 12, 1887.

4. "Reports of the Officers of District Assembly 50 for the Term Ending December 31, 1887," (Detroit, 1888); Detroit *Evening News*, June 8, September 5, 1887; *Advance and Labor Leaf*, September 24, 1887; DLL; Detroit *Unionist*, June 3, 1887.

5. Ibid. Bauer, an iron molder, and Stuermer, the cigarmaker, (later expelled). Andrew Forbes was a longtime leader of the sailors' union, a regional organization of Great Lakes sailors. Both Strigel and Long had some leadership experience in the Crispins, but the national organization of the Crispins was essentially defunct by the late 1870s.

6. Forbes, Strigel, and Long. Long's experiences as a Crispin local and state leader had been in Massachusetts, not Detroit.

7. See note 4.

8. David Boyd to A. Inglis, July 22, 1938, LC; *Evening News*, March 9, 1890.

9. *Labor Leaf*, June 23, August 11, September 1, 1886.

10. Detroit *Evening News*, September 3, 1886; *Labor Leaf*, September 8, 1886. According to the *News*, there were 155 delegates; the total vote on Egan was only 143, leaving 11 abstentions, assuming Egan could not vote himself.

11. Ibid.

12. *Labor Leaf*, September 8, 15, 1886. O'Reilly's unsavory political associations were discussed in the *Labor Leaf* in 1885, and a key article was reprinted in the September 22, 1886, issue. A short biography of O'Reilly can be found in *Chronology of Notable Events* (Wayne County Historical and Pioneer Society, Detroit, 1890), p. 419.

13. *Labor Leaf*, September 15, 22, 1886.

14. *Labor Leaf*, September 22, 29, October 6, 13, 1886; "The Labor Champions," newspaper clipping in Ross Scrapbook (vol. 1, p. 19), Burton Historical Collections, Detroit Public Library. Grenell excused the appointment in his Autobiography by arguing it gave him time to devote to the movement. He was chosen on Egan's suggestion as a neutral candidate in order to settle differences between two rival Republican factions who wanted the job.

15. *Labor Leaf*, September 29, 1886.

16. *Labor Leaf*, October 15, 1886.

17. Ibid., September 1, 18, 22, October 20, 1886; Detroit *Evening News*, November 2, 1886. O'Donnell took a management position with the Peninsular Stove Company in 1887 until his appointment later that year as a customs official.

18. Data for the analysis of the 1886 election comes from Wayne County Election Records and a sample drawn from the 1880 manuscript census and data provided by Olivier Zunz. For a discussion of these sources, see the Note on Sources at the end. The conclusions are based on a series of multiple regression equations, partial correlations, and analysis of sample precincts.

Beta weights for regression equations were as follows: With Germans, skilled workers, unskilled workers, and a dummy variable for factories struck in May 1886, in the equation, beta weights are:

unskilled workers	.362
skilled workers	.217
Germans	.300 (significant only at .1 level
Factory location	.138 with one tailed t test)

With Germans, working class (i.e., skilled and unskilled workers), and factory location, beta weights are:

working class	.425
Germans	.302
Factory location	.136 (significant at .1 level)

19. I.e., $R^2_{wc} = .3899$; partial R^2_{wc} correcting for German working class equals .2050; German working class thus explains 47.4 percent of the effect of percent working class on labor vote. This is consistent with results of regression equations cited in note 18.

20. Wayne County Election Records, 1886, Burton Historical Collections, Detroit Public Library.

21. Detroit *Evening News*, November 2, 3, 1886.

22. Comparing the values predicted by multiple regression equations to the actual labor vote, the mean residual for these precincts is -11.2, while the mean residual for other German working-class precincts is $+5.5$. In other words, given the ethnic and class composition of the first four precincts, they would have been expected to register a mean labor vote 16 points higher if they behaved like the other German working-class precincts. In the latter case the total ILP vote in these precincts would have been 378 votes higher than it was. I have no other explanation for the unusual behavior of these precincts, and the presumption that the low labor vote was the result of the Goldwater gang is also substantiated by the fact that such key leaders of the Goldwater group as Gustav Herzig and Charles Erb lived in the neighborhood. The estimate of a 400-vote influence also comes close to matching the vote totals of local SLP candidates in the early 1890s when the SLP again began running its own candidates.

23. *Labor Leaf*, November 3, 1886.

24. *Labor Leaf*, October 27, 1886; Detroit *Evening News*, June 8, 1887. Long and Haire were Irish-born, Devlin was second-generation Irish.

25. Detroit *Evening News*, September 10, 1887; *Advance and Labor Leaf*, November 5, 12, 1887. Between September and November, the Labor party had changed its name from Independent to United.

26. *Advance and Labor Leaf*, November 5, 12, 1887.

27. Ibid.

28. *Labor Leaf*, May 3, 6, June 9, August 4, November 17, 1886.

29. *KLDB*. Two additional mixed assemblies were predominantly made up of employees in a single factory. Some other assemblies officially designated as mixed have been classified as trade because they were industrial unions made up of related trades in a particular industry or factory. LA's 7749 and 8104, for example, both carworkers' assemblies, were officially designated mixed, but they have been considered trade here because they included several crafts in a single factory. See chapters 3 and 4 for more detailed descriptions of the trade origins of the Knights and relations between the Knights and the unions.

30. For a more detailed discussion of the background to the cigarmakers' dispute, see Philip S. Foner, *History of the Labor Movement in the United States*, 2 vols. (New York, 1947), 2:133–36; John R. Commons, *History of Labor in the United States*, 2 vols. (New York, 1918), 2:412; Norman J. Ware, *The Labor Movement in the United States, 1860–1895* (New York, 1929), pp. 258–79; and Richard J. Oestreicher, "Solidarity and Fragmentation: Working People and Class Consciousness in Detroit, 1877–1895" (Ph.D. dissertation, Michigan State University, 1979), pp. 380–90. The Progressives eventually returned to the International after the Richmond GA expelled all cigarmakers who were dual cardholders, Progressive as well as International. See Commons, 2:412.

31. *Labor Leaf*, May 26, 1886; Oestreicher, pp. 387–90.

32. *Advance and Labor Leaf*, February 19, 1887.

33. *Advance and Labor Leaf*, February 19, 1887.

34. Ibid. The timing of the change of editors coincided precisely with the beginning of the expulsion controversy and led to a dramatic reversal of editorial policy. The change was apparently part of a power play on the part of the administration faction in the district assembly, an interpretation later substantiated by both Labadie and Burton. The editorship changed hands several more times over the next two years as contending factions continued to struggle for control.

35. *Advance and Labor Leaf*, February 26, 1887.

36. *Advance and Labor Leaf*, March 5, 19, 26, April 9, 23, 30, 1887.

37. *Advance and Labor Leaf*, February 26, March 12, April 23, July 16, 1887; *Reports of the Officers of District Assembly 50 for the Term Ending December 31, 1887* (Detroit, 1888), pp. 4–5; "Men Who Make Your Cigars," clipping in Detroit Labor Leaders File, LC.

38. *KLDB*; "Among the Molders," clipping, LC.

39. *Advance and Labor Leaf*, April 16, 23, 30, May 6, 1887.

40. *Advance and Labor Leaf*, February 26, June 11, 1887; David Boyd to A. Inglis, September 5, 1938; Detroit *Evening News*, June 6, 1887.

41. *Advance and Labor Leaf*, March 19, August 27, 1887.

42. *Advance and Labor Leaf*, February 26, 1887.

43. Ibid.

44. Ibid.

45. *Advance and Labor Leaf*, April 30, May 6, June 11, 1887.

46. *Advance and Labor Leaf*, May 14, 1887; Detroit *Evening News*, June 3, 1887.

47. Detroit *Evening News*, June 7, 8, 1887.

48. *Advance and Labor Leaf*, June 11, 18, 1887; Detroit *Evening News*, June 3, 4, 1887.

49. Detroit *Evening News*, June 8, 9, 1887.

50. *Evening News*, July 14, 21, 1887; *Advance and Labor Leaf*, July 16, 1887.

51. Detroit *Evening News*, June 6, 1887; *Advance and Labor Leaf*, June 11, 1887.

52. *Labor Leaf*, March 31, 1886.

53. "Powderly Belabored," clipping in Knights of Labor-History File, LC.

54. *Labor Leaf*, December 29, 1886.

55. *Labor Leaf*, May 5, 1886.

56. *Labor Leaf*, May 19, June 2, 16, 1886.

57. August Spies to Labadie, September 7, 1886, LC.

58. *Labor Leaf*, June 30, July 7, 1886; Labadie reminiscences in Knights of Labor-Michigan File, LC.

59. *Labor Leaf*, August 29, September 8, 15, December 29, 1886.

60. *Labor Leaf*, January 26, 1887.

61. *Advance and Labor Leaf*, April 23, 1887.

62. T. V. Powderly, *Thirty Years of Labor* (Columbus, Ohio, 1889), pp. 544–45. Ware, pp. 317–18.

63. *Proceedings of the Knights of Labor Michigan State Assembly*, 1887, pp. 37–40; *Advance and Labor Leaf*, August 6, 1887; Detroit *Evening News*, August 4, 1887. The state assembly defeated resolutions denouncing the "usurpation" of power by the GEB and criticizing Powderly's salary increase, but passed a resolution endorsing Powderly.

64. Barry to Labadie, June 14, July 24, 1887, LC; Powderly to John Devlin (date illegible, c. January, 1887), TVP.

65. *Advance and Labor Leaf*, July 16, August 6, 13, 1887. For a discussion of pro- and anti-Powderly factions at the state level in the Michigan Knights see my M.A. thesis, "The Knights of Labor in Michigan: Sources of Growth and Decline" (Michigan State University, 1973), pp. 51–71.

66. *Advance and Labor Leaf*, August 6, 1887.

67. *Advance and Labor Leaf*, August 13, September 10, 1887; Detroit *Evening News*, August 10, September 22, 1887.

68. The Minneapolis GA is described in Ware, pp. 318–19; Foner, 2:162–4; Henry David, *The History of the Haymarket Affair* (New York, 1958), pp. 413–18. Labadie's account of the convention is found in clippings

in the Knights of Labor-History File, LC, and his official *Report* of the GA published by District Assembly 50, LC.

69. Ibid; *Proceedings of the Knights of Labor General Assembly*, 1887, pp. 1723–25.

70. Knights of Labor-History File, LC; David, pp. 416–18; Notes on Executive Board Meeting, December 12, 1887, TVP. Barry and Bailey complained of difficulty in getting the floor to speak.

71. Labadie's *Report*, LC; Knights of Labor-History File, LC. Evidence of Powderly's socialist past had already been discussed both in the *Advance* and the Detroit *Evening News* in September. See chap. 3.

72. David, p. 417–18; *Advance and Labor Leaf*, October 29, 1887. The manifesto of the Provisional Committee appeared in a wide variety of newspapers including the Detroit *Evening News*, October 24, 1887.

73. Powderly to Edwin F. Gould, Esq., November 18, 1887; Powderly to P. J. St. Clair, Esq., November 19, 1887, TVP.

74. Knights of Labor-History File, clipping from the Ohio Valley *Budget*, November 5, 1887 (Ehmann was editor), LC.

75. Charles F. Seib to Labadie, November 23, 1887, LC; Seib to Labadie, December 30, 1887, LC; manifesto from the office of the Provisional Committee of New York and Vicinity, January 14, 1888, TVP.

76. Charles H. Litchman to Powderly, November 12, 1887, TVP. Ultimately per capita tax was paid for 437,000.

77. *Advance and Labor Leaf*, October 29, 1887; "Powderly Belabored," Knights of Labor-History File, LC; Seib to Labadie, December 30, 1887, LC.

78. Powderly to Dewey, October 23, 1887, TVP.

79. *Advance and Labor Leaf*, October 29, November 5, 1887; A. M. Dewey to Powderly, October 24, 1887, Dewey to Powderly, November 25, 1887, TVP.

80. John Devlin to Powderly, November 16, 1887, TVP.

81. Dewey to Powderly, November 3, 1887; *Advance and Labor Leaf*, November 5, 1887; "Powderly Belabored," LC. Copies of the *Report* can be found in the Labadie Collection. For Labadie's earlier estimate of the Chicago anarchists, see his letters to Richard Ely cited in Sidney Fine, "The Ely-Labadie Letters," *Michigan History* 36 (March 1952): 1–32.

82. "Powderly Belabored," LC; *Advance and Labor Leaf*, November 19, December 3, 1887; Dewey to Powderly, January 20, 1888, TVP.

83. *Advance and Labor Leaf*, December 17, January 14, 1888; Devlin to Powderly, November 26, 1887, Devlin to Powderly, January 20, 1888, TVP; Detroit Labor Leaders Data File.

84. *Advance and Labor Leaf*, January 14, 21, 1888; Devlin to Powderly, January 20, 1888, TVP. Vicars's election temporarily seemed in doubt because of a legal technicality. He was ineligible because his local assembly had just withdrawn from District Assembly 50 to join a national trade assembly.

Powderly was more than willing to grant a special dispensation allowing Vicars to serve.

85. *Advance and Labor Leaf*, January 28, 1888.

86. Robert A. Rockaway, "The Laboring Man's Champion: Samuel Goldwater of Detroit," Detroit Historical Society *Bulletin* (November 1970): 4–9; *Advance and Labor Leaf*, December 31, 1887, May 19, July 21, September 1, October 13, 1888; *Proceedings of the First Annual Convention of the Michigan Federation of Labor*, 1889.

87. *Advance and Labor Leaf*, February 11, August 18, September 29, October 6, 13, 1888.

88. Official membership in good standing on July 1, 1886, was 4,679 (*Proceedings of the Knights of Labor General Assembly*, 1886, pp. 326–28.) In March 1887, District Assembly 50 claimed 8,000 (*Advance and Labor Leaf*, March 19), but Grenell argued in December 1887 that less than 70 percent had been in good standing (*Advance*, December 10). However, Grenell was trying to demonstrate that the Knights were not declining, raising doubts about his credibility. DMW Long claimed 3,200 in the officers' *Reports* in January 1888, but the financial secretary reported only 2,467 in good standing based on October 1887 per capita tax. It is not clear whether the latter figure includes LA's in the process of transferring to national trade districts or not. Thus, taking verifiable per capita tax figures, the decline was 4,679 to 2,467; taking unverified claims, 8,000 to 3,200.

89. *Proceedings of the Knights of Labor General Assembly*, 1887, 1888. The 1887 *Proceedings* gave District Assembly 50 2,620 on October 1, 1887. The 1888 *Proceedings* credited only 2,527 on the same date.

90. *Onward*, December 1, 1888; *Advance and Labor Leaf*, December 24, 1887, July 27, August 10, 1889; *KLDB*; *Labor Day Review*, 1891, 1892. District Assembly 50 claimed twenty LA's in August, 1889, but there were still thirty-six LA's in Detroit (including suburbs) in 1890. LA 8775, which joined NTD 226, had 307 members in July 1888 (1889 SA *Proceedings*). Other trades joining NTD's included shoeworkers, book binders, brass workers, machinists, and shipcarpenters.

91. *KLDB*; Foner, 2:165; Detroit *Evening News*, August 31, 1890; *Journal of the Knights of Labor*, January 7, 1892; Detroit *Evening News*, November 20, 1891, June 6, 1892; John Devlin to Powderly, April 22, 1892, TVP.

92. *KLDB*; Detroit City *Directory*, 1894; *SBLS*, 1894, p. 383. A small group of glassworkers at Delray, a Detroit suburb, stuck with the Knights until the early 1900s, while a group of local shoecutters affiliated with a KL National Trade District briefly in 1910.

93. McGregor Scrapbook, LC; typewritten account of the Knights of Labor by J. Labadie, 1926, LC.

94. *Labor Leaf*, September 15, 22, 29, October 13, December 29, 1886; *Advance and Labor Leaf*, March 5, 12, April 23, 1887.

95. *Advance and Labor Leaf*, January 28, 1888.

96. *Advance and Labor Leaf*, April 23, August 20, 1887, April 7, 1888.

97. *Advance and Labor Leaf*, January 28, November 24, 1888.

98. Detroit *Evening News*, September 3, 1886; *Advance and Labor Leaf*, March 19, 1887, January 14, 1888; *Reports of the Officers of District Assembly 50* (Detroit, 1888); *Proceedings of the Knights of Labor General Assembly*, 1887; *Labor Day Review*, 1892; 1892 estimates based on estimates of locals in the *Labor Day Review*. Some locals may have been omitted.

99. *SBLS*, 1903, p. 334.

100. *Advance and Labor Leaf*, April 7, 21, July 7, 1888; November 2, 1889.

7

THE LEGACY OF THE 1880s:
Detroit Workers in the 1890s

The Knights of Labor collapsed nearly as quickly as it had risen, bringing most of the formal institutions of the oppositional subculture it had nurtured down with it. But dreams die hard. Parts of the moral code and cultural practice of an oppositional subculture remained as a legacy incorporated into the popular culture of Detroit's working class. Yet except for the small minority of the city's workers who remained active in trade unions, these values were not sustained by a reinforcing network of associations transcending neighborhood and workplace. Ethnic cultures continued to be the most important source of identity and group commitment.

The result was an inconsistent pattern of behavior. Throughout the 1890s workers engaged in industrial disputes, were quick to take to the streets in marches and demonstrations, and quick to appeal to a vision of class solidarity, asking and expecting widespread and direct support from workers who were not involved in their conflicts. The forms and style of such direct actions clearly show the resonance of 1886—a memory of a brief moment shaping workers' perceptions of strategy, tactics, and moral posture for more than a decade after.

Class Solidarity and Working-Class Cultures

However, the responses to such appeals to class solidarity were quite mixed. Sometimes broad sections of the city's working class responded in ways that suggested the moral postures of strikers, the memories and code they appealed to, were indeed part of a workers' culture. But at other times, the same workers rejected appeals for solidarity, refused to honor boycotts, crossed picket lines, or fought fellow workers. Workers were neither consistently class conscious, nor consistently lacking in class consciousness. Rather they approached each concrete situation as individuals with multiple identities and loyalties, choosing the response that seemed appropriate to the occasion.

In the streetcar strike of 1891, acts of solidarity seemed appropriate to most workers. The streetcar company was widely disliked for its poor service as well as its poor treatment of its work force. Company executives had been wrangling with popular Mayor Hazen Pingree over service and fare structures for months. The geographic dispersal of streetcar lines provided ample opportunity for workers to take action with little fear of reprisal or arrest. Given an almost universally unpopular and easily vulnerable target, and an implicit (and sometimes explicit) sanction of worker actions by the business and political leaders who had been fighting for better streetcar service, working-class support for the streetcar strikers was overwhelming, bringing the streetcar management to its knees in only four days and provoking Robert Reitzel to only half-mockingly proclaim that "the World Revolution must emanate from Detroit."[1]

Streetcar workers on the privately owned City Street Car Company had been organized in the city's second largest Knights of Labor assembly between 1886 and 1890. The assembly lapsed after repeated conflicts in 1890, but former assembly leaders reorganized as the Street Railway Employees Mutual Benefit Association the following April. The company immediately fired fifteen organizers, declaring its commitment not to "turn the control of the business over to a few professional agitators."[2] In the ensuing strike, although the union had enrolled less than a third of the work force and had virtually no funds or organization, streetcar men were quickly able to frustrate the company's attempts to maintain even token service with a small force of loyal drivers and supervisory personnel. Cars had to be escorted by police through hostile crowds gathered around car barns. As most people boycotted the streetcars, people on street corners greeted empty cars with cries of "Traitor! Scab! Turncoat!" By the second day, newspapers reported gatherings of 1,500 or more blocking cars at key intersections and several scab drivers were dragged off the cars and severely beaten. Even four-man police escorts on each car leaving the barns could not keep the cars running as the crowds charged cars, and the police had to hold them off with drawn revolvers while drivers hitched the horses at the other end to reverse directions and return to the barns.[3]

Just as the car builders' strike had stimulated widespread imitation in 1886, the streetcar strike provoked a host of spontaneous sympathy strikes as workers began leaving their factories to parade through the streets in military rank as they had done five years before. Two hundred striking stove workers gathered at the city limits and marched downtown where they were joined by another 500 Detroit Stove Works workers marching under a red flag. Other sympathy strikes took place at the Detroit Lubricator Works; Baldwin's, McGraw's, and Pingree and Smith's shoe factories; and the Detroit and Michigan Radiator Works. Iron workers leaving one factory after the afternoon shift spent two hours ripping up two blocks of tracks in front of their shop.[4]

By Friday, the fourth day of the strike, the Trades Council made plans for a Saturday mass march to unite the various spontaneous actions taken by workers around the city. But the march proved unnecessary. That evening, after Mayor Pingree categorically refused to call in the state militia to clear the streetcar lines, the streetcar company capitulated, agreeing not only to rehire the fired organizers, but also to recognize the Street Railway Employees' Association as the exclusive bargaining agent for all its employees and to grant the association union shop status. The Saturday morning solidarity march became a victory parade.[5]

The breadth and strength of the support for the streetcar men was the product of more than class solidarity: middle-class patrons angry at poor service joined the crowds blocking streetcars, downtown businessmen helped to collect a strike fund, and the city administration appeared sympathetic to the strikers.[6] Yet the actions of thousands of workers whose support made the streetcar men's victory possible demonstrate the continuing belief in a code of solidarity. Arrest statistics reveal the overwhelmingly working-class composition of the crowds who blocked the streetcars' paths; the form of protest was clearly reminiscent of other working-class crowd actions, not middle-class protest.

Working-class support was both extensive and intense. Sympathetic workers were willing not only to contribute to the strike fund, to accept the inconvenience of a boycott, but also to strike themselves, to battle police and to risk arrest on the streetcar men's behalf. Such support cut across occupational and ethnic boundaries. A list of twenty-four people arrested for strike activities included a butcher, a shoemaker, a bricklayer, a tailor, five metal workers, three clerks, a messenger boy, a porter, and radical editor Robert Reitzel. Those arrested included several Irish, Scottish, and German names as well as one Italian and a Pole. Only one of those on the arrest list was a streetcar worker.[7]

But the working-class response to two other strikes that same spring was quite different. News of the streetcar men's victory provoked a shorter-hours strike at the Michigan Car Works on Saturday, April 25, 1891—the day of the streetcar men's victory march. At noon, when the men quit work for lunch, they learned the outcome of the streetcar strike, and at one o'clock many refused to reenter the plant. At 1:30 the plant managers blew the whistle again, hoping to stimulate a back-to-work move, but instead the men responded by marching from department to department, just as they had done in 1886, urging those who had gone back to work to join them in a strike.[8]

The instigators were probably hoping to use the excitement surrounding the streetcar strike to continue the tradition of May Day mass shorter-hours strikes. The tradition had been renewed in 1890 when 2,000 carpenters and other building trades workers had deserted all the city's building sites for an eight-hour strike, and rumors of another round of May Day strikes had been circulating for several weeks before the streetcar strike. With the spectacle of sympathy strikes and mass car blockings the week before, and May Day approaching the following week, it is not surprising that some car workers could hope to instigate a series of shorter-hours strikes as they had done in 1886.[9]

But this time the scenario was quite different. Carshop molders and machinists refused to join the strike. When carshop workers marched to the Detroit Spring Works, a subsidiary of the carshop, the workers there ignored them, and when 1,000 strikers gathered at the plant gates the following Monday, an estimated 300 workers crossed their picket lines and entered the plant. The largely Polish and German crowd battled police, but their appeals for solidarity did not sway the English-speaking molders, who complained to reporters that they wanted to go to work but were intimidated by the violence. The strike limped on for several days, but all efforts to broaden it failed. Three hundred of the striking workers were fired as the company resumed normal operations.[10]

The contrast between the response to the carworkers' appeals for solidarity and the response to the streetcar workers the week before was remarkable. Polish and German carshop laborers had struck expecting to reap the benefit of the enthusiastic solidarity that had propelled the streetcar workers to victory. Yet the same metal trades who had been disproportionately represented in the arrest lists and sympathy strikes the week before proved most resistant to their appeals. The carwork's machine shop and foundry had been the last to shut down, and they were the first to resume operations. By Thursday, April 30, over 400 workers had reentered the Michigan Car Works foundry when only eighty others had resumed work in the rest of the complex.[11]

We do not have a breakdown of the composition of the car works' work force, but newspaper accounts suggest division both by skill—highly paid metal trades versus largely unskilled yard laborers—and ethnicity—unskilled laborers were primarily Poles and Germans while the foundry workers were described as English speaking. Names of those speaking at strike meetings and arrested at plant gates indicate the ethnic split; all but two of twenty-six such names were German or Polish. And this image was confirmed by the editor of the *Michigan Volksblatt*, who contrasted the moderation of city authorities during the streetcar strike with the forceful police actions against the carshop workers: "This time it will not be handled so moderately, as in the street car strike . . . this time the military will be called. Naturally—that one was mostly Americans, but here there are only Poles and Germans—therefore it doesn't matter if a few are beaten down.[12]

A stonecutters' strike in June revealed equally contradictory examples of solidarity and fragmentation. Stonecutters struck citywide on June 1, demanding an increase in the union wage scale. When contractors imported thirty-seven Italian stonecutters from New York during the third week of the strike, union members met the Italians at the station, explaining the situation. The Italians agreed to join the strikers; "No, no ve no Scab," explained one of them in broken English. Yet two weeks later the stonecutters had fractured along ethnic lines into four hostile groups. One group had split off from the stonecutters' union to form a dual Progressive Union, which returned to work on the employer's terms. A few days later twenty German stonecutters also returned to work and formed yet another stonecutters' union. The remaining regular union members, mainly English and Scottish trade union veterans, pledged to continue the struggle, but they too were demoralized when the union president, a young doctor who had worked his way through medical school as a stonecutter, broke ranks and returned to work. Each group blamed the others for the collapse, agreeing only on their mutual hostility to the Italians. The Italians had left town in mid-June, hoping to find work at "the Soo" (Soo Locks at Sault Ste. Marie), but when they arrived there the largely French-Canadian work force refused to work with them. They straggled back to Detroit in early July only to find that with the strike over local employers no longer wanted them, and local stonecutters supported the employers' decision despite the Italians' gesture of solidarity only weeks before. "Italians don't count," declared one local worker, "they are not stonecutters at all. One good man can do as much as half a dozen of them." Another justified the employers' decision by claiming that "the Italians cannot cut the stone used here." [13]

The streetcar strike showed that under some circumstances appeals to solidarity could kindle a widespread response. Many other events in the 1890s suggest that that response was not simply the product of the peculiar circumstances of the streetcar strike. The Knights' code of egalitarianism and mutuality had outlived them, legitimating direct action tactics like strikes, marches, and boycotts and communicating the idea that all workers had a moral responsibility to honor each other's grievances. In 1892, when forty-five bakers struck against forced night work, over 125 local grocers signed a boycott pledge as Trades Council committees systematically canvassed all the city's retail grocers, and mobs of workers attacked the delivery wagons of the struck firms. Master bakers admitted that they were running at less than three-quarters of capacity, and most firms agreed to rescind the night work order. A saloonkeeper across from the Michigan Stove Works who served scab bread found his dinner business dropped by three-quarters. After three days he signaled his surrender when he hung a large union bread sign over the bar. [14]

Other boycotts like the cigarmakers' boycott of 1895 or a boycott of several theaters in 1899 and 1900 in response to disputes with their stagehands received similar mass support. Workers demonstrated a commitment to egalitarianism and mutualism in other ways as well. Polish street laborers, for example, agitated in 1894, in the midst of a bitter depression, for equal division of street work among unemployed workers and maintainance of predepression wage scales. A demonstration against introduction of piecework at one construction site led to the tragic Connor's Creek incident in which three workers were killed and a score seriously injured when a construction foreman and a small group of policemen opened fire on protesting workers. [15]

Yet while such actions indicated widespread support for the principles of solidarity, most boycotts were only partially effective. The bakers lost their strike, despite the initial success of their boycott, after the four largest employers cut bread prices to stimulate sales and break the boycott. A newsboys' strike against a 50 percent cut in the *News* price in 1893 was broken quickly, and there is no evidence that their boycott plea had any marked effect on sales. In 1891, Polish and German carshop workers and the Italian stonecutters embraced the code of solidarity only to find their English-speaking compatriots rejecting it.[16]

The divisive conflicts among the stonecutters and carshop workers were not isolated incidents. In the months surrounding these strikes Detroit daily newspapers reveal abundant examples of intraclass hostilities and rivalries between ethnic groups, between occupations, and between skilled and unskilled within occupations. Working-class Polish Catholics were bitterly divided between followers of Father Kolasinski and those who supported the new Polish parish recognized by the bishop. The Kolasinski question repeatedly led to barroom brawls in Polish neighborhoods. The anti-Kolasinski faction was itself divided over the priest assigned to their church. Father Rochowski, despite his Polish name, was accused of being a German Pole who could not speak proper Polish. Rochowski was supported by a small faction of German Poles, but most of his congregation petitioned the bishop to remove him and threatened to boycott pew rentals, the parish's main source of income, until their request was granted. Widely distributed anti-Rochowski circulars declared, "So long as the world exists a Pole will not become the brother of a German." The Rochowski affair had wider repercussions as Polish street laborers complained that Irish coworkers threatened them with violence for "making trouble" with Bishop Foley.[17]

Several unions reported serious internal conflicts over ethnicity and religion. The Street Railway Employees Association nearly split in two in January 1892 when eighty Protestants, members of the nativist and anti-Catholic Patriotic Sons of America, met as a separate faction to nominate an anti-Catholic slate in upcoming union elections. The following year two rival slates of officers each claimed authority over the union, leading to a temporary split. Bricklayers also split over nativism. A local independent union of 205 bricklayers, which required U.S. citizenship as a condition of membership, refused to join the 100-member local of the International Union because the International "admits foreigners" who "take work away from us." Dockhands split into the lily-white longshoremen's union and an integrated stevedores' union. The tailors' union debated whether its official documents should be printed in English only or English and German. The vice president of the largely immigrant cigarmakers' union declared that the U.S. should "shut out all foreign immigration" because immigrants "don't seem to understand" unionism. The English-speaking

branch of the Socialist Labor party complained that the party's difficulties were all the fault of the Germans, but socialism was finally
spreading "in spite of" them.[18]

Serious intraclass conflict was not confined to such ethnic and religious hostilities. Several trades were torn by bitter rivalries between
subcraft groups. Shoecutters, for example, split off from the boot and
shoeworkers' union in October 1891. Machine molders and regular
ironmolders had a running feud including mutual accusations of scab-
bing on each other. Carpenters were divided between the Brotherhood
and the Amalgamated Association, and despite the decline of the
Knights of Labor, both the ironmolders and the shoeworkers reported
continued discord with the Knights in 1891.[19]

The picture is thus quite mixed: the workers who fought police in
behalf of the streetcar workers, the stove workers who refused to patronize a saloon selling scab bread, the Italian stonecutters who honored the stonecutters' picket lines, the Polish street laborers who called
for equal division of available street work, the working-class theater
goers who refused to patronize boycotted theaters in 1899 all demonstrated that the concept of solidarity had been effectively communicated to workers of many trades and nationalities. But the evidence of
bitter conflicts between workers is also unmistakable. Detroit workers
in the 1890s displayed high levels of both class solidarity and intraclass fragmentation.

This coexistence seems to fly in the face of many notions about
class solidarity. Why would workers who respond positively enough to a
class appeal to risk their own well-being and safety in behalf of other
workers also display such high levels of antagonism to each other? Perhaps we are simply talking about different individuals, and if we disag-
gregated such categories as "streetcar men" or "the metal trades," we
would find that the nativists who threatened the welfare of the Street
Railway Association had not been active during the strike or that the
ironmolders who battled police and built barricades across the streetcar
tracks were not the same individuals who ignored the carshop laborers'
appeals for solidarity. Lacking more than fragmentary data about individual behavior during these events, it is impossible to say for sure.
But while such reasoning may not be entirely inappropriate, it is an
insufficient explanation. The patterns of available evidence suggest in
too many ways that the phenomena of solidarity and fragmentation co-
existed, not only temporally, but also in the behavior of specific individuals. It was, for example, at the Detroit Stove Works, where striking

carshop laborers futilely clashed with police as they appealed to the stove workers to join their shorter-hours strike, that the wave of sympathy strikes for the streetcar men had begun the week before.

The contradiction is real. To explain it we must understand how and why workers made decisions in particular circumstances. What are the sources, at an individual level, of what we are calling solidarity and fragmentation? What is it about the way people lived that would lead workers to practice class solidarity sometimes and to fight with fellow workers at other times? The answers are to be found in the multiple networks of association in which they functioned as they attempted to solve their basic problems, the competing cultural systems we have already described.

Workers did not face their problems as isolated individuals. Our very understanding of what is problematic is drawn from our relationships with other people. But Detroit's workers did not live in a society where most workers shared a single set of common values and traditions. Workers came from many different ethnic and cultural backgrounds. Their experiences as workers gave them some common ground, but when workers met across a gulf of widely diverging cultures, such common ground occupied only a narrow range of often very recent experience. Thus, while they had some common experiences in the oppositional traditions they had worked out over the previous decades, such traditions were fragile, competing with many other loyalties. Simultaneous participation in competing cultural systems gave workers alternative approaches, alternative frames of reference, for dealing with each situation they faced.

From this perspective, the mixed responses of Detroit workers in the 1890s make sense. In a period of intense enthusiasm like the mid-1880s, the immediacy of conflicting loyalties temporarily receded, but as the excitement passed and the reinforcing network of an oppositional subculture atrophied, class loyalties once again had to compete with other alternatives. The feelings behind a surge of solidarity like 1886 did not disappear, but workers weighed their choices more carefully.

The daily realities of workers' lives involved continuing sources of antagonism which produced a latent reservoir of hostility to employers, to symbols of authority, to the social inequities of society. This submerged undercurrent of dissatisfaction could periodically reveal itself in impressive displays of class solidarity. But the same experiences that created such class anger also taught workers the realities of the power relationships in society and the dangers of rash action. Covert forms of resistance such as the stint, the informal agreement to limit output to a specified level, usually involved relatively little risk. Strikes were far more severe tests of courage and the willingness to make sacrifices.

In contrast, personal mobility and ethnic solidarity did not demand the same risks. Often, instead of antagonistically confronting the middle or upper classes, these strategies involved mobilizing some members of those classes on one's behalf. If such avenues had been closed, then perhaps class solidarity would have been the only feasible strategy for workers to pursue. But the evidence of working-class participation in, and even occasional leadership of, the organizations of other cultural systems demonstrates that that was not the case. Moreover, the patterns of economic development continued to produce sharp differences in the economic experiences of workers. While a large fraction of the city's work force faced near starvation in the mid-decade depression, for example, the wages of many skilled trades remained stable.

It is not surprising, then, that workers usually tried to avoid strikes. Some grievances could be solved in other ways; even when that was not true, the risks of action might outweigh the possible benefits. But when opportunities presented themselves to express underlying anger, particularly if the situation suggested that the risks of doing so were not excessive, many people eagerly seized the chance. The streetcar strike was exactly such a situation. Geographic dispersal reduced the risks of action while endorsement of the strikers by several prominent businessmen constituted a tacit approval of workers' actions. The sympathy strikes which followed were "quickie" affairs lasting a few hours. Given the atmosphere in the city, no employer risked more serious conflict by discharging such sympathy strikers.

In contrast, the workers at the carshops and stove factories the following week faced a much more difficult decision when some of their fellow workers raised the shorter-hours cry. In both industries workers had fought management for more than a decade over a variety of in-plant issues, generally with little success. The shorter-hours strike of 1886 had been totally defeated. The managers of these factories had consistently taken punitive actions against strikers and union activists—as the Michigan Car Works did again to those who struck in 1891. The short strikes in sympathy with the streetcar workers had been ignored by the companies, but many workers must have recognized that mass shorter-hours strikes would involve an extended struggle with a poor chance of victory. Under such circumstances, English-speaking skilled workers, even those who had just supported the streetcar workers, must have found it tempting to respond to a crowd of unskilled Germans and Poles not as fellow workers worthy of the obligations of the code of solidarity, but as hotheaded foreigners who did not understand the principles of American workmen. If the situation could be analyzed according to the symbols of their ethnic cultural systems rather than those of the workers' subculture of opposition, the dilemma of choosing between moral violations or a losing strike could be avoided.

The stonecutters similarly fell back on ethnic identity to retreat from the difficulties of earlier class action. The stonecutters' multiethnic work force had begun their strike with an impressive display of the power of the code of solidarity. They shut down all the major building sites in the city that had employed stonecutters, and when the Italian strikebreakers were brought in, they, too, honored the code. Class solidarity had demonstrated its strength. But the stonecutters faced a well-organized group of building contractors. They maintained a united front, refusing to bargain or negotiate. As the strike entered its sixth week, many stonecutters began to doubt whether it made sense to continue for the extra quarter a day they had demanded from their employers. If they went back to work now at the old wage, they would lose nothing but the wages they had already lost by striking. Why add to the damage by continuing the strike? These arguments divided stonecutters along ethnic lines. For the British trade union veterans, such an ending had symbolic consequences that outweighed monetary considerations; the overriding issue for them was the employers' refusal to recognize the union by engaging in negotiations. Such refusal violated traditions going back to Chartism and before, their image of themselves as artisan-citizens who expected their employers to treat them as equal members of a republican polity. The stonecutters of other nationalities, without the same tradition, were not persuaded. When the British workers insisted on continuing the strike, the other stonecutters abandoned class organization, and their ethnic systems provided an escape route: go to the employers as national groups, blame the British for the trouble, and humbly ask for the old jobs back.[20]

Thus, the coexistence of solidarity and fragmentation was the product of an economically and culturally divided work force. Judging from the frequency of newspaper accounts, the significance of these divisions increased in the 1890s. These conflicts were aggravated by the struggle for jobs in the mid-decade depression, an increase in nativist agitation, and a shift in immigration patterns away from the predominantly German, British, and Irish mix of the previous decades toward a preponderance of southern and eastern Europeans. Such divisions did not do away with the realities of the class relationship, but workers who functioned in multiple and competing cultural systems would respond differently on different occasions. Without a network of common institutions to bridge cultural divisions on a regular daily basis, the legacy of the 1880s seemed at times like only an occasional memory.

Political Alliances

The security of property rights does not rest upon courts
and bayonets so much as it does upon a contented people.

Hazen Pingree, c. 1895[21]

The memory, however, was sufficiently vibrant to alter class relations in several important ways. The repeated spectacle of public disorder—strikes, mass marches, picket line battles—had a profound impact on prevailing visions of America, permanently burying the idea that the exceptional nature of American society automatically protected America from the European horror of class war. It would be easy for us, recognizing the tenuousness of working-class solidarity, to underestimate the psychological impact of these events on contemporaries, but to do so would be a mistake. Working-class unrest in the 1880s created a working-class presence in the minds of all strata in American society, even when the reality of working-class consciousness was far more contradictory than many people realized.

The tone and content of public rhetoric shifted. Newspaper editors who criticized the very existence of all labor organizations in the early 1880s adopted a far more conciliatory tone by the late 1880s and early 1890s, differentiating between radicals and what they considered more responsible conservative unionists and recognizing the legitimacy of many working-class grievances. Corporate leaders who seemed to disregard such legitimate grievances were harshly criticized. The editors of the *Evening News*, for example, denounced Henry Clay Frick, the manager of Andrew Carnegie's Homestead Steel Works, after the gun battle during the Homestead strike in 1892, holding him personally responsible for the deaths because of his refusal to bargain with the union. Works like Edward Bellamy's *Looking Backward* and Henry Demarest Lloyd's *Wealth Against Commonwealth* were widely read and seriously discussed by businessmen, politicians, ministers, and editors. A significant minority of business and political leaders became convinced that they had a responsibility to exert positive leadership to prevent the outbreaks that had already occurred from developing into the more profound social crisis predicted by people like Bellamy and Lloyd.[22]

The decline of the Knights and many of the oppositional institutions that had surrounded them did little to abate this fear of potentially more serious conflicts. Hardly a year passed in Detroit without renewed public manifestations of the working-class presence. The carpenters' eight-hour strike in 1890 had involved a full month of mass marches and skirmishes with police. The 1891 streetcar and carshop strikes mobilized even larger crowds, rivaling those of 1886. The bakers' boycott in 1892 produced almost daily reports of scuffles between strikers and scabs, boycotters and nonunion delivery men. And with the onset of depression in 1893, unemployed demonstrations, marches, and battles like the one at Connors' Creek were common occurences.[23]

The most important business leader who responded positively to the working-class presence was Mayor Hazen Pingree. Pingree had been one of the primary antagonists of the Knights in 1885 and 1886. His brother had threatened to fire workers who had talked to the *Labor Leaf* after stories appeared about working conditions in their shoe factory in 1885; the firm had hired Pinkertons to spy on the Knights and report names of members who were subsequently fired; and the company had been the object of a national boycott during the 1885–86 strike. But in 1886 Pingree agreed to sign a contract with the Knights, and by the end of the decade he had agreed to the union shop provisions that had been one of the major sticking points in the earlier conflict. Perhaps with the pride of a self-made man Pingree had bristled at the idea of surrendering some of the control of the firm he had built, but the experience of the strike at his own company as well as the many other strikes of the mid-1880s led him to rethink his assumptions about industrial relations.[24]

His own experiences gave him more basis for empathy with workers' problems than most industrialists. He came from a poor family, a rarity among Detroit factory owners. His father had been an itinerant cobbler, and Pingree had worked as a cotton-mill hand and shoecutter before starting his own small shop. His own success gave him confidence in the ultimate fairness of the system, but his background and early experiences also made him sympathetic to workers' arguments. In the late 1880s he began reading Richard Ely's books on the labor move-

ment. Ely argued that trade unionism was a necessary and justified response of the workers in an advanced industrial system and a barrier to
more destructive radicalism. In an age of large factories, few workers
could hope to duplicate Pingree's career; most would inevitably remain
wage workers regardless of their determination and talents. Unless
means could be developed for adjusting the inevitable grievances and
conflicts that would emerge, workers would become permanently alienated and grow increasingly susceptible to radical doctrines.[25]

By the end of the decade Pingree had been convinced that orderly
negotiations between businessmen and responsible union leaders were
both necessary and justified. Property rights could only be secure if
justice were also secure, and ultimately "the unity of labor is the safety
valve of the civilized globe," the only prevention of "the dreadful remedy" of revolution.[26] While Pingree's position was still undoubtedly a
minority view within the business community, many other previously
nonunion firms followed his example of negotiating written contracts
with trade unions, a major departure from business practices in the
early 1880s and before. Until the 1880s, the union contract had been a
rarity. Even in de facto union shops most unions had maintained union
wage rates and work rules by ordering all union members to refuse to
work at less than union scale and to refuse to work alongside of non-
unionists. Most contracts were initially no more than a formal recognition of existing practices, but union leaders generally considered such
recognition as a major step toward acceptance of the legitimacy of
workers' rights to bargain over the terms and conditions of employment.[27] In 1889 Pingree was drafted as the Republican mayoral candidate by a coalition of business leaders who sought a new face to
overturn the Democratic machine and institute a mild program of
conservative reforms. Recognizing the existence of ethnic as well as
working-class grievances, Pingree campaigned actively for the ethnic
votes that had often been ignored by previous Republican candidates
and was swept into office with an overwhelming victory. As he grappled
with problems of municipal corruption, poor public services, inequi-
table tax assessments which favored corporations and the well-to-do,
and upper-class resistance to administrative changes, Pingree's thinking appeared to shift further to the left, alienating many of his original
business supporters, but endearing him to his working-class and ethnic
constituencies.[28]

Pingree was by no means anti-business or anti-corporate, but his
programs anticipated Progressive notions of using state action to regu-

late the business system in the interests of order and efficiency and to force overly narrow-minded businessmen to behave more responsibly.[29] His response to the 1891 streetcar strike was an excellent example. He was hardly pro-union, as some of his most enthusiastic labor supporters argued. He ordered the police to attempt to keep the streetcars running in the face of the hostile crowds and allocated extra manpower to the effort, joining police escorts himself. But at the same time, he refused to call in the state militia to break the strike as the streetcar company requested, ignoring the criticisms of newspaper editors for his failure to do so. Instead he pressured the streetcar company to negotiate with the union, personally acting as the mediator. His actions, labor supporters argued, had been the key to union victory. By 1893, Pingree had moved closer to these labor and liberal supporters as Judson Grenell joined his personal staff and Joseph Labadie became a city water inspector. Both the People's party and the SLP endorsed his 1893 reelection bid.[30]

Pingree's career illustrated the qualitative change in the attitudes of a segment of Detroit's economic and political elites as well as much of the new middle class, a change that was a harbinger of the national coalition that emerged as the Progressive movement in the following decade. Many employers were quite unimpressed and still steadfastly refused to deal with unions, but the presence of other people like Pingree, such as clothing manufacturer Hamilton Carhart, who had come to accept trade unionism and the broader need of state action to maintain the stability of the system made new political coalitions possible.

Labor leaders who were willing to accept positions as junior members in such a political alliance now had a viable strategy for winning many of the limited reforms that had eluded them up to this time: factory inspections, safety codes, workmen's compensation. Many labor leaders, especially the German socialists, argued that such coalitions were a trap—a means of coopting labor's power without altering the basic structure of class relations. To some degree they were right. Discontented workers, especially the nonunionized majority, were starting to look to liberal reformers like Pingree for political leadership and redress of grievances instead of to the labor movement. A labor movement representing only a small minority of the increasingly ethnically diverse work force would be hard pressed to convincingly present itself as the voice of the working class, especially when liberal reformers seemed more able to deliver concrete benefits to the nonunionized majority of the working class.

The support of sympathetic business leaders like Pingree was nonetheless welcomed by a majority of labor organizers. Native Protestant and other Anglo-Saxon labor leaders, especially, were early and enthusiastic Pingree supporters. The Pingree coalition was the very embodiment of their still vibrant republican tradition, the alliance of artisan-citizens with honorable manufacturers to defend the republic from the twin forms of corruption—alien anarchists and nonproductive monopolistic speculators. Equally important, the failures of the late 1880s convinced many labor leaders that liberal reform had more realistic chances for changing the industrial system than socialist agitation. Even some radical labor leaders who had predictably expressed initial doubts about Pingree were swept onto the Pingree bandwagon on this basis by his second and third terms in office. Perhaps this is what the reformist leadership of the Knights had had in mind all along, but such a reformist alternative had not really been available before the upheavals of the 1880s. Without the specter of 1886, it seems unlikely that men like Pingree would have moved in the direction of liberal reform when they did. The larger legacy of the 1880s was, thus, in part ironic. By demonstrating the working-class presence workers had helped to create new coalitions which would make the reemergence of an independent working-class political movement more difficult.

Detroit's Labor Movement in the 1890s: The Triumph of Pure and Simple Unionism

Even before the mid-decade depression threw thousands out of work, the labor movement faced rough going. Most of the core of organizers whose energies had sustained the movement throughout the 1880s had become disillusioned by the setbacks of the late 1880s, and they dropped out of active participation in the movement. Some went into politics. Sam Goldwater, for example, abandoned his earlier objections to collaboration with capitalist parties to become a Democratic alderman. Others left their trades for business or journalism.

Labadie was in and out of the printers' union as he went from job to job: a newspaper foreman, a junior editor, city water inspector. He still wrote occasionally for local and national labor periodicals, but the local movement treated him like a crank, an old-timer (although he was only in his forties in the 1890s) to be trotted out on ceremonial occasions to tell amusing stories, but not someone to be taken seriously. When the Michigan Federation of Labor held its annual convention in

Detroit in 1894, Labadie, its first president and one of its creators, was reduced to the role of toastmaster at a banquet for ex-delegates.[31] Although he still considered himself a radical, his writings reflected profound pessimism, cynicism, and disillusionment. Now converted to the individualist anarchism he had gleaned from Benjamin Tucker's *Liberty*, he wrote editorials denouncing socialism as "the philosophy of the mentally indolent" and espousing the virtues of individual incentive and initiative as the only source of social progress. Every person "should attend strictly to his own affairs," he wrote, and unions should confine themselves strictly to immediate economic interests.[32]

Grenell's later career was not unlike Labadie's. He had occasionally worked as a labor reporter and editorial writer for the Detroit *News* since 1884. By the early 1890s this part-time activity had blossomed into a full-fledged journalistic career, first as a labor news editor, then managing editor of the paper's Sunday edition, and a series of editorships at other papers. While he continued to be active in reform politics, serving on Pingree's staff, campaigning for the single tax, and fighting for municipal ownership of streetcars, he permanently left the labor movement after 1891.[33] Like Labadie, Grenell grew cynical about workers' capacity for perception and action. "The people know how to produce wealth, but the mass are still babes when approaching the subject of its scientific and equitable distribution. Yet on every hand are to be seen examples of bad economic conditions resulting from ignorantly imposed customs and laws." The average worker was not class conscious and had no conception of equity; he was satisfied, "so long as . . . [he] can purchase with his daily wage the things to which he is accustomed."[34]

They were not exceptions. The turnover in labor leadership was nearly total within less than a decade. While a few of the 1880s activists continued to hold local union offices, especially in the smaller craft unions, hardly any of them held significant offices in either the Trades Council or the larger local unions. Among the sixteen officers, executive committee members, and trustees of the Trades Council in 1897, only John Strigel had been an important labor leader in the 1880s. Another had been a Knights of Labor local assembly official. None of the other fourteen had even been mentioned as a labor leader in the labor or daily press before 1890. Of the more than 200 local delegates to the Trades Council in 1897, only six were mentioned before 1890.[35]

The activists of the 1880s had been convinced they were making history, that the cooperative commonwealth was just around the corner. Few were prepared for a sustained and indecisive struggle. When their expectations were not fulfilled, many people reacted bitterly. As things started to go wrong, members of all of the factions adopted a scapegoat mentality. Substantive criticisms were lost amidst crude and often irrelevant personal attacks. Labadie and Tom Barry, for example, in their critique of the Knights' other national leaders, interspersed their arguments against cowardice in the case of the Haymarket anarchists, mishandling of strikes, and violations of internal democracy, with charges that Powderly had displayed excessive vanity by allowing his picture to be printed in the order's journal or that Hayes had submitted a personal laundry bill to be paid by the order. Administration supporters could point out that Barry had requested more money in travel funds than most of the other board members. Amidst such petty backbiting, important criticisms were lost, and many members must have concluded in disgust that all of the leaders were corrupt.[36]

An experienced and disciplined cadre of radical labor agitators drifted away from the movement. Those who remained, as well as the majority of the new cohort of labor leaders, drew mainly negative lessons from the experiences of the 1880s: ambitious schemes of social reconstruction and inflammatory postures of mass insurgency should be avoided. In this emotional and political atmosphere, native and Irish-born activists in particular tended to resolve the ambiguities of their political cultures by abandoning the more radical variants of native republicanism on the one hand and nationalism on the other. Several prominent native, Canadian, and British labor leaders who had embraced the universalist republicanism of the Knights in the mid-1880s were prominent in local nativist organizations by the early 1890s, while key Irish Catholics, whose flirtations with radical nationalism had helped steer them toward the ILP and the artisan-reformer faction of the Knights, shifted firmly back into a safely Irish Democratic mold by the 1890s.

The disillusionment of many former Knights of Labor organizers was mirrored by a wider disillusionment among the masses of participants in the 1880s. They had joined the Knights amid promises of the millenium apparently only to be used. An MFL organizer complained in 1894 of the cynicism he constantly faced as he tried to organize former Knights. Workers say, he complained, "there is no good in it [the labor movement]. I once belonged to the Knights of Labor . . . I paid my dues regularly and yet I never reaped any benefit . . . I don't see any use of joining and trying again—I know it will be the same as before."[37]

A stable and loyal core of craft unionists remained. The total union membership of slightly over 7,000 in 1892 was virtually the same as the combined union and Knights of Labor membership had been in late 1887. It remained between seven and eight thousand throughout the 1890s, including the worst years of the mid-decade depression, but as the work force continued to expand rapidly, such stable membership meant that the labor movement represented a declining proportion of the city's workers. At the 1886 peak, combined union and Knights of Labor membership had topped 20 percent of the work force; perhaps a third of the industrial workers were unionized. By 1892, the percentage had fallen to 8.2 of the work force; by 1901, to 6.2 (see figures 1 and 2).[38]

The movement's ability to maintain a stable membership during the most severe depression in American history up to that time was a major achievement. Unions had always virtually collapsed during previous depressions. Their ability to survive this time indicates a qualitative change in attitudes about organization. For the minority of convinced unionists, labor organization had been accepted as a permanent part of their lives. They maintained their membership even during layoffs and hard times; they participated regularly in union affairs. About one-quarter of the printers' union membership was present and voting at typical union meetings in 1898; an average of 77 percent voted in elections for local and international union officers. In the thirty-five-member woodcarvers' union, attendance at meetings in 1899 averaged 52 percent.[39]

But while union stability and regular membership participation had been established in many crafts, the meaning of union membership had shifted. The unions, and the immediate economic benefits they had demonstrated they could win for some trades, were becoming ends in themselves, rather than means to some larger vision of class solidarity and social change. For example, in a local union president's "Agitator's Dream," published in 1895, his most utopian vision of future Detroit, every product has a union label, every worker belongs to a union, every politician is a trade unionist, and the Trades Council headquarters is the city's most imposing building, but there is no mention of any change in the system of production or social organization, no mention of a cooperative commonwealth. The change in emphasis was not complete;

240

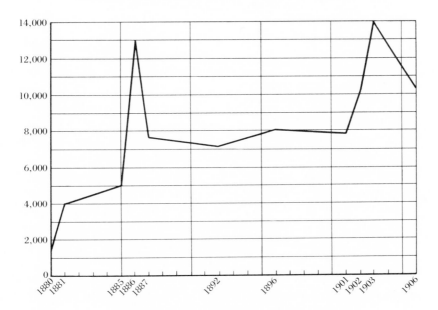

Figure 1. Union Membership in Detroit, 1880–1906

Sources: Detroit Trades Council File, LC; Detroit *Evening News*, September 3, 5, 1886; Detroit *Post and Tribune*, October 17, 1880; *Labor Day Review*, 1892; Detroit *Times*, April 10, 1881; *KLDB*; Knights of Labor General Assembly *Proceedings*, 1888; State Bureau of Labor Statistics, *Annual Report*, 1896, p. 245, 1903, p. 334, 1904, p. 168; Jacob Solin, "The Detroit Federation of Labor, 1900–1920," M.A. thesis, Wayne State University, 1939, p. 13.

Notes: Totals for 1886 and 1887 are combined totals of Knights of Labor and trade unions. They may include a small number of dual members thus counted twice. The 1886 figure is a newspaper estimate, substantiated by contemporary Knights of Labor officials, but not verifiable by more objective sources. It is consistent with other data on levels of participation such as the size of the 1886 Labor Day demonstration, but using the July 1886 per capita tax figures on DA 50 would yield a total about 3,000 lower. Local Knights of Labor officials based the higher figure on further growth after July 1, 1886.

German radicals maintained an unswerving socialist faith, and they continued to find English-speaking allies and converts. Most unionists continued to use a rhetoric of social reform.[40]

Actual union practice, however, was far more narrowly circumscribed than this rhetoric would suggest. Most labor leaders had decided that political activities, given an ethnically and politically divided membership, were divisive. Unions should avoid participation in politics. Even some of the socialists argued that the question of socialism should be separated from daily union affairs. W. D. Mahon, the socialist president of the street railway employees union, the city's

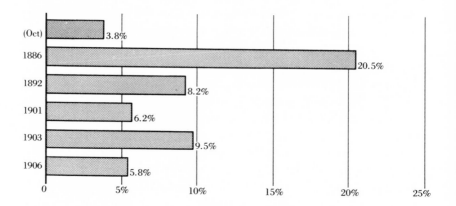

Figure 2. Union Membership as Percentage of Work Force, Detroit, 1880–1906

Sources: Union membership: Figure 1. Workforce: *Tenth Census*, 1880, vol. 1, p. 876; *Eleventh Census*, 1890, vol. 1, pt. 2, p. 664; *Twelfth Census*, 1900, Abstract, p. 124; *Thirteenth Census*, 1910, vol. 4, p. 166.

Note: The size of the work force was estimated by extrapolation from census figures.

largest union, explained, for example, that he had voted against the socialist Plank Ten of the proposed AFL program at the 1894 convention, even though his union had instructed him to vote in favor. Mahon feared that debates over socialism would disrupt the union, and he did not want his union "torn up for the next two years by a useless discussion."[41]

While Michigan unions outside of Detroit still urged political action during the depression and supported the Peoples party at Michigan Federation of Labor conventions in the mid-1890s, most Detroit delegates opposed these political activities.[42] In 1899, when the MFL elected L. W. Rogers, an active socialist, its president, several Detroit unionists including Jerry Sullivan, president of the Building Trades Council, and Sam Marcus, editor of the *Detroit Sentinel*, a short-lived labor weekly, campaigned for his impeachment. Rogers, Marcus argued, would "degrade the Federation . . . Between the contending principles [socialism and trade unionism] there is no possible reconcilement. The fight between them is to the death." The impeachment proposal was rejected and both the Building Trades Council and the Central Labor Union passed resolutions of support for Rogers, but the incident reveals the growth of an important antiradical minority within the movement: never before had any sizable segment of the local labor movement argued that socialists were unfit for union office.[43]

The movement maintained a rhetorical commitment to universal organization, but in practice little organizing took place. Unions that had attempted to organize women, blacks, and unskilled immigrants in the 1880s abandoned their commitments to racial and sexual equality and class unity. Most of the union locals with sizable female membership were holdovers from the Knights of Labor, and the Trades Council seemed lukewarm about further organization of women workers. In the 1880s, the Knights' DA leaders had actively supported the women in Florence Nightingale Assembly, who organized a series of assemblies for women workers. By the late 1890s, former women organizers were relegated to more traditional roles. Rose McBrearty, for example, one of the Florence Nightingale Assembly's original leaders, became the librarian of the Trades Council's reading room. Unions were nearly gone from factories with a preponderance of unskilled immigrant workers like the railroad carshops. While the Knights had had large locals in the carshops, in 1893 the State Bureau of Labor Statistics found only twenty-two union members among 1,066 carshop workers they interviewed.[44]

Union racial policies were also less progressive in the 1890s than they had been in the 1880s. The Knights emphasized racial equality in membership policies, employment, and political action, and local Knights of Labor leaders had criticized the order's national leadership for its failure to adequately defend black workers in the South. But when the Knights' longshoremen's assembly, which had a large black membership, switched to the Trades Council in 1891, it formed separate white and colored locals without any objections from the Trades Council.[45]

The German radicals who criticized these policies were even more isolated from the rest of the labor movement than they had been before. While they kept up a sniping attack at conservative and exclusionary policies, they had little impact on the dominant trends within the movement.[46] Increasingly the labor movement represented a native and old immigrant base of craft workers in small-scale light industries like printing, construction, clothing, and tobacco, and a collection of transportation workers like streetcar and railroad workers, also disproportionately drawn from native and old immigrant stock.

Labor organizers recognized that they were cut off from much of the city's working class and that the movement was exercising a declining influence in the political and cultural life of the city. Labor Day parades no longer drew the crowds they had in the 1880s. Few workers read the labor press: two attempts to revive the English-language labor press in the 1890s folded for lack of support.[47] The daily newspapers no longer considered labor union activities major news. In 1898, the Trades Council tried to revive the earlier enthusiasm for the annual Labor Day celebration, but they complained that all of the daily newspapers were completely ignoring their plans. In the late 1880s, advance reports of Labor Day events had run as full-page stories. In 1898, the Trades Council had to print 25,000 of its own advertising circulars to compensate for inadequate press coverage. By 1900, writers in the *Labor Day Review* were looking back nostalgically to the 1886 parade, which they described as the largest in the city's history. The movement of the mid-1880s had consistently been able to mobilize an entire subculture which went beyond the ranks of dues-paying union members for boycotts, public demonstrations, political and cultural activities. In the 1890s, just the opposite was the case: Labor Day turnouts were consistently much smaller than official union membership totals.[48]

The narrowing of union objectives had been an immediate response to the collapse of the Knights and disillusionment which followed. Most organizers were convinced that the Knights had failed because they had tried to do too much too fast. In an ethnically and economically diverse population, they believed, unions had to limit themselves to a lowest common denominator—the immediate economic interests all workers had in common—or face similar internal disruptions and disintegration. But in the long run this perspective hurt the movement's capacity to mobilize the popular support and enthusiasm that were essential even for successful organizing around specific trade union objectives.

In the early 1900s, as Detroit was transformed into the symbolic center of modern industry, the labor movement was left behind. Union membership doubled between 1901 and 1903, but the expansion was mainly confined to the traditional craft sectors. When employers responded with a series of open-shop employers' associations and a nonunion hiring agency in 1903, the organizing drives collapsed and union membership fell back from 13,800 in 1903 to 10,000 in 1906 (see figures 1 and 2). Unable to crack the burgeoning automobile industry, ancillary mass production, and heavy industries, the labor movement became increasingly peripheral to the industrial life of the city. Detroit became the least unionized major city in the country. Frank X. Martel, the Detroit Federation of Labor president during the World War I era, looked back to the 1890s as a golden era in comparison. "Before the turn of the century, Detroit was regarded as a good union town," but in 1920, Martel claimed, there were less than fifty functioning unions in the city.[49]

It is ironic that historians have tended to view the Knights as an expression of middle-class reformism and have treated the growth of the AFL as the rise of a more genuinely working-class perspective. In Detroit, just the opposite was the case. The Knights at their peak in Detroit represented an independent working-class subculture. The AFL survived after the Knights were gone, but in relative terms it never rose, it declined. The largely unorganized work force was far more ethnically and economically fragmented than it had been before. The AFL included only a small and unrepresentative segment of the fragmented working population.

Socialist and radical alternatives were equally unsuccessful. The IWW led one major automobile strike in Detroit in 1913, but the brief outburst had no permanent impact. The organization probably never had more than two or three hundred members. The Socialist party did only slightly better. Debs's peak vote in Wayne County, 4.1 percent in 1912,[50] was lower than the percentage the SLP's mayoral candidate had received in 1877 (6.0), less than a third of the ILP totals of the mid-1880s. Not until the 1930s would there again be a strong labor movement in Detroit or a significant working-class political presence.

NOTES

1. *Der Arme Teufel*, April 25, 1891. For background on the transit issue see Melvin G. Holli, *Reform in Detroit, Hazen G. Pingree and Urban Politics* (New York, 1967), chap. 3.

2. "Reports of the Officers of DA 50 for the Term ending December 31st, 1887," (Detroit, 1888), p. 12; *KLDB*; *Sunday News*, January 10, 1892; *Evening News*, April 18, 1891.

3. *Evening News*, April 20, 21, 22, 23, 1891.

4. *Evening News*, April 23, 24, 1891; Holli, pp. 38–41. Holli emphasizes public dissatisfaction with the streetcar company as the source of crowd actions and discounts the importance of class solidarity.

5. *Evening News*, April 23, 24, 25, 26, 27, 1891.

6. *Evening News*, April 22, 23, 24, 25, 1891; Holli, pp. 39–40. Down-

town businessmen may have supported the strike because they thought poor transit service hurt their business, but when they were interviewed by reporters, they emphasized the excessively long hours and low pay of the streetcar men, not grievances over service, as their reason for supporting the strike.

7. *Evening News*, April 22, 24, 1891.

8. *Evening News*, April 25, 26, 1891.

9. *Evening News*, April 18, 20, May 3, 9, 13, 15, 17, 20, 25, 29, June 6, 7, 14, 15, 18, 19, 21, 23, 24, 1890, April 18, May 1, 1891.

10. *Evening News*, April 27, 28, 29, 30, June 12, 1891.

11. *Evening News*, April 30, 1891.

12. *Evening News*, April 27, 28, 29, 30, 1891; *Michigan Volksblatt*, April 28, 1891.

13. *Evening News*, June 16, 21, July 1, 2, 5, 6, 8, 1891.

14. *Evening News*, March 21, April 26, 27, 28, 29, May 7, 12, 15, 16, 19, 22, 27, June 10, 17, 19, 20, 28, July 3, 8, 18, 1892.

15. *The Union Label* (Detroit), September 14, 1895; *The Detroit Printer*, April 24, 1896; *Der Herold*, September 15, 1899; Minute Book, Detroit Typographical Union No. 18, Archives of Labor and Urban Affairs, Wayne State University, October 23, 1898, September 3, October 21, 1899; Lawrence D. Orton, *Polish Detroit and the Kolasinski Affair* (Detroit, 1981), pp. 172–81; Holli, pp. 64–65. Union work rules were also designed to equalize allocation of available work. The printers, for example, prohibited members from accepting overtime while other members were out of work. Each printer had to submit his time sheet to the union representative in his shop and violators faced stiff fines.

16. *Evening News*, May 27, 29, June 28, July 3, 18, 1892, February 15, 17, 1893.

17. *Evening News*, December 13, 1890, July 20, 1891, June 13, 15, 17, 18, 20, 21, 24, 26, July 13, 18, 1891, February 17, 1892.

18. *Evening News*, October 25, November 27, 1891, January 10, 31, March 20, September 4, 1892, January 1, March 1, 3, 1893.

19. *Evening News*, October 9, 1891, May 10, 17, 20, June 7, September 6, 20, 1891.

20. *Evening News*, June 21, July 1, 2, 6, 8, 1891.

21. Undated speech, Pingree Papers, Burton Historical Collection, Detroit Public Library.

22. *Evening News*, July 8, 1892; *Industrial Gazette*, December 28, 1894, February 15, 22, 1895; Holli, pp. 54–55.

23. Orton, pp. 172–81; Holli, pp. 64–65; *Detroit Sentinel*, May 8, 1897.

24. *Labor Leaf*, December 31, 1884, January 7, May 6, 13, June 10, 24, July 4, October 28, 1885; *Columbian Labor Day Review*, 1893, p. 26. See chap. 4 for discussion of the strike. David Boyd, who worked for Pingree and Smith during these years, argues that even in 1885–86 Pingree was not as

antiunion as his actions appear, but the conduct of the KL negotiators antagonized him. David Boyd Papers, LC.

25. Holli, pp. 3–7, 43; Richard T. Ely, *The Labor Movement in America* (New York, 1890), esp. chaps. 4 and 5.

26. Undated speech, Pingree Papers.

27. There are no reliable figures on the prevalence of union contracts, but they are rarely mentioned in discussions of union activities in the daily and labor press before the mid-1880s and with increasing frequency thereafter. Before 1881 the level of union membership was so low that such contracts must have been rare. From the mid-1880s onward, union membership was stable in many industries and unions had long-term relationships with many employers. The DA 50 Officers' *Reports* (p. 12) notes "satisfactory settlements" with more than a dozen firms in 1887, but it is unclear whether that meant written contracts in all cases. For a discussion of how union work rules functioned in the late nineteenth century, see David Montgomery, "Workers' Control of Machine Production in the Nineteenth Century," *Labor History*, 17 (Fall 1976): 485–509.

28. Holli, pp. 16–21, 52–57.

29. See for example his speech to the Detroit Chamber of Commerce, November 2, 1895, and a letter to Dwight Warren, July 18, 1894, Pingree Papers.

30. Pingree to Dwight Warren, July 18, 1894, Louis P. Ganger to Pingree, October 4, 1893, Pingree Papers; *Evening News*, April 21, 23, 24, 25, 27, October 5, 9, 1891; Holli pp. 61–62, 138–41; Grenell, "Autobiography," pp. 53–55, 59.

31. *Evening News*, July 5, September 6, 1891; *Detroit Sentinel*, May 23, 1898; Robert A. Rockaway, "The Laboring Man's Champion: Samuel Goldwater of Detroit," *Detroit Historical Society Bulletin* (November 1970); *Evening News*, May 18, 1890, January 1, 1891, October 9, 1892; *Detroit Sentinel*, May 19, 1897; *Industrial Gazette*, December 14, 1894.

32. Joseph Buchanan to Labadie, December 30, 1893, LC; *Industrial Gazette*, December 14, 1894.

33. Judson Grenell, "Autobiography," pp. 38–44, 51–55, 74.

34. Grenell to Labadie, undated, LC; *SBLS*, 1908, pp. 349–50; For further details on the later careers of Labadie, Grenell, and other 1880s activists, see Oestreicher, "Solidarity and Fragmentation," pp. 467–71.

35. *Labor Day Review*, 1897; DLL. It is likely that some additional Trades Council delegates held minor union offices before 1890. There is no list of council delegates during the 1880s to use for systematic comparison.

36. McGregor Scrapbook, LC; Barry Scrapbooks, originals in possession of Barry family, microfilm copy at Michigan Historical Collection, Ann Arbor, Michigan; *Advance and Labor Leaf*, January 7, October 20, 1888; *Organic Law of the Brotherhood of United Labor*.

37. *Industrial Gazette*, December 14, 1894; *Labor Day Review*, 1892,

p. 43. For a more favorable retrospective on the legacy of the Knights, see J. D. Flanigan in *SBLS*, 1896, pp. 235–36.

38. See sources of figures 1 and 2, also Jacob Solin, "The Detroit Federation of Labor, 1900–1920" (M.A. thesis, Wayne State University, 1939), p. 13.

39. Minute Books, Detroit Typographical Union No. 18, 1898; Minute Book, International Woodcarvers' Association, Local Detroit, 1899, Archives of Labor and Urban Affairs, Wayne State University.

40. Henry C. Barter, "The Agitator's Dream," in the *Industrial Gazette*, February 22, 1895.

41. *Industrial Gazette*, December 21, 1894.

42. *Industrial Gazette*, December 14, 1894.

43. *Detroit Sentinel*, January 21, 28, February 11, 1899; *Der Herold*, January 27, February 3, 1899.

44. *SBLS*, 1893, pp. 736, 780; *KLDB*; *Labor Day Review*, 1892, 1893, 1897.

45. *Labor Leaf*, March 31, April 21, 28, December 22, 1886, July 23, 1887; *KLDB*; *Evening News*, September 6, 1887; *Labor Day Review*, 1897, pp. 38, 45.

46. Evidence of discord between German radicals and other trade unionists can be found in nearly every issue of *Der Herold*, the CLU organ in 1899, and from the other side in the *Detroit Sentinel*.

47. The *Industrial Gazette* lasted for less than six months in late 1894 and early 1895 and the *Detroit Sentinel* lasted about two years at the end of the decade. *Der Herold* (a German socialist weekly with extensive labor coverage), in contrast, had a stable and slightly expanding readership from the later 1890s through the early 1900s.

48. *Labor Day Review*, 1900, p. 29; *The People* (Detroit), August 19, 1898; *Detroit Sentinel*, August 13, September 10, 1898. The 1898 parade drew 6,000, about half the 1886 parade, but the largest "in years" according to the *Sentinel*.

49. *SBLS*, 1903, p. 334, 1904, p. 168; Solin, pp. 13, 104–6. Frank X. Martel, "Progress in Detroit," *American Federationist*, 62 (May 1955): 18; Martin Marger, *The Force of Ethnicity: A Study of Urban Elites* (Detroit, 1973), p. 27; Employer's Association of Detroit scrapbooks, 1904–6, Burton Historical Collections, Detroit Public Library.

50. *Michigan Manual*, 1913 (Lansing, 1913), p. 673.

CONCLUSION

Between 1875 and 1900 Detroit was an economically and ethnically diverse city. Workers who had come from different traditions continued to live and work in different circumstances. But industrialization also brought workers together, taught them the need to cooperate, and created possibilities for common action. Beginning in the late 1870s, a group of activists tried to use these lessons to create a movement that would give workers a set of common ideals and improve all of their lives. The impulse for that process was the emerging subculture of opposition; its organizational focus was the Knights of Labor.

By 1886 the movement appeared to be on the verge of success. The strikes and demonstrations of that year and the dramatic expansion of the Knights of Labor shook the foundations of the city's social system. New loyalties seemed to be developing. But the tensions of the resulting crisis, as well as the underlying differences in workers' experiences and traditions, led to paralyzing factionalism at the same time that the movement provoked a fierce counterattack from employers. The movement fell apart.

With the destruction of the Knights and the whole network of complementary institutions which had made up the subculture of opposition, new loyalties could not be cemented into permanent patterns of behavior. Class consciousness cannot exist in the abstract, without vehicles of meaningful expression; older loyalties reasserted themselves. Despite that destruction, the events of the 1880s left a legacy. Even without the framework of a unifying organization like the Knights of Labor, the memories of the 1880s were repeatedly sufficient to bring workers into the streets again in the 1890s, and the continuing threat of class conflict forced a renegotiation or at least a modification of the existing social contract. Businessmen like Hazen Pingree became convinced that unbridled acquisitive individualism had to be restrained. If social peace were to be maintained, workers had to be guaranteed min-

249

imal standards through processes of orderly negotiation and political reforms.

The labor movement of the 1890s had a place in such a scheme, but certainly not the one envisioned by the activists of the 1880s. Negotiations and union standards did not a cooperative commonwealth make. And unsure of the wisdom of the mass mobilization which had opened the door to partial recognition of union bargaining rights, Detroit unions were not very effective in maintaining a position of even limited union power as the scale of industrial production was transformed in the early 1900s.

What happened in Detroit in these decades happened in many other places in industrial America. The Knights of Labor expanded dramatically in the mid-1880s in nearly every large city and major industrial town in the United States. The strike wave which stimulated the organization's rise was also a national phenomenon. Local labor parties challenged major party politicians in more than two hundred cities and towns, often more successfully than in Detroit. Labor mayoral candidates drew nearly a third of the vote in elections in New York City and Chicago. Across America the "labor question" became one of the central political topics of the day. But nearly everywhere in the next decade, as in Detroit, the combination of bourgeois counterattack and internal factionalism spelled doom for the Knights of Labor and crippled the elan and optimism that had characterized the labor movement in the mid-1880s. The retreat was not always as marked as in Detroit, and in many cities, union membership rebounded quickly after the mid-1890s depression. The relative decline and paralysis of Detroit's labor movement after the turn of the century was an extreme case. Unions continued to be powerful political, cultural, and economic forces in such cities as Chicago, Cleveland, and Milwaukee. Yet in most cities, even in labor strongholds, unions found it increasingly difficult to respond to the social and structural changes which accompanied the rise of large scale mass production after 1900. While national union membership grew rapidly in absolute numbers in the late 1890s and early 1900s, that growth did not match the growth of the industrial work force. In 1886, the combined Knights of Labor and trade union national membership had reached at least one million and represented more than 15 percent of the nonagricultural work force. In 1910 total union membership of 2.1 million represented only 15.3 percent of nonagricultural wage earners (see figure 3). Only after 1917 would the proportion of the work force that was unionized clearly ex-

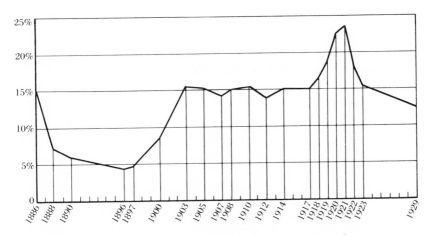

Figure 3. Percentage of Unionization of Nonagricultural Employees,
1886–1929[1]

Sources: Union membership:[2] 1886: Leo Wolman, *The Growth of American Trade Unions* (New York: National Bureau of Economic Research, 1924), pp. 21, 31; Commons, et al., *History of Labor in the United States* (New York: MacMillan, 1918), p. 396; George E. McNeil, *The Labor Movement: The Problem of Today* (New York: M. W. Hazen Co., 1891), chaps. 12–14.
1888–1896: Wolman, McNeil; Knights of Labor General Assembly *Proceedings*.
1897–1933: *Historical Statistics of the United States* (Washington, D.C., 1960), pp. 97–98, D. 736.

Workforce:[3] 1886–1899: *Historical Statistics of the United States*, "Gainful Workers: 1820–1940," total of columns D 60, 61, 62, 63: mining, manufacturing, construction, transportation, and utilities, p. 74.
1900–1929: Stanley Lebergott, *Manpower in Economic Growth* (New York: McGraw-Hill, 1964), p. 513, nonfarm employees.

    1. Union membership totals include Canadian members, but this discrepancy hardly affects the slope of the graph. In 1910 and 1920, when separate Canadian statistics are available, Canadian members made up only 1.8 and 3.3 percent respectively of the total membership of U.S. based unions.
    2. Union membership statistics before 1900 are problematic. Wolman estimates 1,000,000 as the peak figure for the 1880s based on 703,000 for the Knights, 138,000 for the AFL, and another 150,000 or so for unaffiliated trade unions like the railroad brotherhoods. But McNeil, a contemporary source, estimated 600,000 trade union members based on interviews with union leaders. While McNeil's estimate may include some exaggeration, Wolman does not provide any argument to justify his lower estimate. The figure of one million in 1886 may be too low.
    3. Excludes domestic servants. Size of workforce before 1900 determined by extrapolation from census years. Definitions of gainful workers used before 1900 and nonfarm employees after 1900 are slightly different. See sources above.

ceed that of 1886, and by the end of the 1920s, it would once again fall close to 10 percent. Well over half of all union members in the early 1900s were found in industries like construction, printing, and clothing, still characterized by small-scale, relatively unmechanized production, or in transportation, where the railroad brotherhoods representing the running trades had reached an accommodation with many of the major railroads. Unions were nearly absent from basic industries like steel, auto, chemicals, and textiles.

Thus what happened in either Detroit or the nation does not sustain the Wisconsin School's contrast between the alleged success of the supposedly practical trade unionists of the AFL and the supposedly fuzzy-minded visionaries of the Knights. Perhaps more importantly, neither classical Marxist theories of modernization nor non-Marxist modernization theories emphasizing tensions between tradition and modernity are completely adequate to understand what happened either. Industrialization in Detroit did not lead to the increasing proletarianization and class polarization that late nineteenth-century Marxists had expected, but to continuing and even increasing diversity of occupational experience and social position. When polarization did occur momentarily in the mid-1880s, it did not happen because development of the forces of production had wiped out differences between workers, but rather in spite of those differences. Tendencies toward both solidarity and fragmentation continued into the 1890s.

The theory of tradition versus modernity also provides insufficient insight. The people who marched and struck in 1886 were demanding a different version of modernity as much as they were protesting violations of customary rights. The sense of solidarity that moved them was based on recently learned ideals as well as traditional habits. The issues which divided them were outgrowths of industrial diversity as well as ethnic variations.

Solidarity and fragmentation were intertwined and coexisting parts of the same whole, both as much the products of the processes of industrialization, urbanization, and social change we call modernization as the new machines, new buildings, and new ways of living. Economic growth attracted workers of varied backgrounds, increased economic diversification, and provided economic opportunities which gave doctrines of individual mobility continuing plausibility. But industrialization also led to new work methods and work rhythms, created new forms of interdependence, new patterns of cooperation. If class consciousness were to emerge, it would have to emerge into a situation in which the potential for both solidarity and fragmentation were simultaneously increasing.

But class consciousness as a social phenomenon is not simply a set of abstract propositions to which people can indicate their agreement or disagreement as if they were participating in an opinion survey.

252

Most people do not begin to think about the world differently, do not begin to act upon such thinking, until they begin to see meaningful ways of acting. Class consciousness cannot develop without concrete vehicles for its expression. *More people were class conscious in Detroit when it seemed more possible to be so.*

People must search for such possibilities within the constraints in which they find themselves: the internal constraints—culture—which tell them what is right, and the external constraints of social reality. But this is not simply a passive process. If the possibilities for consciousness are dependent upon concrete vehicles for expression, then people's actions are the decisive factor in the development of those possibilities because it is through their own actions that they create such vehicles.

Detroit's workers did not create the cooperative commonwealth. They did create vehicles—the Knights of Labor and the subculture of opposition—based on a new vision of industrial life. Many of their hopes went unfulfilled, yet as they tried to remake their lives according to this vision, they helped to change the cultural and political terrain of Detroit. But through their own actions they also helped to destroy the vehicles which had suggested new possibilities, and thereby helped to limit those possibilities. Perhaps there is a lesson there.

A Note On Sources

In an age of spiraling publishing costs, it does not seem worthwhile to repeat all of the sources already cited. Readers wishing to know the sources on which this study is based should consult the notes. A listing of many of these sources can be found in the bibliography of my dissertation, while an excellent general bibliography on Detroit can be found in David Katzman's *Before the Ghetto*. It does seem useful to alert readers to the strengths and limitations of the most important primary sources and especially to the ways the limitations may have affected my conclusions.

General Social and Economic Structure

My understanding of Detroit's social and economic structure comes primarily from three sources: daily newspapers, reports of the State Bureau of Labor Statistics and state factory inspectors, and the United States Census (both manuscript and published census volumes). In addition I benefitted from the careful research of Olivier Zunz, who generously provided me with data from his 1880 census sample and an advance copy of his manuscript. His book, *The Changing Face of Inequality*, is the best introduction to the social structure of late nineteenth-century Detroit.

Daily newspapers were a particularly valuable source. The *Evening News* was consistently most useful, and I skimmed all issues published during the time period of the study. Other papers generally gave far less attention to working class and ethnic life, and I read them only intermittently for comparison with the *News* coverage of major events.

Published census volumes were also essential. However, the methodological biases and inaccuracies of the census have been well documented by social historians. Readers are urged not to assume that statistical evidence based on the census is more reliable than the order of magnitude.

State Bureau of Labor Statistics Reports are even more problematic. The samples, especially in the earliest reports most essential as sources for the 1880s, were neither random nor systematic. Often respondents were simply those who were willing to cooperate or were conveniently located for the bureau's limited staff. The bureau's activities and very existence were controversial political issues. The Michigan labor movement had lobbied for its creation, provided many of its initial personnel, and supported its activities. Antiunion employers opposed the agency. The law establishing the bureau was ambiguous about its powers to force employers and citizens to cooperate with its investigations. Early directors generally chose not to push the question. The possible implications of these factors are obvious, but the reports are so rich with detailed information not only about wages, hours, and working conditions, but also about the quality of working-class life, that they were essential sources. Wherever possible, I attempted to corroborate the bureau's findings with other sources or to use individual level data.

Ethnic Cultures

Much of the information on ethnic cultures was gleaned from the sources cited in the previous section. Beyond that, the quality and availability of primary documents produced by individuals or organizations who were part of ethnic cultures varied considerably. Such variations undoubtedly shaped my perceptions. For example, the virtual absence of distinctively Canadian or British primary sources certainly contributed to the impression that these groups functioned as part of the same cultural system as native whites.

For each of the major ethnic cultures other than native whites there were major gaps in the sources available. Since nearly complete runs of several German daily and weekly newspapers are still extant, these gaps were probably least serious for the Germans. I read all issues of *Der Arme Teufel* (Robert Reitzel's radical and free-thought literary journal) published between 1884 and 1892, all issues of *Der Herold* (independent radical weekly and official organ of the German unions) between 1898 and 1900 (the only years before 1900 still extant), and selected issues of the *Michigan Volksblatt* (German Democratic daily) and *Detroit Abend-Post* (German Republican daily) throughout the 1880s and 1890s. Unfortunately I was unable to locate any surviving copies of the *Arbeiter Zeitung* (the German labor daily of the early 1890s).

For Poles the situation was not nearly so fortunate. I do not read Polish, and even if I did, only very scattered copies of the local Polish press still survive. A variety of secondary sources on Detroit's Polonia helped to augment newspaper accounts and census materials, but in every case their treatment of evidence gave grounds for suspecting the reliability of some parts of the works. My conclusions about Detroit Poles must thus be taken as tentative.

For the Irish, in addition to daily newspapers, census volumes, and scattered stories in *The Irish World*, I depended on JoEllen Vinyard's *The Irish on the Urban Frontier: Nineteenth Century Detroit, 1850–1880.*

Labor Movement

The starting point for examination of the local labor movement is the Labadie Collection at the University of Michigan, which contains nearly complete runs of all of Detroit's labor papers from the late 1870s through the early 1890s and an extensive selection of other documents and private correspondence between Labadie and other movement figures. Further important documents and newspapers not in the Labadie Collection can be found in the Burton Historical Collection of the Detroit Public Library, the Knights of Labor Papers (Catholic University and microfilm edition—some items at Catholic University are *not* included in the microfilm edition), the Socialist Labor Party Papers, the Henry George Papers (in the New York Public Library), the executive office files of the Michigan State Historical Commission, and the Wisconsin State Historical Society. Judson Grenell's unpublished autobiography, a particularly important document not previously consulted by scholars to my knowledge, is in the Archives and Historical Collections of Michigan State University. The Archives of Labor and Urban Affairs at Wayne State University has some important local union minute books for the late 1890s, but beyond that little of value for this period.

Despite this relative abundance, some important gaps remain. The Labadie Collection, the most significant collection for this part of the study, is heavily skewed towards Labadie's activities and personal interests. The other sources do not completely remedy that emphasis. The labor press, for example, was largely a product of Labadie's circle and is biased in much the same direction as Labadie's personal papers.

Thus, I know more of the internal details of the movement during the 1880s than during the 1890s, more about the Knights of Labor than about some of the most important trade unions, more about labor radicals than conservatives.

Working-Class Life

Using all of the sources previously cited it was possible to give an overall picture of working-class life, but beyond the general trends that emerge from quantitative sources it is difficult to find qualitative evidence about working people who were not connected either to the labor movement or to formal ethnic organizations, i.e., about the majority of Detroit workers during most of these years. There are some interviews in the State Bureau of Labor Statistics Reports and daily newspapers, some useful case histories in the records of the Detroit Association of Charities. Nonetheless, except by inference, I know relatively little, for example, about the opinions and aspirations of antiunion workers or casual laborers.

Labor Voting Analysis

The analysis of labor voting trends discussed in chapters 4 and 6 is based on election returns in the Wayne County Election Records (Burton Historical Collection) and profiles of election precincts created by combining data from Olivier Zunz's 1880 census sample, my own sample of the 1880 manuscript census, and a series of descriptions of each precinct published in the *Sunday News* in the summer and fall of 1891. Comparison of 1880 samples with the 1891 descriptions made it possible to estimate how the composition of precincts changed between 1880 and 1884 and 1886. Verbal descriptions of the ethnic composition of neighborhoods found in the 1890 Census (volume 4, part 2, pp. 219–27) were also useful.

Of the sixty-one precincts in the analysis, data for eighteen came primarily from my samples of the manuscript census, thirty-seven primarily from Zunz's census sample, and six primarily from the *Sunday News* articles. The sampling methods of these three sources varied, and this may have affected the results. For the eighteen precincts I sampled, I sought to create a random sample of approximately 100 males over twenty-one for each precinct. In most precincts this meant a 20 percent random sample, but for very large precincts, I lowered the percentage and in a few small precincts increased it. In some neighborhoods, census takers did not include street addresses. While some of these individuals could be placed in the correct election precinct by cross-checking the names in city directories, this was not always possible. This was especially true in the fourteenth, fifteenth, and sixteenth wards, which were outside the Detroit city limits in 1880.

Zunz's original sample was constructed quite differently. He selected clusters of a square block and two facing frontages and included everyone living in each cluster. Professor Zunz extracted the relevant data on all males over twenty-one living in each cluster and provided me with the results. I then placed each cluster in the correct election precinct. Since the election analysis was not a central objective of this study, it did not seem worthwhile to spend hundreds of hours creating samples for precincts when someone else had already done so, but it should be clear that the samples based on Zunz's data include *all* of the potential voters in *part* of the precinct rather than a sample of the entire precinct. Sample sizes for these precincts range from twenty-seven to 220, but only six precincts have sample sizes below forty, and only five are above 150. The final six precincts were in those neighborhoods where census takers did not include street addresses, and sufficient numbers of potential voters could not be located by cross-checking with city directories. For these precincts, I used the estimates of class and ethnic composition found in the *Sunday News* articles. The *News* estimates were based on extensive interviews with precinct workers of both parties, but obviously are not scientific samples.

Where possible, I cross-checked the results for selected precincts derived from each source and the results were similar. However, the values assigned to each precinct for the percentage of German workers are less reliable than the other variables and probably biased slightly upward. The percentage of German workers in each precinct was calculated as a percentage of the number of potential voters for whom both occupation and ethnicity (including parents' birthplace) could be identified, rather than the entire number of potential voters in the sample for that precinct. In a few cases this method yielded a percentage of German working class slightly *higher* than the percentage of Germans in the precinct, an obvious impossibility. In general the estimates of German working class are probably a couple of percentage points too high.

Index

Note on the Author

Richard Oestreicher holds a Ph.D. in history from Michigan State University and teaches at the University of Pittsburgh. *Solidarity and Fragmentation* is his first book.

Books in the Series

Worker City, Company Town: Iron and Cotton-Worker Protest in Troy
and Cohoes, New York, 1855–84
DANIEL J. WALKOWITZ

Life, Work, and Rebellion in the Coal Fields: The Southern
West Virginia Miners, 1880–1922
DAVID ALAN CORBIN

Women and American Socialism, 1870–1920
MARI JO BUHLE

Lives of Their Own: Blacks, Italians, and Poles in Pittsburgh, 1900–1960
JOHN BODNAR, ROGER SIMON, AND MICHAEL P. WEBER

Working-Class America: Essays on Labor, Community, and American Society
EDITED BY MICHAEL H. FRISCH AND DANIEL J. WALKOWITZ

Eugene V. Debs: Citizen and Socialist
NICK SALVATORE

American Labor and Immigration History: 1877–1920s: Recent European Research
EDITED BY DIRK HOERDER

Workingmen's Democracy: The Knights of Labor and American Politics
LEON FINK

Electrical Workers: A History of Labor at General Electric and Westinghouse,
1923–60
RONALD W. SCHATZ

The Mechanics of Baltimore: Workers and Politics in the Age of Revolution,
1763–1812
CHARLES G. STEFFEN

The Practice of Solidarity: American Hat Finishers in the Nineteenth Century
DAVID BENSMAN

The Labor History Reader
EDITED BY DANIEL J. LEAB

Solidarity and Fragmentation: Working People and Class
Consciousness in Detroit, 1875–1900
RICHARD OESTREICHER

Counter Cultures: Saleswomen, Managers, and Customers in
American Department Stores, 1890–1940
SUSAN PORTER BENSON